BRITANNICA ET AMERICANA

Dritte Folge · Band 33

herausgegeben von
WOLFRAM R. KELLER
ANDREW JAMES JOHNSTON

The Return of the Historical Novel?

Thinking
About Fiction and History
After Historiographic
Metafiction

Edited by

ANDREW JAMES JOHNSTON
KAI WIEGANDT

Universitätsverlag
WINTER
Heidelberg

Bibliografische Information der Deutschen Nationalbibliothek

Die Deutsche Nationalbibliothek verzeichnet diese Publikation
in der Deutschen Nationalbibliografie;
detaillierte bibliografische Daten sind im Internet
über *http://dnb.d-nb.de* abrufbar.

COVER ILLUSTRATION

Tommy Atkins and his mates return from Dunkirk.
Frank Capra (still from Why We Fight)

ISBN 978-3-8253-6721-3

© 2017 Universitätsverlag Winter GmbH Heidelberg
Imprimé en Allemagne · Printed in Germany

Gedruckt auf umweltfreundlichem, chlorfrei gebleichtem
und alterungsbeständigem Papier.

Den Verlag erreichen Sie im Internet unter:
www.winter-verlag.de

Contents

6

Acknowledgements

We would like to thank Winfried Fluck, Therese Fuhrer, Ursula Kocher, Joachim Küpper, Ansgar Nünning, Wilhelm Schmidt-Biggemann, Stefan Willer and all contributors to this volume for their enthusiastic participation in the lecture series on the Historical Novel at Freie Universität Berlin in the Summer Term 2011. We are grateful to Wolfram R. Keller for his editorial advice and support, and to Elena Radwan and Dilan Güngör for their invaluable help in preparing the manuscript. Last but not least, many thanks are due to Martin Bleisteiner, Sven Durie and Jan-Peer Hartmann for their support throughout this undertaking.

Berlin, August 2016
Andrew James Johnston and Kai Wiegandt

ANDREW JAMES JOHNSTON, KAI WIEGANDT

Introduction

The historical novel is marked by a chequered critical history. As a genre, it has been haunted by what one might, half-seriously stealing from Derrida, call "The Spectre of Lukács". Few other theorists have been as influential as the twentieth-century Hungarian Marxist in shaping our critical perception of historical fiction. Arguably, there is only one other theoretical approach that can be said to rival Lukács in its influence on our views of the historical novel, and that is the concept of 'historiographic metafiction', a notion introduced by the Canadian critic Linda Hutcheon in 1988. Until fairly recently, it was these two perspectives that all but dominated attempts to conceptualize the genre. But things seem to be changing: the last decade or so has seen the advent of new ways of thinking about the historical novel. It is in the freshly developing discussion of the genre that this volume seeks to participate.

György/Georg Lukács's Marxist view sees the historical novel in very specific ideological terms and, consequently, affords it a very particular – and surprisingly brief – space in literary history. Central to Lukács's unabashedly teleological scheme of things, set down most comprehensively in his monograph *The Historical Novel* (1937), is a narrative of origins. The historical novel in its 'true sense' was invented by Sir Walter Scott (1771-1832), with *Waverley* (1814) constituting the first example. But after little more than two decades, according to Lukács, the genre's most salient features were already being absorbed into the social realism of Honoré de Balzac. Hence, the historical novel as one would commonly understand it, that is a novel set in the (distant) past, effectively became obsolete. From Balzac (1799-1850) onwards, historical fiction was drained of its aesthetic and intellectual relevance since the genre's central principles as developed by Scott migrated into the kind of realism cultivated in the bourgeois novel. For, as Lukács argues, the historical novel's particular legitimacy in history derives from the genre's capacity for imaginatively analyzing the ways in which a given period's social conditions shape human experience. And this capacity is best expressed when the genre deals with eras marked by momentous change and cataclysmic rupture: "the portrayal of a total context of social life, be it present or past, in narrative form" (Lukács, *The Historical Novel* 242). The historical novel's realism is encapsulated, in an especially poignant fashion, in the typical construction of its protagonists whom Lukács has famously called – rather unflatteringly – "mediocre heroes". Instead of employing the great personalities from history – e.g. Caesar, Cromwell, Napoleon – as the central stars of its cast, the historical novel as invented by Scott uses utterly fictitious characters as its protagonists. Their lives are powerfully affected by the historical developments depicted, but this always happens in a manner supposedly characteristic of their times.

Thus, the protagonists' actions have next to no impact on the general course of historical events. Indeed, the protagonists in question are made to look rather ordinary – hence their supposed mediocrity: fairly intelligent and usually endowed with more than a modicum of ethical sensibilities, but without being in any way special: "as central figures they provide a perfect instrument for Scott's way of presenting the totality of certain transitional stages of history" (Lukács, *The Historical Novel* 35).

Paradoxically, Lukács's teleological account of the genre's absorption into Balzac's social realism results in the historical novel's abandonment of what one would conventionally assume to be the 'historical': the genre's link to periods set in the (distant) past. As displayed by Balzac's fiction, the historical novel's capacity for representing and analyzing the social imprint on human experience was being further refined by novels narrating contemporary, or at least, near-contemporary events: "The classical historical novel arose out of the social novel and, having enriched and raised it to a higher level, passed back into it" (Lukács, *The Historical Novel* 242). From a Marxist point of view, novels clearly set in the past, in periods untouched by living memory, were thus rendered superfluous. Little wonder then that after 1848, the year that saw the failure of so many of Europe's democratic bourgeois revolutions, the historical novel purportedly entered a period of rapid decline – and the bourgeois realism Lukács sets so much store on was soon to follow suit. Indeed, as Lukács argued, the actual emergence of a subgenre of historical fiction set in the distant past clearly testified to that decline. For these later historical novels, the "turbulence of the times" was, if at all, merely "used as a pretext for revealing human-moral qualities" (Lukács, *The Historical Novel* 243).

Even though nowadays the majority of critics would probably not accept Lukács's position in its totality, quite a few of his accusations against the post-1848 development of historical fiction continue to stick, depriving the genre of much of the prestige it seems to have enjoyed during the 19th century. And some of Lukács's larger perspectives on historical fiction, such as his fundamental claim that the genre's aesthetic and intellectual legitimacy stems from its ability to critically interrogate the total complexity of social experience in conditions of change, have recently been championed by theorists such as Perry Anderson and Fredric Jameson.[1] In fact, Jameson pushes Lukács's argument to its limits when he contends that in today's economic and political conditions the social purposes that lend legitimacy to historical fiction are best served by a conscious thematic focus on the future, on the "Science-Fictional inasmuch as it will have to include questions about the fate of our social system, which has become a second nature" (Jameson, 'The Historical Novel Today' 298). Nor is this all: not only did Lukács's influential history of the genre significantly contribute to considerably devaluing the historical novel set in the distant past, but it also helped to open up a massive analytical chasm between historical fiction, on the one hand, and modernism with its avant-garde aesthetics and formal experimentation, on the other. Moreover, as a consequence of its emphatically teleological thrust, Lukács's account of the historical novel ignored or even scorned the vast majority of novels set in the distant past. Under

---

[1]   Perry Anderson, 'From Progress to Catastrophe.' *London Review of Books* 33-15 (July 28, 2011): 24-28; Fredric Jameson, 'The Historical Novel Today, Or, Is It Still Possible.' *The Antinomies of Realism*. London: Verso, 2013. 259-313.

the impact of Marxism, the historical novel proper was relegated to the realm of the middle brow, if not the trivial.

The second influential perspective on the historical novel, though radically different from Lukács's interpretation in nearly every way, did not exactly improve matters. This second important account of historical fiction is encapsulated in Linda Hutcheon's much-celebrated postmodern concept of 'historiographic metafiction' (*A Poetics of Postmodernism* 105-23). Coined in 1988, the term refers to a decidedly self-reflexive type of fiction that uses metafictional strategies in order to highlight the problematic nature both of fictional and of non-fictional historical writing. Novels belonging to this school self-consciously employ devices such as parody, pastiche or anachronism while simultaneously experimenting with intertextuality in all its manifestations. A list of well-known English-language examples would include John Fowles's *The French Lieutenant's Woman* (1969), William Kennedy's *Legs* (1975), Salman Rushdie's *Midnight's Children* (1981), Graham Swift's *Waterland* (1983), A. S. Byatt's *Possession* (1990), Michael Ondaatje's *The English Patient* (1992) and Thomas Pynchon's *Mason and Dixon* (1997).

Linda Hutcheon did not perceive historiographic metafiction simply as the perfect expression of a specifically postmodern approach to history, but rather as giving voice to some of the fundamental principles of postmodernism themselves. Postmodernism, Hutcheon contends, radically questions the teleological narratives supposedly associated with the modernist perspective and insists that all (historical) knowledge is mediated by discourse. The notion of the postmodern appears, therefore, to be perfectly embodied by a fictional mode playfully fragmenting historical experience while at the same time insisting on the ultimate inaccessibility of historical truth by drenching its narrative in intertextual effects and using parody and pastiche to undermine any sense of historical authenticity.

The notion of historiographic metafiction as the later twentieth-century's principal form of self-reflexive historical fiction did not, however, meet with unanimous approval. In his detailed analysis of a broad range of historical novels, Ansgar Nünning demonstrates that, as a concept, historiographic metafiction is decidedly too limited to encompass the many forms of self-reflexively narrating history in fiction that evolved after classical modernism. Nünning has shown convincingly that even in conditions of postmodernism there are many examples of the historical novel that possess a remark-able degree of self-reflexivity and aesthetic complexity, without, however, fulfilling the (full range of) criteria attributed to historiographic metafiction.[2]

Further, though somewhat implicit, challenges to historiographic metafiction's criti-cal preponderance were levelled in the form of a fundamental criticism of the totalizing assumptions either voiced by poststructuralist theorists themselves or else associated with postmodernism in art and literature. In *Doing Time* (2000), the feminist critic Rita Felski draws attention to the way critics supporting the notion of postmodernism either as an aesthetic style and body of theory or, alternatively, as a fully-fledged era in

---

[2] Ansgar Nünning. 'Crossing Borders and Blurring Genres: Towards a Typology and Poetics of Postmodernist Historical Fiction in England since the 1960s.' *European Journal of English Studies* 1-2 (1997): 217-238; Ansgar Nünning. *Von historischer Fiktion zu historio-graphischer Metafiktion*. LIR 11. 2 vols. Trier: Wissenschaftlicher Verlag Trier, 1995.

cultural history stay fettered to a form of teleological history that views historical time
as a linear succession of chronological stages (6).[3] These stages, Felski posits, imply an
inevitable logic of sequence and simultaneously enforce the notion of a unified whole of
historical experience: "Within such a framework, homogeneity and sameness become
all-important, and dissident or contradictory historical currents are banished to the side-
lines of analysis" (11). If we accept Felski's critique, then the notion of historiographic
metafiction, too, must inevitably become complicit in this kind of teleological historicism, even as historiographic metafiction claims to be dissolving the epistemological
foundations of both historical fiction and traditional historiography. Moreover, what is
particularly interesting about Felski's critique is that its basic thrust, that is, its anti-
teleological critique of homogenizing approaches to temporality, applies to the Marxist
and the postmodern theorizations of the historical novel in equal measure.

Change did not, however, exclusively occur on the level of theory. Even as the
freshly coined term 'historiographic metafiction' was gaining currency in critical discourse, a new generation of novelists were beginning to betray a growing interest in
historical fiction as a way of gauging modes of historical experience. These authors
returned to a style of fiction much more akin to the traditional forms of the historical
novel, devoting their attention to historical fiction's capacity for probing the alterity of
the past. Although historiographic metafiction, too, has been concerned with the issue of
alterity, the scholarly discussion of historiographic metafiction tended to be overwhelm-
ingly preoccupied with postmodern problems of representation and literary self-
reflexivity. Critics dissecting examples of historiographic metafiction preferred to stress
the inaccessibility of an authentic historical experience, rather than showing interest in
historical experience, however inauthentic, itself. Yet in the very year after the term
'historiographic metafiction' had entered the critical lexicon, the newly developing
interest in historical experience became clearly manifest within the official institutions
of English literature. 1989 witnessed the publication of two important historical novels
evincing a marked swerve away from historiographic metafiction's more radical principles: Rose Tremain's *Restoration* (1989), shortlisted for the Man Booker Prize and
winning the *Sunday Express* Book of the Year award, and Kazuo Ishiguro's *The
Remains of the Day* — which did win the Booker Prize. Different from historiographic
metafiction though they certainly are, these new novels do not constitute a complete
break with postmodern historical fiction. These novels, and many others following in
their wake, too, are informed by notions and styles deriving from historiographic metafiction, even as they redirect their focus to problems such as the otherness of life in the
past. As Rosario Arias explains: "many contemporary historical novels seek to show the
relevance of the knowledge of the past, however problematic this may be" ('Exoticizing
the Tudors' 21). And, in a similar vein, Kate Mitchell has suggested

---

[3]   Felski consciously collapses the two perspectives, since the former tends to "almost always
       smuggle in a historical theory".

... that these novels, while demonstrating a vivid awareness of the problematics involved in seeking and achieving historical knowledge, remain nonetheless committed to the possibility and the value of striving for that knowledge. They are more concerned with the ways in which fiction *can* lay claim to the past, provisionally and partially, rather than the ways that it can not.

(*History and Cultural Memory in Neo-Victorian Fiction* 3)

Indeed, it is not always easy to clearly distinguish between the two types of historical fiction. Consequently, some novels are actually recruited into both camps, and sometimes we can see novels switching from one to the other, as seems to have been the case with Antonia S. Byatt's *Possession*. Byatt herself has refrained from aligning her work with historiographic metafiction, positing, instead, a more general revival of historical fiction in English since the 1960s. Her view self-consciously bridges the shifting gap between historiographic metafiction and other types of historical fiction (Byatt, *On Histories and Stories* 9-35).

As scholars have increasingly begun to train their critical gaze on the issue of temporality itself, some have even argued that, precisely because historical novels are *per se* incapable of avoiding a precarious relation to the past, the genre is ineluctably self-reflexive in regard to its negotiation of temporal otherness. And this is held equally to be true of Scott's earliest examples of the genre and of the most naive of contemporary bodice-rippers. Self-reflexivity is thus elevated to a fundamental characteristic of the historical novel as such. An argument of this nature must automatically reduce the uniqueness of historiographic metafiction.[4] Instead, in many quarters these postmodernist novels are now seen merely to be performing, with a greater degree of emphasis and visible self-consciousness, what the genre has, in fact, been doing all along (Boccardi, *The Contemporary British Historical Novel* 1-27; de Groot, *The Historical Novel* 1-10).

Recent criticism is, thus, increasingly blurring the boundaries between the various styles of historical fiction without, however, erasing the distinctions altogether. Drawing on the newly-established concept of 'Neo-Victorianism', Elodie Rousselot, for instance, has made an interesting bid for theorizing the new(er) type of historical novel as 'neo-historical fiction' ('Introduction: Exoticising the Past' 2). This is a kind of historical novel intensely curious about the temporal otherness of the past and about the different ways in which the past was experienced when it was still the present. This literary approach refuses to view the past as an extended teleological narrative, in which each and every element already has its pre-ordained place within a larger scheme of historical

---

[4]   Thus Jerome de Groot is not overly preoccupied with maintaining the distinctions between historiographic metafiction and other types of historical novels. He states: "Over the past two decades literary novelists have interrogated history in a variety of interesting ways, from Janet Winterson's *Sexing the Cherry* (1989) and *The Passion* (1987) through Margaret Atwood's *Alias Grace* (1996) to Hari Kunzru's *The Impressionist* (2002). Rose Tremain's novel *Restoration* (1989) demonstrated the popularity and the possibility of the literary historical novel, winning various prizes with huge sales. Tremain managed to combine critical acclaim with populist appeal. It is now commonplace for serious fiction writers to produce historical work, where it was not 20 years ago" (De Groot, *Consuming History: Historians and Heritage in Contemporary Popular Culture* 218).

development. Nor does this approach rest content with conceiving of history as an endless succession of simulacra either testifying to the past's mere constructedness or else
to its insurmountable inaccessibility. Rather, what seems to be taking shape is a notion
of the past that seeks to understand temporal difference as a fundamental category of
cultural experience, while recognizing, at the same time, that any awareness of the
otherness of the past must inevitably be directed by the concerns and the discursive
constraints prevailing in the present.

It seems, therefore, that we are entering into a new phase in the critical reception of
historical fiction as the discussion of the historical novel is rapidly becoming more inclusive, more tolerant and, above all, more diverse. It is before the backdrop of these
changes in the critical debate that the contributions to this volume are meant to be read.
Rather than seeing historical fiction as locked in a clear-cut scheme of teleological
succession or assigning to the historical novel specific aesthetic purposes, the articles in
this collection seek to probe deeply into the historical novel's potential for providing
readers not simply with an understanding of how the image of the past is constructed
but also of how attempts to chart forms of historical otherness constitute a specific
mode of cultural experience mediated by literature, even if the historical authenticity
one might nostalgically associate with that project must always elude us.

Cordula Lemke's chapter revisits Sir Walter Scott's contribution to the genre's
development. She discusses Scott's fictional responses to historiography's increasing
demands for scholarly objectivity, the kind of objectivity that banished all fiction to the
realm of literature. Even as Scott seemed to be paying tribute to the new lines of demar-
cation between the factual and the fictional by self-consciously endorsing the factual in
his novels, he was fully capable of creating an illusion of historicity by inventing supposed 'facts'. In so doing, Scott highlighted the textuality and constructedness of
history. As Lemke shows, some of the most important features that were later considered to define historiographic metafiction were already part and parcel of Scott's
poetics. At the same time, Scott's idiosyncratic blurring of fact and fiction allowed him
to fabricate Scottishness as a national identity. While James Macpherson had tried to
create a Scottish national genealogy by writing his Ossianic epic in the style of Homer
and Vergil, Scott attempted something similar by promoting the historical novel as a
new genre.

The next two chapters complicate, revise, and complement the notion of historiographic metafiction: John Fowles's *The French Lieutenant's Woman* (1969) and
Graham Swift's *Waterland* (1983). Claudia Olk reads *The French Lieutenant's Woman*
as one of the earliest Neo-Victorian novels, a genre that, in critical terms, saw its firm
establishment only in recent decades. *The French Lieutenant's Woman*, she argues, is
typical of the Neo-Victorian genre because of the specific theoretical discourses it employs as it adapts its historical material. Palaeontology, evolution and determinism serve
as subjects through which the historical novel reflects upon itself and stages its own
historicity, while it simultaneously reconstructs different Victorianisms in relation to
current theoretical paradigms and aesthetic practices such as a postmodernist pluralization of forms.

Ute Berns, too, discusses *The French Lieutenant's Woman* and the considerable
degree to which many writers of historical fiction have been fascinated by natural
history. She offers an in-depth analysis both of Fowles's novel and of Swift's

Waterland to show how these narratives each address issues of natural history in order to generate alternative models of temporality, models aligned with specific aesthetic, social and political positions. The two novels implicate human history in natural history and thereby qualify as environmentally-oriented works *avant la lettre*. They both trace different conceptions of nature throughout history and thus contribute to the body of literary works ecocriticism is interested in. One of Berns's principal claims is that while historiographic metafiction in general takes great pains to deconstruct the grand narratives of human history, the two novels in question re-assemble and re-value various aspects of history, amongst other things: of natural history. As they draw on natural history's temporal patterns, these novels modify and re-conceptualize perspectives on human history while questioning the very boundary between human and non-human history.

Russell West-Pavlov and Kai Wiegandt both turn to postcolonial versions of the historical novel, demonstrating how these reinvigorate what used to be a predominantly European genre. In his reading of *The Gunny Sack* (1989) by Tanzanian-Canadian writer M. J. Vassanji, West-Pavlov shows that this novel 'provincializes' the European historical novel. Yet this is a gesture that must not be taken as being typical of postcolonial writing. Salman Rushdie's *Midnight's Children* serves as a case in point: through generally linking the novel to the Western canon, and particularly to Sterne's *Tristram Shandy,* Western critics have successfully assimilated the novel into the discourse of European Literature. Vassanji's historical novel, by contrast, refuses to be chained to specific historical narratives and keeps its connections to history tenuous. In his defense of hybrid ethnic entanglements as a viable model for the future of African polities, Vassanji rejects linear genealogies and avoids models of historiography incapable of embracing fractured, zig-zag cartographies of past, present and future. In relocating the genre of the historical novel outside Europe, Vassanji questions the connections between national history and individual life-story that lie at the origin of the European historical novel. *The Gunny Sack* shows that it is possible to write historical novels without reference to a national paradigm and without an individual subject as their principal synecdoche.

As Wiegandt shows, J. M. Coetzee's *The Master of Petersburg* (1994) – a novel about Dostoevsky's inquiry into his stepson Pavel's death – goes beyond historiographic metafiction, too, albeit in a very different way. The protagonist's manipulative treatment of his dead son's traces testifies to the constructedness of history, and is also symptomatic of what this novel identifies as the basic pattern of history: the struggle between generations. On the one hand, this struggle takes place between the fictional Dostoevsky and Pavel and on the other, as though refracting literary history, between Dostoevsky and a Coetzee who is rewriting Dostoevsky's novel *Demons*. The novel's recurring motifs of parricide and of the father devouring his own child have their historical equivalents in Petersburg's rioting students and the violence of the tsarist police's retaliation.

The historical novel's proximity to fictional biography forms the specific focus of Helga Schwalm's and Heike Hartung's contributions to this volume. Both chapters examine how history and life writing have been brought into dialogue in recent as well as very recent British fiction. Schwalm's analysis focuses on the ways in which historical novels are capable of negotiating the possibilities and epistemological frames of historiography as much as those of life writing. Insofar as such novels fictionalize 'real' events or actual people from the past, they operate as historical novels; but inasmuch as they fictionalize the lives of 'real' persons, they operate as biographical novels; and they operate as metafiction as they call attention to their own status as text or fiction. Reinventing the past as fiction, these texts still insist on the inevitability of historical and biographical narration. They do so by employing different strategies of rehabilitating the figure of the Romantic author. Peter Ackroyd's *Chatterton* (1987) and Alan Massie's *The Ragged Lion* (1994) demonstrate a simultaneous figuration of the author as collective and authentic subject, whereas Julian Barnes's *Arthur & George* (2005) reveals the author as the precarious centre behind a seemingly conventional double plot.

Hartung compares the oeuvres of Julian Barnes and Ian McEwan with regard to their treatment of life in time and in history, and demonstrates how their recent work departs from the postmodern paradigm that dominated their earlier books. Both authors invest the narrative voice with a powerful sense of authority. McEwan dramatizes childhood, whereas Barnes focuses on old age and dying, but in their focus on the catastrophes and failures of ordinary lives, as well as in their timescapes, they explore, in a similar fashion, the temporal dimensions of evolutionary and geological, historical and individual time in order to envision specific versions of the contemporary. The third-person voice of McEwan's *On Chesil Beach* (2007) and the unreliable narration of Barnes's *The Sense of an Ending* (2011) both produce the effect of a displacement of history; the first through an extended reflection on a spoiled beginning, the second in the inconclusiveness of a retrospective search for meaning. While Barnes's and McEwan's novels differ in their attitudes to contemporary science's materialist approach to consciousness in time, both writers are centrally concerned with reassessing contemporary life in time.

Like Hartung, Andrew James Johnston detects a conscious turning away from (post)modernist literary practices in Ian McEwan's recent fiction. He reads *Atonement* (2001), a novel relating the fictional author Briony Tallis's bedevilled attempts to 'atone' through fiction, as a complex intertextual meditation on the narrative evocation of penitential desire. McEwan scrutinizes the difficult relationship between narrative and ethics through the prism of Chaucer's *Canterbury Tales*, a text that self-consciously exploits and combines the paradoxes of the frame tale narrative with those of confessional discourse. Just as Chaucer's narrative more than once performatively en-genders a longing for redemption by actually withholding that very redemption, Briony Tallis makes her readers experience the emotional and ethical urgency of her desire for atonement by framing atonement as impossible: because, in determining her characters' ultimate fates, she has practically assumed a godlike position, there remains no higher entity capable of forgiving her. But the very fact that, despite this ineluctable impasse, she continues to strive for atonement, validates the seriousness of her penitential desire, and takes the novel's final part beyond the mere artfulness of a postmodern parlour game. As it borrows aesthetic devices from medieval story-telling, *Atonement* proves to be a historical novel in a variety of senses, not only a novel set in the past and about the past but also a novel reactivating ethical and emotional discourses from (literary) history.

Renate Brosch's and Margitta Rouse's chapters, finally, take the present volume to the most recent generation of historical novels, novels which likewise participate in discourses of premodernity. Demonstrating how the novel creates a unique experience of intersubjectivity for the reader, Brosch reads Hilary Mantel's *Wolf Hall* (2009), arguably the most successful historical novel of the new century, in the terms of reader-response criticism. At first glance it seems that the novel tells the success story of capitalism and the transformation of the incipient nation state's financial administration by figuring Thomas Cromwell as a hero. The narrative of political success the story appears to be affirming is undermined, however, by the psychology of an inter-subjective reading of the proto-capitalist protagonist, a psychology that we, as the novel's readers, cannot resist. Realizing that we have been complicit in constructing him as a hero the way we *wish* to see him rather than confronting the questionable aspects of his character, we are alerted to the ease with which our judgments can be misled. Privileging both the experience of intersubjectivity and the examination of ethical choices this experience entails over metafictional historiography, *Wolf Hall* is indicative of the historical novel's departure from its long-reigning postmodernist paradigm as seen by Hutcheon and others. Readers willing to tackle the novel's dense, complex and sometimes opaque deixis, where the reference of the pronoun 'he' must constantly be inferred, are rewarded with substantial affective involvement. We enter Cromwell's mind only to ultimately reject egocentric subjectivity in favour of an alter-native focus on an intersubjective construction of identity.

This volume concludes with Rouse's reading of Jim Crace's novel *Harvest* (2013) as an elegy both on the genre as Scott conceived it, and on the genre in its various post-modern, meta-fictional guises. Crace's novel pictures the destruction of a temporally and topographically unspecified rural village community by the advent of novel methods of farming, and criticizes the Scottian historical novel's tendency to promote progress and a sense of national belonging no matter how tragically competing forces impact on individual lives. Crace eschews the postmodern tendency that seeks to rescue the historical novel through telling the stories of the marginalized, the forgotten and the dispossessed. Ultimately, that model, too, Rouse argues, relies on narratives of progress. *Harvest* offers an alternative to the historical novel's politics of time by blending reali-stic and fantastic modes of narrating the past with their related temporalities, and by suffusing them with biblical temporalities introduced only to be deconstructed soon after. The novel adapts multi-temporal modes of storytelling already to be found in medieval literature.

Works Cited

Arias, Rosario. 'Exoticizing the Tudors: Hilary Mantel's Re-Appropriation of the Past in Wolf Hall and Bring Up the Bodies.' *Exoticizing the Past in Contemporary Neo-Historical Fiction*. Ed. Elodie Rousselot. Basingstoke: Palgrave Macmillan, 2014. 19-36.

Boccardi, Mariadele. *The Contemporary British Historical Novel: Representation, Nation, Empire*. Basingstoke: Palgrave Macmillan, 2009.

Byatt, Antonia S. *On Histories and Stories*. Cambridge, MA: Harvard University Press, 2001.

De Groot, Jerome. *Consuming History: Historians and Heritage in Contemporary Popular Culture*. Abingdon: Routledge, 2009.

De Groot, Jerome. *The Historical Novel*. London: Routledge, 2010.

Felski, Rita. *Doing Time: Feminist Theory and Postmodern Culture*. New York: New York University Press, 2000.

Hutcheon, Linda. *A Poetics of Postmodernism: History, Theory, Fiction*. New York & London: Routledge, 1988.

Jameson, Fredric. 'The Historical Novel Today, Or, Is It Still Possible.' *The Antinomies of Realism*. London: Verso, 2013. 259-313.

Lukács, Georg. *The Historical Novel*. Trans. Hannah and Stanley Mitchell. Introduction by Fredric Jameson. Lincoln: University of Nebraska Press, 1983 [1937].

Mitchell, Kate. *History and Cultural Memory in Neo-Victorian Fiction: Victorian Afterimages*. Basingstoke: Palgrave Macmillan, 2010.

Rousselot, Elodie. 'Introduction: Exoticizing the Past in Contemporary Neo-Historical Fiction.' *Exoticizing the Past in Contemporary Neo-Historical Fiction*. Ed. Elodie Rousselot. Basingstoke: Palgrave Macmillan, 2014. 1-16.

CORDULA LEMKE

Scott-land and the Invention of the Historical Novel: Walter Scott's *Waverley*

Scotland – the land of myths and fairy tales: it evokes images of misty mountains, treacherous moors and dark cities where ghosts, monsters and shady figures strike terror in the hearts of unsuspecting people and obscure Celtic rituals unfold their magic powers. It is a land where rough clans lead bloody wars and hold raucous feasts. There is always an old storyteller sitting at a crackling peat fire telling tales of times long gone to whisky-swigging tourists, a pub where songs of 'auld lang syne' create a nostalgic feeling of belonging.

Scotland's other side is easily forgotten in these Arcadian myths of unspoiled nature. The exoticist perspective spread by tourists all over the world is countered by the pragmatic empiricism of the thinkers of the Scottish Enlightenment, like the philosopher David Hume, who held a strong belief in the scientific potential of history and denigrated religion as superstition, or the economist Adam Smith whose thoughts on the 'invisible hand' of the market are still influential today. Thus, it comes as no surprise that in addition to the many colourful tales an apparently dry genre like the historical novel has its roots in Scotland. In Georg Lukács's definition of the historical novel Sir Walter Scott is seen as the prototypical representative of the genre if not as its inventor (Lukács, *Der historische Roman* 37). Although it has often been claimed that the novel as a genre has had close affinities to history from its very beginnings and that a realist mode of writing cannot be conceived of without a historical background to support it, we still look to Walter Scott's *Waverley* novels if we want to define the genre.

At the time Scott wrote his novels two concepts of history were struggling for supremacy: antiquarianism and historiography. Eighteenth century antiquarianism is mainly based on a desire to collect all things antique. The focus lies less on an attempt to explain historical events and progress than on providing hard historical facts to those looking for all-encompassing explanations. However, the aim of collecting swerved from its documentary aspect towards a collecting for collecting's sake. Although antiquarians usually set out with a goal in mind, like tracing their family line or the history of their village, they were easily side-tracked by the sheer wealth of their material and let themselves be swept into various new directions by their excitement for the material past (Stagl, 'Homo Collector' 47).

Historiography dates back to antiquity itself. It has come a long way from the mythical descriptions of Herodotus who peppered history with anecdotes, through the lengthy national epics which explain the facts of nation building by recourse to the world of the gods. The idea of storing data in archives in order to create a semblance of objectivity originated from medieval historiography, although historical data were then overtly employed to support political and religious aims. During the era of Enlightenment it was claims of rationality and objectivity that determined historiographers' perspectives. Turning away from the all-encompassing force of a divine plan predetermining historical progress, historiographers focused on 'Man' who, despite his fallibility, was deemed responsible for the running of the world. And in order to create an increasingly better world, he needed instructions. As has often been stated, historiography seemed to offer criteria by which 'Man' could satisfy his desire for improvement, for a steady development towards a better and more civilized state of society (Manning, "Walter Scott" 145). Thus, historiography had to follow strictly scientific methods in order to fulfil the requirements of objectivity.

Since fiction can emphasize entertainment more than edification, tension between antiquarians and historians was constantly on the rise. Antiquarians were enthusiastic about every material aspect of history and displayed an undiscerning veneration for all historical artefacts. This provoked historians to deny antiquarians the capacity of distinguishing between fact and fiction. They regarded documents collected by antiquarians as an indiscriminate jumble of mythical legend and historical fact. But as historians came to put more store by tangible evidence during the Enlightenment, the two warring factions began to converge, as antiquarians went beyond their voracious collecting of artefacts and began to interpret their treasures themselves. At the same time, the imaginative thrust of the historiographic enterprise was gradually superseded by the ambition to reproduce historical events as faithfully as possible. Both historians and antiquarians began to cling to what they perceived as historical fact and relegated all fictionality to the realm of literature (Harmsen, *Antiquarianism in the Augustan Age* 24).

This vacuum between fact and fiction is precisely the site where the historical novel was going to evolve. Every definition of the genre focuses on this close tie between fact and fiction: The historical novel prominently deploys confirmed historical events as an intertext peopled with an altogether fictitious cast of characters. Though readers are supposed to learn about history, information is not imparted in the form of straightforward instruction. Rather, the course of history is experienced and suffered through the eyes of the characters. This emotional response to historical events is at odds with such academic ideals as critical distance and objectivity. As subjective moral judgment and emotional preference are allowed to assume relevance, the well-guarded dividing line between the public and private spheres becomes permeable. What is more, as soon as different characters are given voice, a variety of perspectives emerges which not only introduces a moment of suspense into historical processes but opens these processes up in a fundamental way by inviting revision and qualification from the different characters and their different perceptions. Needless to say, the new readings which are thus produced are still based on the raw material of historical fact. But while history takes its inexorable course, the characters are free to handle it in their own idiosyncratic ways and add their own perspective.

A striking example of this tension is Walter Scott's preface to the first edition of his novel *Waverley; or, 'Tis Sixty Years Since* of 1814. Here, emotions are seen as the paramount object of investigation: "by throwing the force of my narrative upon the characters and passions of the actors; – those passions common to men in all stages of society and which alike agitated the human heart" (Scott, *Waverley* 5). Scott, then, is less concerned with the historical events in themselves, which he strategically misrepresents (Pittock, 'Scott as Historiographer' 151), than with the different emotions they cause and which determine the way in which the engagement with those events are handled. As he goes on to explain, he chooses to disregard the feelings of his contemporaries and to turn to a different epoch because he believed that earlier generations were less civilized in treating of these emotions. Even though he admits that the emotions as such do not disappear in the course of time, he believes that their intensity decreases with every succeeding generation and that they are thus less potent didactically and less edifying morally.

Much as Scott is here appropriating the core of Scottish Enlightenment thought, he has some significant reservations. Even though he suggests that history follows a linear course along the different stages of humankind, he assumes human character traits to be immutable. Still, historical contemplation can be instructive and can foster more civilized forms of behaviour and a general improvement:

> Some favourable opportunities of contrast have been afforded me, by the state of society in the northern part of the island at the period of my history, and may serve at once to vary and to illustrate the moral lessons which I would willingly consider as the most important part of my plan, although I am sensible how short they will fall of their aim, if I shall be found unable to mix them with amusement, – a task not quite so easy in this critical generation as it was 'Sixty Years Since'.
>
> (Scott, *Waverley* 5)

Like the historiographers of his time, Scott pursues moral ends, but he chooses different means. He seeks to educate not by presenting objective data, but by eliciting sympathy for his characters and, importantly, by entertaining his readers. Against the truth-claims of Enlightenment historiography, Scott therefore believes in the greater didactic force of fiction.

According to Scott, the didactic potential of historiography is situated at the intersection of fact and fiction and derives its force from the transgressions which are everywhere taking place in historical novels. Jerome de Groot defines this movement between the two poles of fact and fiction as 'faction' (de Groot, *The Historical Novel* 5). The term aptly describes the way in which the historical novel embeds authoritative data in its fictional world, thereby infusing this world with 'truth'. The novel, which was in the early nineteenth century regarded as a lesser literary genre and quite unfit for a male readership, was thus rehabilitated by being married to the academic discipline of historiography. In his autobiographical 'General Preface' to his *Waverley* novels of 1829, Scott describes this development in terms of a personal rescue:

> I was plunged into this great ocean of reading without compass or pilot [...] Familiar acquaintance with the specious miracles of fiction brought with it some degree of satiety, and I began by degrees, to seek in histories, memoirs, voyages and travels, and the like, events nearly as wonderful as those which were the work of imagination, with the additional advantage that they were at least in a great measure true.
>
> (Scott, *Waverley* 350)

Having discarded the unwanted influence of the 'miracles of fiction', Scott sets out to look for events that could as well be fictional within historiography. His method is therefore emphasizing fictionality. Rather than relegate historical facts to the rank of socio-cultural background or period flavour, Scott decides to introduce historical events into the heart of his novels and thereby succeeds in reconciling fact and fiction. He ends up producing precisely the kind of novel he was envisioning as a young man. As the historical novel leaves the sentimental novel and its stigma of effeminacy behind, its new-won factuality confers on it a semblance of facticity.

Unlike 'facticity', the term 'factuality' implies that facts may, indeed, be fictional. Their textuality aligns them with the constructedness of fiction and Scott points out unlikely and even miraculous events to be found in older historiographical texts. The textuality and constructedness of history is a pivotal tenet of the postmodern genre of historical fiction which has come to be known as historiographic metafiction. This subgenre reflexively draws attention to the way in which a comprehensive textuality allows the line between fact and fiction to blur. Today, there is a tendency to see this reflexivity as a unique marker of postmodernity. However, Scott was already writing in a similar vein (see Kerr, *Fiction against history* 17). In *Waverley*, which is going to serve as my example, we find the very debate between historiography and antiquari-anism and even an argument about the merits of fiction in the dissemination of historical information presented in the text by Waverley's uncle and aunt. Moreover, *Waverley* sports an omniscient narrator who never tires of telling the reader about the exact nature of the genre to which the novel belongs.

This metafictional device set Scott's novels apart and he could be sure that he would be credited with having produced a major innovation. Even though he did not, at first, choose to acknowledge authorship of the Waverley novels, Scott used his preface to the first edition of 1814 to proclaim that the novels represent an entirely new genre. The very choice of name for his protagonist is a sign of this novelty:

> I must modestly admit I am too diffident of my own merit to place it in unnecessary opposition to preconceived associations: I have therefore, like a maiden knight with his white shield, assumed for my hero, WAVERLEY, an uncontaminated name, bearing with its sound little of good and evil, excepting what the reader shall be hereafter pleased to affix to it.
>
> (Scott, *Waverley* 3)

What Scott is trying to pass off as an act of modesty soon stands revealed as a self-confident and emphatic claim. He is, in fact, turning against the tradition of the novel as a genre, which at the time is still in its infancy. While his predecessors were detained by such issues as 'fashion' and 'manners', Scott opts for the heroic mode and describes 'passion' (Scott, *Waverley* 4-5). This is the new beginning which causes him to seek an unsullied virgin name for his novel's protagonist.

Much as researchers never tire of denying the Waverley novels' claim to being the first historical novels and of citing the examples of the likes of Defoe and Richardson as earlier authors interested in questions of historical plausibility, Scott still tends to be regarded as the founder and prime innovator of the genre. Lukács's enormously influential monograph on the historical novel has greatly contributed to Scott's eminence within the canon. But Scott's preface to *Waverley* shows that his position is not merely an edifice constructed by literary scholars but that he was very much an active agent in the building of his own legend. By carefully marking his distance from his peers and by describing his search for the name of his protagonist as a wiping of the genre's slate, Scott is doing everything to claim the invention of the historical novel for himself. As I want to show here, his claim of being the first, the founder, the inventor includes even the subject matter he writes about.

Considering Scott's proclamations about the importance of historical distance, it is remarkable to see that the plot of his first novel predates its composition by a mere sixty years. Hence the novel's subtitle which recurs throughout as a refrain: 'Sixty Years Since'. The explanation for this short time span given in his preface of 1829 relates to very personal reasons. Seeing the economic failure of a novel set in the Middle Ages which a friend of his had published, Scott decided to look towards a different epoch, even though his true fascination did lie with the Middle Ages (Scott, *Waverley* 354), a fascination which was later going to produce the highly successful novel *Ivanhoe*. In *Waverley*, Scott focuses on a central epoch of Scottish history whose didactic value he inscribes by the refrain 'Sixty Years Since': the Jacobite rising of 1745 and the campaign of Bonnie Prince Charlie, known to his enemies as 'The Young Pretender'.

Scott's novel is intimately linked to the fate of Scotland as a nation which, by the time Scott was writing *Waverley*, had changed dramatically compared to the eighteenth century. In 1707 Scotland finally agreed to the 'Union of Parliaments' with England after 1603 had seen the 'Union of the Crowns' when the Scotsman James VI succeeded the childless Queen Elizabeth I on the English throne as King James I of England. Social and economic hardship struck Scotland during the seventeenth century. When England refused to improve the terms for Scottish trade, the Scots threatened to terminate the Union of the Crowns – a measure which only served to exacerbate the situation since England went on to enforce even more severe sanctions against an already weakened Scottish trade. At the same time, England was eagerly promoting the Union of Parliaments in order to strengthen its hold on Scotland. The union was a highly controversial issue since there were fears that Scotland might end up no more than another English colony. It was only when England agreed to guarantee free trade to Scotland and when both the rights of the Calvinist Church of Scotland and the integrity of the Scottish legal system were recognized that the Union was at last implemented.

It has often been argued that it was fear of English colonization that gave rise to the Scottish desire for a strong national identity. Upon closer inspection, however, one can see that national identity was, in fact, a project of the Scottish Lowlands who were looking towards the Highlands for typically Scottish traits. Lowland culture was closely modelled on the English drawing room while the Highlands could easily be identified by religion, clothes, the clan system and the Gaelic language. Though at the beginning of the eighteenth century the Lowlands were still given to despising the Highlands, sentiment soon became anti-English above everything else. The Highlands offered a remarkable range of characteristics which could be deployed in a bid to distinguish the Scots from their English neighbours and Highland culture soon came to be appropriated, colonized and subordinated to Lowland interests. This process is often described as the invention of a Scottish national identity (see Devine, *The Scottish Nation* 232-33).

An early instance of this process can be found in James Macpherson's so-called 'translation' of the songs of Ossian. Macpherson collected ballads from the Highlands and worked them into a more or less coherent epic structure by liberally adding material of his own. Being a Highland Scot himself, Macpherson reprocessed Highland culture in a way which was supposed to prove Scotland's predominance on the British Isles and his heroic epic played a major role in the constitution of Scottish national self-confidence. But Macpherson's creativity has often been seen as a blatant act of forgery and this charge has undermined not only the prestige of the literary text, but also put the basis of Scottish national identity into jeopardy. This is where Scott sought to intervene. When the report of the Highland Society concluded that Macpherson's methods had indeed been improper, Scott, who at the time was still a poet noted for his commitment to the cause of Scottish national identity, did not attempt to challenge the Society's verdict. He was, however, eager to rehabilitate Macpherson's epic writings as a great and important literary achievement. The general dismissal of Macpherson's contribution to Scotland's national identity left a vacuum to be filled by new suggestions and Scott was only too happy to offer his input. His great success in this field made sure that he was to become not only the founder of the historical novel, but also the inventor of Scottish identity. Scott's decision to have his first historical novel address the events of the battle of Culloden opened up the possibility not only of establishing the historical relevance of those events, but of actively shaping the way in which they were interpreted and of effectively disseminating his view through the popularity of the novel.

The plot of *Waverley* can be seen as a straightforward English victory. Scott's novel is set before the backdrop of the battle of Culloden of 1746 and treats the ill-fated attempt of the Jacobite Highlands to place Charles Edward Stuart on the British throne. Waverley, an English gentleman and soldier whose support of the Jacobites is patently founded on his misguided interest in a Highland beauty named Flora, fights alongside Flora's brother, the noble but wily Highland chief Fergus Mac-Ivor, against the English and for Bonnie Prince Charlie. After the defeat at Culloden Waverley has to sort out his allegiance and marries the Lowland girl Rose Bradwardine in what appears to be an act of private colonization. This comprehensive subjection is reconfirmed by the way in which the Scots are described: Rose's father, the Baron of Bradwardine, comes across as quaint, Rose is a naive damsel who has fallen head over heels for the handsome soldier Waverley, and Bradwardine's friends are hopelessly drunk cowards. The Highlanders, by contrast, are depicted as animalistic thieves or as scheming noblemen. There are, thus, no Scottish traits on offer here which might serve to protect a Scottish identity against English hegemony.

However, Waverley himself is less strong than this colonial reading might suggest. From the start he is shown as mild and pleasant, but also as effeminate and chaotic. As has often been stated, his is a character who is very aptly named (see McCracken-Flesher, 'Scott's Jacobitical Plots' 50): when he chooses to remain in the Highlands rather than return to his English regiment, this is an example of his 'wavering honour' (Scott, *Waverley* 126). The literature he read as an impressionable youth is to blame:

[...] he was losing forever the opportunity of acquiring habits of firm and incumbent application, of gaining the art of controlling, directing and concentrating the powers of his own mind for earnest investigation [...].

(Scott, *Waverley* 12)

The flaw in Waverley's character is traceable to his enthusiasm for fiction, for romances, and to his unruly reading which was not disciplined by the truth which historiography had to offer. When Waverley arrives in Scotland, his reading determines his perception and he cannot help seeing the land through romance-tinted glasses:

Three or four village girls, returning from the well or brook with pitchers and pails on their heads, formed [...] pleasing objects, and with their thin short-gowns and single petticoats, bare arms, legs, and feet, uncovered heads and braided hair, somewhat resembled Italian forms of landscape. Nor could a lover of the picturesque have challenged either the elegance of their costume, or the symmetry of their shape [...].

(Scott, *Waverley* 33)

Waverley's positive approach to Scottish society is shaped by his affinity to the non-teleological charm of romance writing, to what Robin Maynard calls Waverley's 'Castle-Building' (Maynard, *Walter Scott* 17). He encounters Scotland with an openness and candour which does not figure in the improvement which was being expected from historiography.

Unlike the Englishman Colonel Talbot, whose contempt for all things Scottish the novel regards as typically English, Waverley is curious about Scottish society which he expects will conform to the world of his beloved romances. And Scotland does, in fact, deliver: Waverley is introduced to any number of Scottish legends and myths, he meets Donald Bean, the Scottish Robin Hood, he experiences an at least seemingly romantic and naive clan and in matters of the heart he finds himself counselled by a veritable prince. To Waverley, even the ongoing war is a romantic rebellion and he enjoys the sketching of landscapes during the campaigns. Needless to say, the women he meets in Scotland are likewise subjected to his romantic rewriting: He describes Rose as a naive, rural beauty who lives in a tower taken straight from the pages of a gothic novel and his first encounter with Flora takes him to a 'land of romance' (Scott, *Waverley* 105) where, like Macpherson's Ossian, the Highland beauty sits on a mossy rock and sings ballads about the greatness of Scotland. Even though reality is insistently making itself felt, Waverley stubbornly abides by his romantic vision. He may recognize Fergus for the scheming character he is and he may discover that Donald Bean is a common crook, but he is prepared to forgive all in defence of the romance which he has himself created.

Waverley holds on to his view of Scotland right up to the point when he returns to England after the lost battle. He explicitly ends the romance with a memorable statement: "[...] he felt himself entitled to say firmly, though perhaps with a sigh, that the romance of his life was ended, and that its real history had now commenced" (Scott, *Waverley* 283). This sentence tends to be read as a turn towards realism (see Lagan, 'The Context of Romanticism' 70). It seems that Waverley is turning away from his romantic infatuation with the Highlands and with Flora in favour of the more down-to-earth girl Rose and the reality of domestic life. However, it remains unclear why

Waverley's lament which initiates this turn should lead to his return to Scotland, especially since he names Rose as part of his Scottish romance. The teleology of Enlightenment historiography would demand that his abandoning of the Highlands indicate an abandoning of a more primitive state of humankind in order to assume the responsibilities of a civilized Englishman after being officially banned from entertaining any further contact with people from Scotland.

But Waverley is not one to renounce his romantic dreams which – pace Gottlieb – do not differ greatly from his dreams before his apparent conversion (Gottlieb, *Walter Scott and Contemporary Theory* 20). Barely a few weeks back in England, he decides to return to Scotland and to his beloved Rose, fully aware that this trip may well cost him his life. There is precious little left of his newly-won realist outlook when he supports the irrational tartan-mania of a fellow Englishman whom he meets along the way. Never having been particularly political, Waverley may now have turned his back upon the political cause of the Highlanders, but he is tangibly less at ease with the historical realism of his English home than he is in Scotland, where there is always ample space for fiction alongside the historical facts. His respect for the quaint figure of Bradwardine is an early indication of this attitude:

> But although Edward and he differed *toto coelo*, as the Baron would have said, upon this subject, yet they met upon history as on a neutral ground, in which they claimed an interest. The Baron, indeed, only cumbered his memory with matters of fact; the cold, dry, hard outlines which history delineates. Edward, on the contrary, loved to fill up and round the sketch with the colouring of a warm and vivid imagination, which gives light and life to the actors and speakers in the drama of past ages. Yet with tastes so opposite, they contributed greatly to each other's amusement.
>
> (Scott, *Waverley* 57)

From the start, the two are representatives of the two poles of fact and fiction which come together in the historical novel, and the wedding of Rose and Waverley towards the end of novel nicely captures this link. Waverley and Bradwardine are the ideal combination of authors to produce historical novels, and the union between the Bradwardines and the Waverleys serves as an emblem of the successful composition of historical fiction.

Still, Waverley figures in the creation of a Scottish national identity when, as an Englishman, he does not share any of the needs and concerns of either the Highlands or the Lowlands. This is where Scott's keen antiquarian interest in family trees becomes relevant. As he writes in his autobiographical fragment: "Every Scottishman has a pedigree. It is a national prerogative as inalienable as his pride and his poverty" (qtd. in Scott, *The Complete Poetical Works of Sir Walter Scott* IX). Scott adored family trees, and this fascination is nowhere more in evidence than at Abbotsford, Scott's mock-medieval dream home in the countryside of the Scottish borders. The entrance is stuffed with all manner of antiques from medieval swords and instruments of torture right up to Highland collectables of the eighteenth century. But the visitor's gaze is soon drawn towards the ceiling and its impressive array of family crests. Scott's own crest is prominently displayed above the door to his study and the arrangement suggests that all the other crests are somehow closely related to Scott's family. If you are a visitor to

Abbotsford, your guide will be quick to fill you in on the backgrounds to the many eminent Lowland families, but when asked about the sheer abundance of families, he will also happily concede that many of the crests quite simply do not have a family behind them. Scott put so much store by family trees and crests that he simply made them up. His creative handling of genealogies puts the above quotation in perspective: The fact that every Scotsman has a pedigree does not necessarily mean that that pedigree is going to be Scottish. More often than not, its Scottishness will have been a fabrication. The question is: How can this idiosyncratic handling of history be conducive to the strengthening of a national identity?

Private ties are an important step on the way towards a Scottish nation, and the Scottish part of the pedigrees does not have to be particularly long, old or noble, as long as it is recognizably Scottish. Bradwardine and his peers look with pride upon their lineages, but claims to their antiquity are repeatedly put in doubt. When the baron ceremonially pulls off Prince Charles Edward's boots, this immediately gives rise to thoughts about a new family crest. Even though the ceremony is the object of general mockery, Waverley sides with Bradwardine:

> Were it not for the recollection of Fergus's raillery, thought Waverley to himself [...] how very tolerable would all this sound [...] and truly I do not see why the Baron's boot-jack may not stand as fair in heraldry as the water-buckets, waggons, cart-wheels, plough-socks, shuttles, candlesticks, and other ordinaries, conveying ideas of any thing save chivalry, which appear in the arms of some of our most ancient gentry.
>
> (Scott, *Waverley* 240)

Not only does Waverley see the baron's point, but he suggests that other crests are likewise the product of a royal whim. Pedigrees, like crests, are thus not mirrors of historical facts, but are changeable constructs. As long as the Scottish component is dominant, even the newly begun line of Waverley and Rose can contribute to a Scottish identity.

Still, Scott insists on the importance of pedigrees even though he is well aware of the malleability of their historical value. Committed both to Scottishness and to the Union with England, Scott had to come up with a form of identity for Scotland which would be flexible enough to accommodate the interests of the Highlands, of the Lowlands and of England. The idea of the genealogical tree offers precisely this form of flexibility. Intermarriage across national borders makes these borders more permeable and serves to create a sense of belonging. The form of national identity which results is strikingly productive: while it can adapt to changes in the historical situation, it still remains recognizably Scottish. In *Waverley*, after all, being Scottish means little more that living in Scotland and being able to cope with the constant adjustments of identity. This form of identity is borne by a strong sense of community and by the many gestures of inclusion and exclusion which a community requires.

Community building is the energy which centrally informs the most striking feature of Scottish identity: hospitality. Waverley witnesses this hospitality both at Bradwardine's house and in the Highlands where Fergus's power as Chieftain is closely linked to his generosity as a host. Celebrations are therefore staged as huge mass-gatherings where everyone is invited, from the highest-ranking members of the clan right down to strangers like Waverley:

> Mac-Ivor, indeed, apologised for the confusion occasioned by so large a party, and pleaded the necessity of the situation, on which unlimited hospitality was imposed as a paramount duty. These stout kinsmen of mine, he said, account my estate as held in trust for their support; and I must find them beef and ale, while the rogues will do nothing for themselves but practice the broad-sword, or wander about the hills, shooting, fishing, hunting, drinking, and making love to the lasses of the strath. But what can I do, Captain Waverley? every thing will keep after its own kind, whether it be hawk or Highlander.
> (Scott, *Waverley* 97)

Collective eating is a sign of belonging and Waverley's accepting of Fergus's invitation is the first step towards his being adopted by the clan. Accepting an invitation requires tolerance of the host, but it does not entail a dismissal of one's own identity. Hospitality is therefore another instance of the flexibility of Scottish identity. The resulting sense of community is given its apotheosis in the novel in a painting which shows both Fergus and Waverley wearing the tartan of the clan. Displayed in Bradwardine's home, this image of Waverley as a son of a Highland clan ends up as an ornament to the home of a Lowland Scot whose daughter married the Englishman Waverley. A person's origin is hence no longer a reliable sign of her or his nationality.

The flexibility I have explained is also at the heart of Scott's choice of genre. Unlike James Macpherson, who tried to create a Scottish genealogy by writing his Ossianic epic in the style of Homer and Vergil, Scott develops the historical novel. Scott's novels have often been regarded as a nostalgic lament for a long-lost romantic Scotland. This nostalgia, which placed Scotland's glory in a distant past, has been ascribed to Scott's unionist stance which in turn has been felt to be the cause of the failure of Scottish identity. But keeping Scott's handling of lineage in mind, one can see that his historical novels are in fact conducive to his notion of identity. In his preface to *Waverley*, Scott is careful to stress the relevance in the present of the historical past he is describing. The narrator never tires of insisting that behaviour 'Sixty Years Since' is in no way different from behaviour in the present or, indeed, in the future. The morality of the past therefore does not lose its validity in the present. Scott's decision to date the origin of his idealized genealogy of the Scottish nation not back to some distant past of old clans and venerable warriors, but to the relatively recent past of the Union, is further proof of the adaptability of this genealogy. Like the family trees of his characters, he keeps the genealogy of Scotland short and therefore open to change.

Scott's historical novels portray the Scottish nation as intricate, flexible and irreducibly open. Scotland's transgressive identity meets every form of alterity with an offer of communication, the only precondition being that Scottishness, howsoever peculiar it may appear, be respected as a valid national identity. This may lead one to think that Scott would be a prominent point of reference for Scottishness in today's world of European integration and globalization which calls for flexibility and adaptability, as Caroline McCracken-Flesher shows (*Possible Scotlands* 10). After all, the national identity which Scott envisages strives for an unbiased individual encounter with the other and for the harmonious and civilized creation of common ground. Still, Scott's achievement is far from universally acknowledged. One reason for this might be the basic design of his historical fiction which proclaims that it is more than mere imaginative writing. In his successful antiquarian blend of fact and fiction he andvances his reading of history which appears almost as authoritative as the historiographic reports of his day. A contemporary of Scott's coined the ironic term 'Scott-Land' which still describes the extent to which Scott's writing influences and, indeed, determines the way in which Scotland is seen today (see Kelly, *Scott-land*) – the extent to which Scott has 'invented' Scotland.

Works Cited

Devine, T.M. *The Scottish Nation: 1700-2000.* London: Penguin, 2000.

Gottlieb, Evan. *Walter Scott and Contemporary Theory.* London: Bloomsbury, 2013.

Groot, Jerome de. *The Historical Novel.* Abingdon: Routledge, 2010.

Harmsen, Theodor. *Antiquarianism in the Augustan Age: Thomas Hearne 1678-1735.* Oxford: Peter Lang, 2000.

Kelly, Stuart. *Scott-land: The Man Who Invented a Nation.* Edinburgh: Polygon, 2010.

Kerr, James. *Fiction Against History: Scott as Storyteller.* Cambridge: Cambridge University Press, 1989.

Lagan, Celeste. "'The Poetry of Pure Memory': Teaching Scott's Novels in the Context of Romanticism." *Approaches to Teaching Scott's Waverley Novels.* Eds. Evan Gottlieb and Ian Duncan. New York: Modern Language Association of America, 2009. 67-76.

Lukács, Georg. *Der historische Roman.* Neuwied: Luchterhand, 1965.

Manning, Susan. 'Walter Scott (1771-1832): The Historical Novel.' *The Cambridge Companion to European Novelists.* Ed. Michael Bell. Cambridge: Cambridge University Press, 2012. 140-158.

Mayhead, Robin. *Walter Scott.* Cambridge: Cambridge University Press, 1973.

McCracken-Flesher, Caroline. *Possible Scotlands: Walter Scott and the Story of Tomorrow.* Oxford: Oxford University Press, 2005.

McCracken-Flesher, Caroline. 'Scott's Jacobitical Plots.' *The Edinburgh Companion to Sir Walter Scott.* Ed. Fiona Robertson. Edinburgh: Edinburgh University Press, 2012. 47-58.

Scott, Walter. *Waverley; or, 'Tis Sixty Years Since.* Ed. Claire Lamont. Oxford: Oxford University Press, 1998.

Pittock, Murray G.H. 'Scott as a Historiographer: The Case of Waverley.' *Scott in Carnival: Selected Papers from the Fourth International Scott Conference, Edinburgh, 1991.* Eds. John H. Alexander and David Hewitt. Glasgow: Association for Scottish Literary Studies, 1993. 145-53.

Scott, Walter. *The Complete Poetical Works of Sir Walter Scott.* Ed. Charles Eliot Norton. Amsterdam: Fredonia Books, 2004.

Stagl, Justus. 'Homo Collector: Zur Anthropologie und Soziologie des Sammelns.' *Sammler – Bibliophile – Exzentriker.* Eds. Aleida Assmann, Monika Gomille and Gabriele Rippl. Tübingen: Narr Francke, 1998. 37-54.

CLAUDIA OLK

Neo-Victorian Novels: Staging Historicity in John Fowles's *The French Lieutenant's Woman*

> What are we faced with in the nineteenth century? An age where woman was sacred; and where you could buy a thirteen-year-old girl for a few pounds […] Where more churches were built than in the whole previous history of the country; and where one in sixty houses in London was a brothel (the modern ratio would be nearer one in six thousand). […] Where the penal system was progressively humanized; and flagellation so rife that a Frenchman set out quite seriously to prove that the Marquis de Sade must have had English ancestry. Where there was an enormous progress and liberation in every other field of human activity; and nothing but tyranny in the most personal and fundamental.
>
> (Fowles, *The French Lieutenant's Woman*[1] 258-259)

The narrator in John Fowles's novel *The French Lieutenant's Woman*, published in 1969, lists a number of formative ambivalences that are commonly associated with the Victorian Age in England. The text expounds the problem of interpreting the 19th century solely as a history of progress and, instead, focuses on double standards, hypocrisy and differences between the public and the private spheres as general characteristics of the era.

These contradictions show how the narrative construction of Victorianism from a 20th century viewpoint and the deconstruction of a harmonizing perspective on the 19th century overlap and mark this inherently twofold angle of observation as a characteristic of the historical novel. As historical novels are both part of the time they are set in and the time at which they are written, they challenge established historical demarcations. Even though Fowles's novel has been criticised by authors like A.S. Byatt as a "diminishing parody"[2] of the 19th century, it may still be recognized as an example of the 20th and 21st century's continued fascination with Victorianism and hence as one of the first Neo-Victorian novels.

The most recent decades in particular mark a revival of Neo-Victorian culture in the media and beyond – a tendency that has even been declared a "post Victorian cultural turn" (Kohlke, 'Introduction: Speculations in and on the Neo-Victorian Encounter' 3) by a number of scholars. In this context, Victorianism does not appear as a constant of cultural history but rather as both the producer and the product of transformational

---

[1] Henceforth "*The French Lieutenant's Woman*" is abbreviated as FLW.

[2] A.S. Byatt states that her own novel *Possession* is, among other things, an attempt "to rescue the complicated Victorian thinkers from modern diminishing parodies like those of Fowles" (Byatt, *Possession: A Reader's Guide* 47).

processes that generally cast doubt on a homogenizing perspective on the 19th century. "The history of the Victorian Age will never be written. We know too much about it", Lytton Strachey had observed in the foreword to his modernistic portrait of the Victorians in *Eminent Victorians* (1918). Nevertheless, attempts to capture Victorianism as a well-known, yet highly heterogeneous culture of reference and to re-write its history pervade 20th and 21st century historiography and literature. In this respect, Neo-Victorian prose fiction is often regarded as closely affiliated with historiography. However, Neo-Victorian novels do not primarily introduce an alternative historiography but they rather explore the extent to which historical narratives define the relation between past and present.

Informed by poststructuralist theory and 'New Historicism', the 21st century's perspective on Victorianism habitually focuses on contradictions, non-linearity and the notion of non-simultaneity. Victorian thinkers and critics, however, were no strangers to the idea of living in a time of transformation, contradiction and far-reaching change. The experience of one's own historicity and the awareness of historical conditionality are characteristic of historical scholarship in the process of its establishment in the 19th century. Not only is Matthew Arnold's sonnet "On Dover Beach" conventionally read as an expression of uncertainty towards the end of the 19th century, but indeed many of the century's formative social, industrial, philosophical and natural scientific developments account for a definition of "The Victorian Age" as an epoch of continuous flux. "We are living in a period of most wonderful transition", Prince Albert stated in his much-quoted "Mansion House Speech" of 1850 given in preparation of the 1851 London World's Fair exhibition. Indeed, few other eras saw comparably greater societal, economic, political and intellectual change than 19th century England. To what extent this change was perceived as a "wonderful transition" by individuals, however, certainly much depends on the historical perspective.

When the eponym of the era, Queen Victoria, ascended the throne in 1837 at 18 years of age, the development of the British railway system ended the age of the stagecoach, and when she died in 1901 after 64 years of regency, the age of the automobile was already in full swing (Sussmann, *Victorian Technology: Invention, Innovation and the Rise of the Machine* 134-135). At the end of her reign, Victoria was Empress of India and governed over a world empire in which the number of her English subjects alone had doubled, and where England's infrastructure had irreversibly changed: London had become the largest city in the world with a population of almost five million people (London County Council, *Census of London 1901* 7).

Current examinations of the 19th century, which encompass processes of adoption, identification and assimilation, and not least of all rejection, range from parody to imitation and describe the dynamics of cultural production as well as an increase of historiographical concepts. At the same time, they include reflections upon narrative techniques of staging the past, which centre on the novel and its specific narrative strategies. According to Mark Llewellyn, 'Neo-Victorian Studies' are opposed to an a-historic aestheticizing and aim towards the discovery of new approaches to the Victorian Age: "[Neo-Victorian is about] new approaches to the Victorian period rather than an attempt to indulge in escapism marked as historical narrative" (Llewellyn, 'What is Neo-Victorian Studies?' 169).

From the perspective of cultural history, the contemporary image of "the Victorians", however, is not only influenced by Neo-Victorian novels but also by omnipresent references to the Victorians in popular culture. Period productions, for instance, like the BBC's series of Elisabeth Gaskell's novel *Cranford* (2007) enjoy great popularity as they present literary works in a positivist way in which 'historical' costumes and settings offer a "re-enactment" that stages the past as the past.[3]

Among the great number of Neo-Victorian films of the last decade, it shall suffice to mention just a few re-adaptations of Victorian texts: *Dorian Gray* (Oliver Parker, 2009), *Sherlock Holmes* (Guy Ritchie 2009, 2012) and *Wuthering Heights* (Andrea Arnold 2010). Neo-Victorian novels, too, have speedily been adapted as screenplays for film and TV productions: *Possession* (2002), *The French Lieutenant's Woman* (1981), or the Neo-Victorian novels by Sarah Waters: *Tipping the Velvet* (BBC, 2002), *Fingersmith* (BBC, 2005) und *Affinity* (ITV, 2008).

Just as remarkable as literary adaptations are films like *The Young Victoria* (2009). It draws on elements of the monarch's biography and offers its viewers insights into the young queen's secret private life, which mainly deal with conflicts between her public responsibility and her female and private sphere of family, love and marriage. As a kind of cinematic *Bildungsroman*, *The Young Victoria* operates on the threshold between historical evidence and fictionalized romance that is not limited to the queen's life but extends across the whole era. Despite its nostalgia, *The Young Victoria* does not only reflect upon the role of women in public but, like Stephen Frear's film *The Queen* (2006), addresses problems of an increased interest in public figures and the very definition of the term public itself, which changed significantly with respect to the establishment of the news media in the 19th century.

The exact reasons for this widespread fascination with the 19th century are difficult to determine. One important factor would be the contemporary stance towards Victorianism, which is marked by both historical proximity and distance. Despite all the differences in mentality and lifestyle, the 20th and the 21st century are still familiar with Victorianism for example through its presence in architecture. In his survey of Neo-Victorian tendencies of adaptation, Mark Llewellyn observes a simultaneously forward- and backward-looking reception: "It does mean opening up aspects of our present to a relationship with the Victorian past in ways that offer new possibilities for simultaneously thinking through where we come from" (Llewellyn, 'What is Neo-Victorian Studies?' 171). Uncompromised by the anxiety of interference, apparent in Modernist views on Victorianism, some critics hold that the late 20th and the early 21st century seem particularly apt to reflect upon continuities and discontinuities without treating the Victorians as mere precursors of modernity.[4]

Nonetheless, many adaptations and rewritings are affected by a romanticized nostalgia that serves to endorse national identity by using stereotypical views of 'Britishness',

---

[3]   See also BBC productions of: *Daniel Deronda* (2002), *North and South* (2004), *Bleak House* (2005), *Jane Eyre* (2006), *Oliver Twist* (2007), *Tess of the D'Urbervilles* (2008) und *Little Dorrit* (2008).

[4]   Such a teleological interpretation can for instance be found in Sweet, *Inventing the Victorians*.

'Merry old England' or a golden age that are continued in popular public-oriented forms of self-staging,[5] as for example in the wake of the 2012 Olympic Games.

Since the 1960s, a significant orientation towards the Victorian era has become discernable both in novels and literary biographies (Robinson, *Narrating the Past* x). Novels like Jean Rhys's *Wide Sargasso Sea* (1966), John Fowles's *The French Lieutenant's Woman* (1969), A.S. Byatt's *Possession* (1990), Graham Swift's *Ever After* (1992), Julian Barnes's *Arthur and George* (2005), but also Peter Carey's *Oscar and Lucinda* (1988) or Margaret Atwood's *Alias Grace* (1996) are considered classics within an expanding canon of Neo-Victorian literature.

But what exactly is a Neo-Victorian novel? Is it potentially every text that was written after 1901, that is set in the Victorian era and that deals either with real Victorians or with characters taken from Victorian texts? In contrast to broad definitions of the genre "as contemporary fiction that engages with the Victorian era, at either the level of plot, structure or both" (Hadley, *Neo-Victorian Fiction* 4), Dana Shiller identifies two main strategies that are conceived as typical of Neo-Victorian narratives:

> [1] Some of these texts imitate Victorian literary conventions, either by creating altogether new stories or by reimagining specific Victorian novels from a new angle [...] [2] while others are more overtly 'postmodern' in style and tone, but concern themselves with Victorian subjects.
>
> (Shiller, *Neo-Victorian Fiction* 1)

Both strategies, however, are not mutually exclusive, so that Neo-Victorian novels describe ways of both narrating the past and of redefining the line between historiography and fiction. Consequently, the Neo-Victorian novel has become a distinct sub-genre within the historical novel, which has already produced a number of sub-genres – the neo-realistic novel, the neo-romantic novel and the neo-Gothic novel – and continues to work with forms and genres like science fiction and children's literature.[6]

Hence, the influence of Victorianism becomes apparent even in works that are not set in the Victorian era, but do imitate the conventions of the Victorian novel as defined by Shiller. This can be illustrated in looking at what has become the Harry Potter industry. J.K. Rowling's novels draw on biographical *topoi* of 19th century narrative prose that are paradigmatic in the novels of Charles Dickens or the Brontës. Similar to Harry's literary ancestors such as Oliver Twist, David Copperfield and Jane Eyre they tell the story of the hard-pressed orphan who stands up to challenges of all kinds in order to eventually find happiness.

In contemporary novels like these, elements from the 19th century are collected, revised and reconfigured. Linda Hutcheon, who coined the term "historiographic metafiction", identifies yet another analogy to the Victorians:

[5]   Louisa Hadley analyzes the ideological way in which Victorian concepts of value were being instrumentalized in the politics of Margaret Thatcher (*Neo-Victorian Fiction and Historical Narrative* 10ff.).

[6]   In opposition to the term 'Post-Victorian', which is preferred by Andrea Kirchknopf et al., the term 'Neo-Victorian' is now well-established (Kirchknopf, 'Re-Workings of Nineteenth-Century Fiction' 68).

> The Victorians had a habit of adapting just about everything – and in just about every possible direction; the stories of poems, novels, plays, operas, paintings, songs, dances, and tableaux vivants were consistently being adapted from one medium to another and then back again. We postmoderns have clearly inherited this same habit, but we have even more new critical materials at our disposal – not only film, television, radio, and the various electronic media, of course, but also theme parks, historical enactments, and virtual reality experiments.
>
> (Hutcheon, *A Theory of Adaptation* xi)

According to Hutcheon, Neo-Victorianism designs the 19th century as an "old curiosity shop" or a kind of "Great Exhibition" of everyday life, in which the Victorians are resurrected and put on display along with the miraculous and grotesque features of their time. Postmodernism here is considered the heir of this tradition that is constantly updated by the extended opportunities offered by new media.

Christian Gutleben holds a similar view. In his *Nostalgic Postmodernism*, he proclaims that in contemporary novels, the narrative process as such has come to an end. In his interpretation, a post-romantic vision of Victorianism appears as an aporia of nostalgic postmodernism. Instead of focusing on the development of narration, this vision is rather regressive since it marks a return to a pre-modern period. The postmodern reshaping of the 19th century on the whole produces a number of paradoxes. Nonetheless, a theory of adaption that conceives of the Neo-Victorian novel exclusively as a kind of musealization or as a nostalgic reminiscence would appear reductive.

What is new about the adaptive practice of Neo-Victorianism, however, is the theoretical analysis of its adaptive processes themselves in which the texts approach cultural history and reflect their own strategies. Neo-Victorian novels are not only documents or memories of the Victorians, but, as a genre, they reconstruct and present different Victorianisms in relation to current theoretical paradigms and interests. Thus, contemporary Neo-Victorian literature does not understand itself as a substitute for the 19th century or as its mere effigy, but recognizes its function as a negotiator that makes the negotiation part of the presentation.

Neo-Victorian narratives are the result of processes of reflexion and transformation that emerge from the interpretation of the Victorian era and its literary production. They maintain a productive dialogue with the Victorian past, reflect upon changes in the contemporary perception of the 19th century and present heterogeneous meanings of Victorianism in and for the present. They are led by a revisionist agenda concerning any conservative understandings of history that are primarily based on documentary practice.

Neo-Victorian narratives are both fictional texts that are deliberately set in the Victorian era as well as narratives that strive to revise a conception of history that would be generally considered as conventional. In A.S. Byatt's *Possession*, for example, this is done by focusing on obscured layers of textual tradition, on unknown biographical links and undiscovered source material. In a similar vein, Sarah Waters's Neo-Victorian novels are narrated from the perspective of marginalized characters, for example when in *Affinity* (1999), *Tipping the Velvet* (1998) or *Fingersmith* (2002) lesbian women appear that were relegated if not entirely excluded from novels published in the 19th century.

In their anthology of Neo-Victorianism, Llewellyn and Heilmann summarize a number of prototypical thematic elements of Neo-Victorian novels:

> Loss, mourning, and regeneration are prototypical preoccupations of the neo-Victorian novel, which often revolves around the re(dis)covery of a personal and/or collective history and the restitution of a family inheritance through the reconstruction of fragmented, fabricated, or repressed memories: a retracing and piecing together of the protagonist's roots which reflects, metafictionally, on the literary 'origins' of the neo-Victorian genre and the narratological traditions it seeks to reshape.
>
> (Heilmann and Llewellyn, *Neo-Victorianism* 34)

Establishing a productive relation to its culture of reference, Neo-Victorian novels thematize the textual and largely hidden relationship between the past and the present by examining lost sources and original texts or by drawing attention to biographical subjects such as identity and familial origin. Questions concerned with the status of 19th century sources, their authenticity and value, are, for example in *Possession,* linked to inquiries into the narrative-discursive identity of the characters, so that the text and the character alternately reflect on their being as text.

The interplay between different dimensions of time as well as their reciprocal pervasion in the Neo-Victorian novel allows itself to stage a form of history and historiography that is always aware of its narrative-textual presentation and that is not prone to a reduction or dissolution of alterity. Neo-Victorian texts therefore play with the reader's need for history, story and plot and the simultaneous need to avoid it. They present integrated, 'round characters' as well as omniscient, heterodiegetic narrators and, at the same time, offer varied performances of subjectivity and fictional genealogy. Narrative unity, order and chronology are evoked only to be undermined by a diversity of voices, the possibility of multiple endings and storylines. Such a work that uses the Victorian era as a culture of reference to evoke conflicting notions of historicity and cast these into a narrative that reflects on its own creative processes is John Fowles's *The French Lieutenant's Woman* (1969) to which I will now turn.

In his earlier works *The Collector* (1963) and *The Magus* (1965), John Fowles (1926-2005) had already experimented with narrative forms. His third novel *The French Lieutenant's Woman* (1969) is a metafictional work that defines its metafiction primarily through its multiple endings and the use of a 20th-century narrator who tells the reader about events in and around the year 1867. Fowles, to be sure, did not invent the strategy of retrospective narration. It had been used by the Victorians themselves, for example by George Eliot in *Middlemarch*, which is set in 1830 but is narrated in 1867. In *The French Lieutenant's Woman*, however, we are dealing with a narrator who, as opposed to the one in *Middlemarch,* openly claims the authorship of his characters and often steps into the narrative. Fowles himself has compared *The French Lieutenant's Woman* to a science fiction novel by suggesting that the attempt to imagine how the Victorians might have lived is similar to picturing life on a different planet. Only that he is looking at the past rather than anticipating the future (Stephenson, *The French Lieutenant's Woman* 12).

The French Lieutenant's Woman is both a historical and an experimental novel. It connects two centuries including their respective concepts of the novel: a teleological-chronological form, chiefly associated with the 19th century, and an anti-essentialist postmodern pluralization of forms. On the basis of this binary constellation, *The French Lieutenant's Woman* examines opposing relations such as the ones between men and women, author and characters and between narrator and reader in order to demonstrate their complex interactions. In doing so, *The French Lieutenant's Woman* is both Victorian and contemporary. It is Victorian because of its rehearsal of subject matters like gender roles, Darwinism, religion and double standards as well as the contrast between urban and rural regions. It is contemporary because of its programmatic use of 20th-century strategies of reflecting, psychologizing and framing these issues.

Primarily, however, *The French Lieutenant's Woman* is a novel that reflects upon its own historicity. This is performed by means of its dual impetus of historicizing fiction and of fictionalizing history. The staging of historicity first of all relies on the novel's temporal setting and its locations. The story is set in 1867, a year that saw John Stuart Mill's demand for female suffrage as well as the publication of Karl Marx's first volume of *Das Kapital* and that represents a focal point of social and historical developments in the 19th century. Fowles additionally historicizes the story through epigraphs and intertextual insertions drawn from historical documents, newspaper articles and literary texts from the 19th century. Preceding his chapters, these quotations are taken from works by Charles Darwin, Karl Marx, Alfred Lord Tennyson or Matthew Arnold, but they are also drawn from Victorian treatises on the poverty of London's urban population, on the situation of women or on the state of education. They mark a form of authorial control over the novel in which the boundaries between fiction and history become paradigmatically penetrable.

Intertextual framing, narrative interjections and footnotes are on occasion presented as direct interpretation aids as for instance: "The stanzas from *In Memoriam* I have quoted at the beginning of this chapter are very relevant here" (Fowles, *FLW* 35). These let the text appear as a quasi-scientific examination, or they ironically comment on the plot when the narrator uses a motto from G.M. Young's *Portrait of an Age* to characterize the protagonist Charles: "Of all decades in our history, a wise man would choose the eighteen-fifties to be young in" (G.M. Young, *Portrait of an Age*) (Fowles, *FLW* 17). These strategies of historicizing fiction show that temporality in *The French Lieutenant's Woman* is neither static nor clearly to be determined, but that it is continuously reinvented, changed and differentiated through the interaction of texts.

At this point, a brief look at the novel's plot seems useful: Charles Smithson, well-to-do bachelor and ardent hobby-palaeontologist, spends a few days with his fiancée Ernestina Freeman in the Southern English coastal town of Lyme Regis. Early on in the novel during a walk, the couple sees a female character standing at the end of a long landing stage – called the Cobb – looking out to the sea. Ernestina informs Charles that the woman is called Sarah Woodruff, an enigmatic governess, who lives the socially stigmatized life of an outsider because of an alleged love affair with a French lieutenant who eventually left her. For her it has become a habit to seek the loneliness of the Cobb to express her melancholy. Despite being engaged to Ernestina and the prospects of promotion that await him at the Freemans' family business after the marriage, Charles is fascinated by Sarah. The two meet twice more or less at random in a jungle-like alternative world to the small town, called the "undercliff", where they spend a moment of passion together that the narrator times at "precisely ninety seconds". In the wake of a momentary and existential insight, Charles sees himself destined to marry Sarah instead of Ernestina and breaks his engagement, unable to avoid the subsequent humiliation. Adding to his misery and aggravation, Sarah disappears and in looking for her Charles travels through Europe and the USA for two years, where he eventually receives a telegram stating that Sarah was found. Sarah is now both an assistant and a model among the group of Pre-Raphaelites around Dante Gabriel Rossetti, and the novel offers two alternative endings to the story after their reunion: either Charles finds happiness with Sarah and their child or he finds out that they have to remain separate for the rest of their lives.

The novel's setting is already richly embedded in literary history. *The French Lieutenant's Woman* is set in Lyme Regis, Dorset – an area on the Southern English coast that is associated with Thomas Hardy's novels *Tess of the D'Urbervilles* and *Jude the Obscure*. *The French Lieutenant's Woman* makes this association explicit in a couple of instances, for example when it is mentioned that the historical Hardy, "great novelist who towers over this part of England" (Fowles, *FLW* 262), fell in love with his cousin in 1867 or when parallels are drawn between Hardy's protagonist Tess Durbeyville and Sarah Woodruff. Jane Austen's novel *Persuasion* (1818), also partly set in Lyme Regis, is explicitly referred to when Ernestina remembers one of its key scenes on one of her walks:

> And look. She led him to the side of the rampart, where a line of flat stones inserted sideways into the wall served as rough steps down to a lower walk. These are the very steps that Jane Austen made Louisa Musgrove fall down in *Persuasion*.
>
> (Fowles, *FLW* 14)

The landing stage is not only a significant location in *Persuasion* but it also introduces Austen's love triangle between Captain Wentworth, Anne and Louisa Musgrove, that serves as an intertextual frame of reference to *The French Lieutenant's Woman*. While Austen's physically fallen woman becomes a metaphorical character in Fowles's novel, his melancholic protagonist Sarah Woodruff finds her counterpart in Austen's hopelessly enamoured Anne Musgrove: "All the privilege I claim for my sex … is that of loving longest, when existence or when hope is gone" (Austen, *Persuasion* 145).

The 'thick description' of intertextual strata, which is recurrent both structurally and thematically, points to another local geological feature of Lyme Regis: its fossils that do not only form the shore's rock composition – the "blue lias" – but that become an important part of the novel's overall metonymical conception. A fossil preserves an instant that is fixed in time, it presents the confinement within a historical moment that is itself part of history. As such it becomes witness to an evolutionary stage of life that is either continued or that marks the end of its kind. As a relict that becomes the exhibit of its own evanescence in a kind of performative self-contradiction, it presents the paradoxical interchange of duration and momentariness, the beginning and the end of history.

The French Lieutenant's Woman is not only full of fossils in this respect. Fossils can be found at many of its places – on church floors, on the landing stage, on the beach and in Charles's room, who, as an amateur palaeontologist, finds his personal Mecca for his scientific endeavours in Lyme Regis. But also some of the characters appear fossilized, as for example the hypocritical Mrs. Poulteney who offers Sarah a position in her household, following the priest's advice rather than acting upon altruistic motives. The Bible-believing Mrs. Poulteney appears as a persistent residuum of an obsolete orthodoxy that she shrewdly knows to instrumentalize for her own purposes in her household. [7]

Fossilized habits and traditionalist attitudes towards questions of gender roles and marriage, in which the past determines historical and social conventions, are characteristic of Ernestina's family and instil in Charles the feeling of being inescapably trapped in them. He calls himself a "living fossil" – a stranded ammonite, "a potential turned to a fossil" (Fowles, *FLW* 321).[8] Ironically enough, it is a fossil, an echinoderm, also known as 'Sanddollar' that becomes the tragic talisman of Charles's and Ernestina's relationship after Charles brings it home as a kind of trophy from one of his expeditions.

The fossil, the objectified outcome from a continuum of time and space is characteristic of a strategy of historicizing fiction in *The French Lieutenant's Woman*: the method of metonymical reduction that makes historical understanding possible. The novel presents significant, objective details that allow the reader to imagine the possible worlds in which the characters move. Any holistic perspective, or an all-encompassing form of understanding is made impossible because it remains tied to the simultaneity of temporal difference.

Moreover, the geological analogy that reflects the novel's staging of history offers a simultaneous and synoptic view of a 'grand récit', in this case the geological master narrative and some of its stages. Fossilized history becomes the emblem for an integration of contrasts. It corresponds to a staging of historicity in the novel that changes between the singular moment as a significant retreat from a temporal continuum and a process-oriented model of temporality. The former happens when Charles euphorically believes to be displaced from a sensualist Here and Now in what comes close to an epiphanic moment: "The world would always be this, and this moment" (Fowles, *FLW* 43), or when he less euphorically realises his fossil-like existence in the inevitability of the Here and Now:

> he saw that all life was parallel: that evolution was not vertical, ascending to a perfection, but horizontal. Time was the great fallacy; existence was without history, was always now, was always this being caught in the same fiendish machine.
>
> (Fowles, *FLW* 200)

---

[7] 19th-century developments, especially in the realms of biology and geology, rejected a literal interpretation of the biblical history of creation and promoted sceptical approaches of critical historical scholarship. In his *Principles of Geology* (1830-1833), Charles Lyell provided evidence that the earth's age far exceeds the space of time that was estimated by calculations based on biographies, reigns of kings and genealogies from the Bible. Robert Chambers developed the thesis of human evolution in his *Vestiges of the natural history of creation* (1844), and Alfred Lord Tennyson, too, discussed the issue of the literal interpretation of biblical material in In Memoriam, the elegy for his old friend Arthur Hallam.

[8] "There was no doubt. He was one of life's victims, one more ammonite caught in the vast movements of history, stranded now for eternity, a potential turned to a fossil" (Fowles, *FLW* 321).

The interplay of different levels and processes of time unfolds both in the dynamics of the narrative structures and in the reflexion of different forms of experiencing time. *The French Lieutenant's Woman* delineates the process of developing an individual sense of time from the 19th until the 20th century in an anti-evolutionary logic because the change described did not necessarily lead to an improvement of people's quality of life.

> Though Charles liked to think of himself as a scientific young man and would probably not have been too surprised had news reached him out of the future of the aeroplane, the jet engine, television, radar: what *would* have astounded him was the changed attitude to time itself. The supposed great misery of our century is the lack of time; our sense of that, *not* a disinterested love of science, and certainly not wisdom, is why we devote such a huge proportion of the ingenuity and income of our societies to finding faster ways of doing things – as if the final aim of mankind was to grow closer not to a perfect humanity, but to a perfect lightning-flash. But for Charles, and for almost all his contemporaries and social peers, the time-signature over existence was firmly *adagio*.
>
> (Fowles, *FLW* 17-18)[9]

The teleological goal – "the final aim of mankind" – like the explicit references to Darwinism mark evolution, determination, freedom and destiny as additional strategies of staging historicity in the novel (Jackson, 'Charles and the Hopeful Monster' 221). *The French Lieutenant's Woman* approaches evolution from a number of perspectives: here, the earth's evolution is closely tied to the evolution of society as well as to Charles's personal evolution, which is rendered as a kind of *Bildungsroman* depicting the change of a 19th-century gentleman to a 20th century existentialist.

Both Charles and the country doctor Grogan, who literally swears by *The Origin of Species*, are educated followers of Darwin's theory of evolution, but when Mr. Freemann, Ernestina's father, promotes the social-evolutionary principle of adapting to one's environment and suggests that in becoming a *homo oeconomicus* even gentlemen need to turn to the world of trade and economic progress (Fowles, *FLW* 227-229), Charles is repulsed: "he was a gentleman; and gentlemen cannot go into trade" (Fowles, *FLW* 277).

Charles is associated with evolution and considers himself determined by society and fate. As his father's sole descendant and as a gentleman, he belongs to a social stratum that faces extinction. At the end he is even forced by Ernestina's father to sign a document renouncing his right to be called a gentleman (Fowles, *FLW* 324), thus sealing his own extinction. Again, it is the fossil that becomes the correlate of his own state of mind: "Personal extinction Charles was aware of – no Victorian could not be. But general extinction was [...] absent a concept from his mind [...yet] he soon held a very concrete example of it in his hand" (Fowles, *FLW* 54).

Charles, however, is not only the victim of evolution or extinction but he also retains some agency. During a visit to his uncle's country estate, Charles accidentally shoots a rare bird of prey, the "immortal bustard", and while he is uncomfortable with the idea of having brought the bird a step closer to its extinction ("one of the last Great Bustards

---

[9]   "One of the commonest symptoms of wealth today is destructive neurosis; in his century it was tranquil boredom" (Fowles, *FLW* 18).

shot on Salisbury Plain" (Fowles, *FLW* 19)), his uncle has the bird stuffed and proudly displayed in a showcase in his study, following the stereotypical habit of the Victorian collector.

As the example illustrates, the fate of all exhibits of ephemerality in *The French Lieutenant's Woman* continues to be determined by chance. Instead of a predetermined, inevitable fate that needs to be fatalistically adhered to, the novel establishes the unknown, the contingent and chance as a narrative necessity.

In order to avoid teleological determinism the narrator, however, like the Darwinist, is confronted with the puzzle of integrating the idea of chance into evolution. The narrative principle thus follows an evolutionary approach: "What that genius had upset was the Linnaean Scala Naturae, the ladder of nature, whose great keystone, as essential to it as the divinity of Christ to theology, was *nulla species nova*: a new species cannot enter the world" (Fowles, *FLW* 53).

If the process of natural selection is not only supposed to be a covert model of predestination or of eternal recurrence of the same, it has to take into account chance, contingency and mutation without totally abandoning the idea of order. In his last epigraph, Fowles adds a version of this thought in reference to his contemporary Martin Gardiner:

> Evolution is simply the process by which change (the random mutations in the nucleic acid helix caused by natural radiation) co-operates with natural law to create living forms better and better adapted to survive.
>
> (Fowles, *FLW* 440)

Here, Fowles offers a self-description of the Neo-Victorian novel, which proves to be a flexible form that, on the one hand, follows traditional narrative principles and, on the other hand, extends these principles through including moments of the unknown. In *The French Lieutenant's Woman*, these are introduced when the novel presents moments of choice about the further continuation of the plot, both on a meta-fictional level and within the story itself.

The narrator involves the reader in these decisive moments, for example when he asks if he should not rather have let Sarah commit suicide at the end of chapter twelve. The twelfth chapter ends with a cliff-hanger: "Who is Sarah? Out of what shadows does she come?" (Fowles, *FLW* 96). This question is then readdressed at the beginning of the following chapter when the narrator answers:

> I do not know. This story I am telling is all imagination. These characters I create never existed outside my own mind. If I have pretended until now to know my characters' minds and innermost thoughts, it is because I am writing in […] a convention universally accepted at the time of my story: that the novelist stands next to God. […] I live in the age of Alain Robbe-Grillet and Roland Barthes.
>
> (Fowles, *FLW* 97)

The narrator combines a paradoxical interchange of two levels of time and links them to certain narrative conventions. In his programmatically postmodern, meta-fictional intervention, he stages himself as an imitation of 19th-century narrators and in mentioning "a convention universally accepted" refers to the beginning of *Pride and Prejudice*.[10] On the one hand, he pretends not to be a typically Victorian omniscient narrator and, on the other hand, he re-establishes himself as exactly such a godlike entity in describing his characters as products of his imagination. Consequently, he takes up both an extra-diegetic and an intradiegetic stance in some scenes, for example when he, as a narrative *alter ego*, assumes the role of the traveller who sits across from Charles on the train – "the prophet-bearded man" (Fowles, *FLW* 388) – or when he appears as the mysterious character who winds his watch back by a quarter of an hour at the end of the novel in order to present the second ending.[11]

The choice between two different ways and the associated metaphorical going astray characterizes the relationship between Charles and Sarah. After his paleontological expedition Charles finds himself in a situation completely unexpected. Because of the rising tide he cannot go back to Lyme via the beach but is forced to climb the cliff and make his way back through the jungle (the undercliff).[12] Instead of more fossils, however, he finds the sleeping Sarah who not only refers to the past in being presented as a Maria Magdalena-character, but also promises a possible future. As Sarah awakens, the narrator hypostasizes the situation by giving it a touch of general inevitability:

> Charles did not know it but in those brief poised seconds above the waiting sea, in that luminous evening silence broken only by the waves' quiet wash, the whole Victorian Age was lost. And I do not mean he had taken the wrong path.
>
> (Fowles, *FLW* 75)

The anticipated future and the consequently forsaken Victorian past are both unclear to Charles in this situation and he is unable to recognize the consequences of his most recent actions. According to the Victorian model, which the narrator follows, the future only grants two options. Either the protagonists will find each other at the end or they will not. A comparable revision of the novel's ending can be found in Charles Dickens's *Great Expectations*. Dickens, following Bulwer-Lytton's advice, changed the original ending of Pip's and Estella's parting to a more conventional happy ending. "But the conventions of Victorian fiction allow, allowed no place for the open, the inconclusive ending; and I preached earlier of the freedom characters must be given" (Fowles, *FLW* 389).

The narrator in *The French Lieutenant's Woman* manages to do both, following the conventions and allowing for openness and innovation by offering the reader two alternative endings and the opportunity to choose one.

The procedure of metonymical reduction and integration of alternatives, even the creation of a new species, are combined in the character of Sarah. Like other female characters of the Brontës' or of Jane Austen's, Sarah is a governess, an educated woman

---

[10] Austen, *Pride and Prejudice* 11: "It is a truth universally acknowledged, that a single man in possession of a good fortune must be in want of a wife."

[11] "And now let us jump twenty months" (Fowles, *FLW* 400).

[12] "But he could not return along the shore. His destination had indeed been this path, but he had meant to walk quickly to it, and then up the levels where the flint strate emerged" (Fowles, *FLW* 55).

with limited funds, who finds respectable employment. She virtually lives within the fictional worlds of novels by Walter Scott and Jane Austen, and her loneliness appears fateful to her: "As if it has been ordained that I shall never form a friendship with an equal, never inhabit my own home, never see the world except as the generality to which I must be the exception" (Fowles, *FLW* 167). On the one hand she is too educated to marry within her own class, on the other she is too poor to ascend to a higher class through marriage. "Where am I not ill placed" (Fowles, *FLW* 241), she asks Charles. The only way for her to rebel against the social reality that surrounds her is to cultivate her life as an outsider, to stage herself as a fictional character and to pretend to be someone she is not: the French Lieutenant's Woman.

Sarah, the melancholic "black figure" (Fowles, *FLW* 15), consequently appears as a 'black box', as the novel's female mystery created by the palimpsestic intertextual structure. She is not an independent subject but an artifice, a character who is solely described from an external perspective. As such she attracts the formation of legends, projections of gender discussions and essentialist attributions. In Sarah's character, the novel does not only describe its own creation of fictional stories but also its strategy by placing itself within a historical context while at the same time overcoming it.

As a consequence, Sarah can be read differently: as a lonely melancholic, criminal, victim, lover or cheat, while, on the other hand, her femininity is mythified through the references to the Pre-Raphaelites. Mrs. Poulteney anathemizes her, Dr. Grogan pathologizes her, and Charles, infatuatedly, notices that "there was a wildness about her […] a wildness of innocence" (Fowles, *FLW* 240).

In his essay "Notes on an Unfinished Novel", Fowles mentions that his novel developed out of a single image:

> A woman stands at the end of a deserted quay and stares out to sea. [...] The woman had no face, no particular degree of sexuality. But she was Victorian; and since I always saw her in the same static long shot, with her back turned, she represented a reproach on the Victorian Age. An outcast.
>
> (Fowles, 'Notes on an Unfinished Novel' 60-1)

The cinematic image of the averted, faceless woman who embodies the contradictions of the Victorian lets Sarah, the French Lieutenant's lover, appear as a work of art. She creates the novel's title and constitutes its central metonymy.

While Ernestina is compared to a realistic illustration ("Ernestina had exactly the right face for her age; that is, small-chinned, oval, delicate as a violet. You may see it still in the drawings of the great illustrators of the time" (Fowles, *FLW* 31)), Sarah has the features of a Pre-Raphaelite model: "full lips, dark eyebrows, dense and wavy hair, and, of course those astonishingly frank eyes".[13] Sarah describes herself as "fiction", as a work of art, that can never be fully understood – not even by herself – because to understand something completely would mean to lose freedom, to acknowledge that one is entirely designed and determined. Charles addresses this issue at the end of the novel:

---

[13]   This characterization is reminiscent of Pre-Raphaelite models like Elizabeth Siddal, Jane Morris, or Alexa Wilding.

"You refuse to entertain my proposal because I might bring you to understand yourself"
(Fowles, *FLW* 354).[14]

Sarah remains distanced, aloof and inscrutable. Her character presents the impossibility of an historical understanding, which would take place simultaneously with the course of events. Thus Sarah is unable to interpret her own situation, or to historicize herself and her origin philosophically, psychologically or biologically: "I am not to be understood even by myself" (Fowles, *FLW* 431), she states with the inability of a new species to understand itself and its novelty.[15] She remains dependent on her story being narrated, read and interpreted.

The on-going process of interpretation ties in with the inability to ever complete the text in reaching a final explanation. The novel's double ending may be viewed as an act of deferral, a refusal of closure that would give all previous action a definite meaning. Constructing the novel's ending as the ultimate goal would bring to a halt the element of freedom and newness in its play with meanings and their historical dimensions.

From this perspective, Fowles's novel itself appears as a relict – a fossil – of early Postmodernism that the author/narrator may not have anticipated.

The French Lieutenant's Woman exposes paleontology, evolution and determinism as strategies in which the historical novel reflects upon itself and stages its historicity. The author/narrator does not only appear as a kind of paleontologist himself who examines species from the past and creates layers of historical tradition in his intertextual relations. In this process, reading and interpreting are not merely understood as mere intake or *imitatio* but always as a performative-constructive act. Reading appears as a way of uncovering these layers of textualized history and of establishing connections between them and the story line. It is in the potentiality of these multifaceted and heterogeneous syntheses that the novel, the textual object lives on. It is not so much the static moment within an evolutionary schema but rather the continuum of material transformations, including the new and the unexplained, that perpetually claim imaginary realization and identify yet unredeemed possibilities of the historical novel.

Works Cited

Austen, Jane. *Persuasion & Northanger Abbey (Two Novels)*. New York: Mondial, 2008.
Austen, Jane. *Pride and Prejudice*. London: Collector's Library, 2003.
Bryatt, A.S. *Possession: A Reader's Guide*. New York: Continuum, 2002.
Fowles, John. 'Notes on an Unfinished Novel.' *Afterwords: Novelists on Their Novels*. Ed. Thomas McCormack. New York: Harper, 1969. 160-175.
Fowles, John. *The French Lieutenant's Woman*. London: Jonathan Cape, 1969.

[14] "Know thyself, Smithson, know thyself!" "I am not made for marriage. My misfortune is to have realized it too late" (Fowles, *FLW* 218); "I am an enigma to myself" (Fowles, *FLW* 220).
[15] Tony Jackson sees Sarah as a new species, "the hopeful monster" within an evolutionary scheme: "evolutionary theory helps us to see the nature of Sarah. She is a suddenly occurring new kind of self, and Charles is the means by which this self secures its survival" (227).

Golby, J. M., ed. *Culture and Society in Britain 1850-1890: A Source Book of Contemporary Writings*. Oxford: Oxford University Press, 1991.

Gutleben, Christian. *Nostalgic Postmodernism: The Victorian Tradition and the Contemporary Novel*. Amsterdam: Rodopi, 2001.

Hadley, Louisa. *Neo-Victorian Fiction and Historical Narrative. The Victorians and Us*. Houndmills, Basingstoke, New York: Palgrave Macmillan, 2010.

Heilmann, Ann and Mark Llewellyn. *Neo-Victorianism: The Victorians in the Twenty-First Century, 1990-2009*. Basingstoke, New York: Palgrave Macmillan, 2010.

Hutcheon, Linda. *A Theory of Adaptation*. New York: Routledge, 2006.

Jackson, Tony E. 'Charles and the Hopeful Monster: Postmodern Evolutionary Theory in *The French Lieutenant's Woman*.' *Twentieth Century Literature* 43 (1997): 221-242.

Kirchknopf, Andrea. '(Re-) Workings of Nineteenth-Century Fiction: Definitions, Terminology, Contexts.' *Neo-Victorian Studies* 1 (2008): 53-80.

Kohlke, Marie Luise. 'Introduction: Speculations in and on the Neo-Victorian Encounter.' *Neo-Victorian Studies* 1 (2008): 1-18.

Llewellyn, Mark. 'What is Neo-Victorian Studies?' *Neo-Victorian Studies* 1 (2008): 164-185.

London County Council. *Local Government and Statistical Dept. County of London. Census of London, 1901*. General Register Office: London County Council, 1903.

Robinson, Alan. *Narrating the Past: Historiography, Memory and the Contemporary Novel*. Houndmills, Basingstoke, New York: Palgrave Macmillan, 2011.

Sussmann, Herbert L. *Victorian Technology: Invention, Innovation, and the Rise of the Machine*. Santa Barbara: ABC-CLIO, 2009.

Shiller, Dana. *Neo-Victorian Fiction: Reinventing the Victorians*. Diss. University of Washington, 1995.

Stephenson, William. *Fowles' The French Lieutenant's Woman*. London: Continuum, 2007.

Strachey, Lytton. *Eminent Victorians*. Introduction by Michael Holroyd. London: Penguin, 1986 [1918].

UTE BERNS

Historiographic Metafiction and the History of Nature: John Fowles's *The French Lieutenant's Woman* and Graham Swift's *Waterland*

Introduction

When we speak of historical novels we tend to think of fictional representations referring to historical persons or events of a specific period of human history. The historical novel is taken to fictionalize whatever specific period it deals with as a facet of the regional or universal history of mankind. Natural history cannot, however, be considered as just another historical period within this scheme. Natural History does not function like the Middle Ages or the Victorian Age, which have recently become a popular setting for British historical novels. Stretching back even further than the history of mankind, the history of nature is usually set off from human history, though the relation between the two has always been of interest to social historians (especially of Marxist denominations) and, only very recently, to historians with an ecological agenda (see Chakarbarty, 'Climate History: Four Theses'). Irrespective of this conventional separation between the history of humans and that of nature, natural history does actually play a role in historical novels, though usually a minor one. There are, in fact, a number of well-known historical novels that have made it their object to foreground natural history – whether cast in social and experiential, or in scientific and speculative terms – and to explore the interrelations between natural and human history.

Authors ranging from Sir Walter Scott to Antonia S. Byatt, and from Patrick O'Brian to John Fowles and Graham Swift have all taken the history of nature and natural environments remarkably seriously. A number of their novels have turned into a principal topic what often appears to serve as a mere framework, and have assigned to natural history both thematic prominence and the power to affect the novel's very form. This article seeks to investigate different functions of the representation of natural history in two of these novels, focusing, in particular, on these representations' potential to generate alternative models of temporality that are aligned with specific aesthetic and social positions, as well as political structures and values. Adopting an ecocritical perspective, Richard Kerridge holds that the authors in question still treat the topic of natural history as "subsidiary to the main concerns of each work" ('Ecothrillers: Environmental Cliffhangers' 243). Yet I argue that novels like Byatt's *Angels and Insects*, the character of Dr Maturin in O'Brian's novels, Fowles's *The French Lieutenant's Woman* and Swift's *Waterland* doubtlessly qualify as "environmentally oriented work" *avant la lettre,* if we abide by Lawrence Buell's criterion that "[t]he nonhuman environment is present not merely as a framing device but as a presence that begins to suggest that human history is implicated in natural history" (Buell, *The Environmental Imagination* 241). Hence the following analysis is meant to contribute not only to an understanding of the historical novel, but in a wider context, to "the broad archive […] now building up, tracing different conceptions of nature and their effects throughout the history and cultures of the world" (Clark, *The Cambridge Introduction to Literature and the Environment* 4).

In the following I will investigate how a particular kind of the historical novel belonging to what has been called "historiographic metafiction" deploys and shapes the history of nature on different levels of the text. John Fowles's *The French Lieutenant's Woman* and Graham Swift's *Waterland* shall serve as my examples. More particularly, I will be interested in how natural history is turned into a point of reference and resource both for the representation and temporal modelling of human history, and for reconsidering the boundary between the histories of nature and of man. I argue that while historiographic metafiction takes great pains to deconstruct the grand narratives of human history, most of which originated in the 19th century, this type of metafiction at the same time re-assembles and re-values various aspects of natural history. In doing so, these novels draw on temporal patterns of natural history to modify perspectives on human history in unexpected ways while simultaneously questioning the boundary of human and non-human history.

Despite their self-reflexive strategies, the re-valuations of natural history as developed in historiographic metafiction continue to pose ideological challenges. After all, for several decades cultural critics of different provenances have fought against discursive strategies of naturalization which have been understood to cement social hierarchies and injustices. By essentializing differences (e.g. of gender, class or race) and treating them as "natural", so the argument goes, writers and scholars endow these differences with a facticity that obscures the full extent of their social constructedness and renders them well nigh unchangeable. Without denying the relevance of this critique, I agree with scholars who argue that this critical discourse itself produces a dilemmatic effect that needs to be addressed. After all, the critical usage of the term "nature" just outlined tends to disregard that nature itself is an object of discourse, engendering manifold discursivizations across history and culture that may be deployed in very different ways –apart from and beyond conferring facticity and bolstering hegemonic structures (see Soper, *What ist Nature?* 7-8). Moreover, as Bruno Latour has pointed out, the facts of nature themselves "are fabricated, […] 'facts are made'" (*Politics of Nature* 95). Hence the identification of "'the natural' with 'the factual' obscures the very 'fabrication' of nature's facticity through prior exclusions of matters of value or concern" (96). Latour's observations about the construction of the "facts of nature" have been taken up and put to good use in ecocritical discussions (see Clark 143-51). However, Latour is also the first to admit that questioning the fact-value-distinction renders more difficult the position of the cultural critic who has to rely on this distinction when rejecting the ideological manipulation of factual evidence (99-100). As we shall see, this discussion also bears on the analysis of natural history in historiographic metafiction. But before I turn to the novels, I will briefly clarify what I understand by the terms "historiographic metafiction" and "history of nature".

When Linda Hutcheon set out to explicate the notion of postmodernism (*A Poetics of Postmodernism*) she coined the term "historiographic metafiction". The concept refers to literary and cultural objects which use strategies of radical self-referentiality and intertextuality among others to re-shape the relation between fact and fiction. In the course of this reconfiguration of fact and fiction the difference between historio-graphical and fictional narratives is both resolutely affirmed and seriously undermined. The novels do not resolve this paradox by positing the superiority of the literary. They insist, rather, on the parity and hybridity of literary and historiographical modes of nar-ration (*A Poetics of Postmodernism*, 105-123).

Taking their cue from Hutcheon, other critics have transferred the term "historiographic metafiction" from a postmodern paradigm in general to that of the historical novel in particular. Thus Ansgar Nünning distinguishes historiographic meta-fiction from other types of the historical novel when he writes "historiographic meta-fiction deals not so much with historical facts as with the epistemological problems attached to the reconstruction of historical events and the writing of history" (*Where Historiographic Metafiction and Narratology Meet* 365). In the 1980s the critical awareness of these problems was fuelled by discussions within the discipline of history itself.[1] In the light of this debate Monika Fludernik considers historiographic meta-fiction simply as an updated late-twentieth-century version of precisely the same genre [as the historical novel modelled on the nineteenth-century realist novel] which has meanwhile adapted to twentieth-century conceptualizations of the novel and of the his-torical (Fludernik, *History and Metafiction* 93).

Adopting this perspective in the following, I will treat twentieth-century historio-graphic metafiction as a standard form of the historical novel that registers, with ingenu-ity and great formal flexibility, the impact of the contemporary discourses of historiography and literary theory.

The term "history of nature" has accrued a much longer history and its meaning has changed enormously in the course of history. In its traditional understanding, "natural history" denotes natural events and their material evidence – e.g. the eruption of a volcano or the fossils in its stratified lava. Yet it also signifies the historiography of natural phenomena, i.e. treatises on volcanic eruptions, descriptions of fossils etc. Last but not least, the term often includes theories, whether speculative or scientific, that try to account for this history. These different notions already point to a significant difference between the history of man and that of nature. While today's historical novels can draw on a disciplinary discourse of human history provided by contemporary historians, a comparable, unified discourse of natural history is not, in fact, available. Instead we find vulcanologists, palaeontologists and biologists investigating volcanoes and fossils in the arena of the natural sciences. This is, of course, to do with the history of the "natural history" which will also be relevant for the discussion of the two novels and needs briefly to be recalled.

The Greek term history, "ἱστορία", means "exploration" (e.g. in Herodotus) , and Pliny the Elder's *Naturalis Historia* (77 A.D.) collected the knowledge of hundreds of

---

[1]   The historian Hayden White and others critically questioned the status of their discipline as an empirical science by emphasizing the peculiarly "literary" strategies of historiography such as narrative emplotment, point-of-view, tropes etc.; see *The Historical Text as Literary Artifact*.

classical authors about different areas of nature such as cosmology, vulcanology, botany, zoology, mineralogy etc. into an encyclopaedia of 37 volumes. In this sense, the term "natural history" was used for systematic or typological accounts of natural phenomena characterized by careful observation and descriptive detail. Yet in the eighteenth century the term began to encompass an additional, dynamic meaning as naturalists started to speculate about catastrophic events such as volcanic eruptions or floods that resulted in massive transformations of the natural world.[2] These and other histories of nature written around 1800 form the starting point of two contradictory developments that are closely intertwined. On the one hand, there evolves a highly speculative discourse of natural philosophy and of the philosophy of history, which proves especially vertiginous in Germany (from Schelling to Goethe to Helmholtz). Yet at the same time we see the emergence of the natural sciences as they differentiate into distinct and rigorously empirical disciplines such as geology, biology, chemistry etc. In Western culture today, the older "natural history" in its descriptive form has been relegated to various sub-disciplines. And the "philosophy of nature", understood as speculative research into the inner laws of nature's history, has given way to the natural sciences that have derived much of their disciplinary ethos from the breach with these older, speculative accounts (see Engelhardt, *Historical Consciousness in the German Romantic Naturforschung* and Lepenies, *Das Ende der Naturgeschichte*). Today, the place of speculative theory has been taken by post-Darwinian scientific theories of evolution.

For the study of the historical novel the discourse of natural history, past and present, thus presents an intriguingly heterogeneous point of reference. It ranges from rich and detailed descriptions of flora, fauna and geological formations to current scientific accounts of these phenomena, and from the speculations of natural philosophy, more or less idiosyncratic and esoteric, to up-to-date theories of evolution. It includes both the description of particular locations on a synchronic level and the discussion of temporal structures in a diachronic dimension.[3] As I hope to show when taking a closer look at the novels by Fowles and Swift, the discourse of natural history proves a rewarding point of reference precisely because of its complex spatial and temporal, material and philosophical, aesthetic and political dimensions. It is the very diversity of this discourse that the novels mine as they figuratively re-imagine and re-evaluate the histories of man and nature, probing the boundaries between the two.

---

[2]   Georges-Louis Leclerc, Comte de Buffon's *Histoire Naturelle* (1749) appeared in France, James Hutton's *Theory of the Earth* (1795) in Edinburgh and Johann Friedrich Blumenbach's *Handbuch der Naturgeschichte* (1779) was published in Germany. In this article I use the words "natural history" and "history of nature" synonymously, even though this does not reflect their historical usage.

[3]   A more narrow concept, focussing on twentieth-century scientific accounts of nature, forms the point of reference of Ursula K. Heise's study, *Chronoschisms: Time, Narration and Postmodernism*, 1997, 33-68.

Natural History in *The French Lieutenant's Woman*: Theories of Evolution and
Epiphanic Revelations

John Fowles's *The French Lieutenant's Woman* is mainly set in the small English
coastal town of Lyme Regis in the Victorian period, yet the protagonist spends time also
in Exeter, London and North America. A worldly-wise gentleman and the son of a
baron, Charles Smithson has become engaged to the wealthy Ernestina Freeman,
daughter of Ernest Freeman, a London merchant and owner of a department store. Soon
after the engagement Charles Smithson is fatally attracted to Sarah Woodruff, a so-
called "fallen woman", and breaks off his socially advantageous engagement to
Ernestina Freeman. Sarah Woodruff, however, withdraws from him, he spends years
looking for her, and when he finally meets her again, the result of this encounter remains indeterminate, because the narrator offers several endings to the novel. One of
them sees Charles and his fiancée married after all, another intimates that Charles and
Sarah become a couple, while yet another strongly suggests that they part again.

Written in 1969, *The French Lieutenant's Woman* is frequently referred to as one of
the first, if not *the* first, British novel explicitly thematizing and foregrounding the relation between novelistic writing and historiography in a mode later to be labelled
"historiographic metafiction" (Onega, *British Historiographic Metafiction* 94). The
fictional world is represented, for most of the time, by an omniscient narrator. Yet while
this narrator unfolds the Victorian world around 1867 in great detail, he also refers non-
chalantly to the twentieth century (e.g. to Henry Moore, the *Gestapo* or the concept of
"sublimation" (Fowles 4, 21, 269)). The narrator conspicuously stages metafictional
transgressions (most obviously in chapters 13, 45 and 61)[4], yet the novel also includes
the historical figure Dante Gabriel Rossetti and his Victorian household as characters –
thus drawing on a defining device of the historical novel tradition since Walter Scott.

In Fowles's historiographic metafiction natural history occupies a central place. It is
associated, first of all, with a stretch of land called "the Undercliff" outside Lyme Regis.
Within the spatial construction of the fictional world, this natural environment, especially the part called Ware Commons, presents a vital refuge for non-conformist behaviour. It thus counterbalances the space of the provincial Victorian town with its
perfidious apparatus of surveillance and repression. The narrator describes, with great
botanical detail, this landscape of bushes and trees on the cliffs that are rich in geological history, and I shall return to these descriptions later. The significance of the
Undercliff, "an English Garden of Eden" (Fowles 67), has engaged Fowles's critics who
have related it to sites of trial and struggle in Romance literature (Loveday, *The
Romances of John Fowles* 68-9) or, more specifically, to Arcadia (Beatty, *The
Undercliff as Inverted Pastoral* 171-9).

On a second level the history of nature figures in Charles Smithson's leisure time
when he collects fossils. The narrator's ironical perspective targets not so much the
gentleman as amateur scientist than the collector's attitude when he attempts to contain
natural history in a recreational diversion. Setting out in his absurd collector's outfit and
armed with a hammer to look for fossils Charles's success remains very moderate (*The
French Lieutenant's Woman* 47-8). This irony not withstanding, the narrator informs us

---

[4]   See the article by Clauda Olk in this volume.

of "natural history's" high standing at the time (49) and critiques Charles's compartmentalizing interest which has him overlook that this history is not confined to fossils. This is made plain by Dr. Grogan, Charles Smithson's most important interlocutor, for whom natural history "is about the living, Smithson. Not the dead" (162). Though Charles initially considers natural history as something he can turn into his hobby-horse, his reflections on nature and evolution eventually affect his whole life.

On a third level of the text, the history of nature explicitly figures as evolutionary discourse. Darwin's theory of evolution forms the object of conversation, the narrator continuously comments on this topic, and the novel's last chapter is actually headed by a quotation from the evolutionary biologist Martin Gardner from 1967. This evolutionary discourse has continued to attract the critics' attention who relate it to the novel's openly anachronistic existentialism, social Darwinism, and to questions of novelistic form.[5]

I am going to approach Fowles's representation of natural history through a discussion of the novel's evolutionary discourse. The novel presents two very different perceptions of Darwinian evolutionary theory, belonging to the 1860s and 1960s respectively. Moving between two historical frameworks, the narrator negotiates a Victorian view on the one hand, and a radicalized twentieth-century view on the other.[6] In the Victorian mainstream version of evolutionary theory man is part of the animal realm and thus lacks a purely divine origin. At the same time he is, however, positioned as the end-point and *telos* of the *Great Chain of Being*, and in some accounts the creation of new species even after the original "act of creation" is deemed possible. Charles Smithson's thoughts as, on a solitary beach, he contemplates the geological strata of Lyme Regis are rendered as follows:

> He knew that *nulla species nova* was rubbish; yet he saw in the strata an immensely reassuring orderliness of existence. He might perhaps have seen a very contemporary social symbolism in the way these grey-blue ledges were crumbling; but what he did see was a kind of edificiality of time, in which inexorable laws (therefore beneficently divine [...]) very conveniently arranged themselves for the survival of the fittest and best, *exempli gratia* Charles Smithson this fine spring day, alone, eager and inquiring, understanding, accepting, noting and grateful.
>
> (Fowles, *The French Lieutenant's Woman* 50)

Mankind's position at the top of this anthropocentric pyramid does not only count as a pleasant confirmation of a superiority already pre-supposed. Considering the survival of the fittest, retrospectively, as an affirmation of the human species also combines conveniently with the Victorian conception of the temporal dynamics of progress. It is

---

[5]   For a discussion of evolutionary discourse and existentialism see Richard P. Lynch, *Freedoms in The French Lieutenant's Woman* 55; Loveday, *The Romances of John Fowles* 65-6 and also Fowles *Notes on an Unfinished Novel* 17; on social Darwinism see Pohler, *Genetic and Cultural Selection in The French Lieutenant's Woman* ; on evolutionary discourse and novelistic form see Conradi *John Fowles* (on "mutant endings" 65) or Tarbox, *The French Lieutenant's Woman and the Evolution of Narrative* on the evolution of narrative.

[6]   This first part of my argument draws on Tony Jackson, *Charles and the Hopeful Monster* here 221-25.

worth noting that the narrator carefully distances himself from Charles's interpretation by pointing out that he "might perhaps have seen" something quite different had he attributed symbolic value to another facet of his perceptions (the stratas' crumbling). This emphasizes the interdependence of scientific discourse and observational data in Charles's construction of natural history.

Charles's view changes on a solitary walk to the Undercliff early one morning, where he experiences an epiphanic encounter with nature. Rather than conceiving of evolution as an improvement of living beings on a hierarchical ladder (as he did earlier, see above), Charles here gains an insight into evolution as moving along a horizontal line, situating living beings next to each other, each perfectly fitting its place. This understanding approximates the non-teleological interpretations of evolutionary theories dominating the twentieth century – a type of interpretation that emphasizes contingency and disruption. According to these "radical" evolutionary theories posited by Stephen Jay Gould and, less radically, by Martin Gardner – they are quoted in the novel's epigram – species do not change gradually due to manifold contingent yet minute changes. Instead, the development of species is brought about by the sporadic appearance of a so-called "hopeful monster". This denotes the contingent emergence of a living being which appears monstrous and presents a massive breach with the *status quo*. Whether or not this being procreates is uncertain – this is a question of hope. But if it does, what will follow is not merely a minimal adaptation but rather an evolutionary leap.

Drawing on this twentieth-century interpretation of evolutionary theory, the critic Tony Jackson presents an elegant reading of *The French Lieutenant's Woman*: On the level of the story, a "hopeful monster" – Sarah Woodruff, enigmatic and unaccountably emancipated – appears in Victorian society. Charles, adopting an existentialist position *avant la lettre,* decides to share her status as an outsider, and readers wishing to find out what becomes of them are left in uncertainty. On the metafictional level, the historiographic narrative shares evolutionary theory's scepticism of any retrospective projection of causality. The novel's deft narrative acrobatics – the narrator throws a coin to decide which ending to present first and sets back the clock – attempt to prevent the retrospective projection of a telos that would obscure the ending's contingency. Hence Jackson argues that in this novel a postmodern theory of an evolution shaped by radical contingency, on the one hand, and the credo of historiographic metafiction, on the other, make a perfect match and together critique "metaphysical absolutes of all kinds".[7]

Considered in the wider context of Fowles's representation of natural history, this argument, for all its ingenuity, remains highly selective, and the novel's purported rejection of metaphysical absolutes does appear compromised. Two passages in particular are worth considering in this context. The first portrays Charles's thoughts and experiences in a momentous encounter with the natural environment that is amply commented on by the narrator, the second describes the narrator's reflections on the temporality of cultural consciousness.

---

[7] Jackson defines a "metaphysical absolute" as "any representation that is taken consciously or unconsciously as entirely self-contained, self-identical, self-present, and therefore outside the realm of culture, history, desire, and ideology" (Jackson, *Charles and the Hopeful Monster* 222).

Despite the novel's overall historicizing strategies, the crucial situation preparing Charles for the choice he will make does not aim to historicize at all –on the contrary. I here refer to the moment when he recognizes 'a universal parity of existence':

> On the slopes above his path the trunks of the ashes and sycamores, a honey gold in the oblique sunlight, erected their dewy green vaults of young leaves; there was something mysteriously religious about them, but of a religion before religion; a druid balm, a green sweetness over all [...]. A fox crossed his path and strangely for a moment stared, as if Charles was the intruder; and then a little later, with an uncanny similarity, with the same divine assumption of possession, a roe-deer looked up from its browsing; and stared in its small majesty before quietly turning tail and slipping away into the thickets. There is a painting by Pisanello in the National Gallery that catches exactly such a moment: St Hubert in an early Renaissance forest, confronted by birds and beasts. The saint is shocked, almost as if the victim of a practical joke, all his arrogance dowsed by a sudden drench of nature's profoundest secret: the universal parity of existence.
>   It was not only these two animals that seemed fraught with significance. The trees were dense with singing birds [...] A tiny wren perched on top of a bramble not ten feet from him and trilled its violent song. He saw its glittering black eyes, the red and yellow of its song-gaped throat – a midget ball of feathers that yet managed to make itself the Announcing Angel of evolution: I am what I am, thou shalt not pass my being now.
>   (Fowles, *The French Lieutenant's Woman* 241-42)

Charles here learns that "nature has no built-in value scale" (Jackson 234) in the sense that his vision runs counter to his earlier conception of a hierarchical Chain of Being crowned by man. Yet what else does this passage convey?

To begin with, the text quoted links the rhetoric of a detailed and celebratory natural history that labels and describes the particularity of flora and fauna (much too long to quote in full) to the figure of an "Announcing Angel of evolution". In this manner, Charles's vision ascribes a number of substantial values to nature – beauty, perfection and the manifold appear to be in evidence and accessible. Furthermore, an ethico-political claim to mutual recognition is here asserted in the look he exchanges first with the fox and then again with a deer. And rather than historicizing Charles's experience of mystery, the text foregrounds the epiphany's spiritual dimension which bridges the centuries to the prehistoric myths of the Druids (see Aubrey, *Introduction* 24). To be sure, this neo-romantic spiritualism is focalized largely through Charles, yet rather than distancing himself from the protagonist's perspective as in the passage where Charles reflects on geological strata (see above), the narrator here is at pains to de-historicize and thus universalize the character's mystical experience.

The crucial device for achieving this is the evocation of the Renaissance painting. Stepping back from the character, the narrator links Charles's epiphany to Pisanello's painting of the conversion of St. Hubert with the claim that Pisanello catches "exactly such a moment".[8] This is all the more intriguing as Fowles's text could be said to do

---

[8]   The painting shows St. Hubert (a similar narrative exists for St. Eustace) facing a Roe carrying Christ on the cross between his antlers; see also Jill Dunkerton et. al. *Giotto to Dürer. Early Renaissance Painting in the National Gallery*. 1991. 276-77.

much more than simply refer to the painting. The lush visual detail in the textual depiction of nature suggests that it might in fact be read as a loose ekphrastic rendering of the natural environment in the painting, a rendering that rewrites St. Hubert's vision of the cross between the deer's antlers in the painting as the protagonist's spiritual yet de-Christianized experience of the natural world. The evocation of the painting at the centre of this lavishly visual passage could even be said to cast this image as a *mise-en-abyme*. The reader would thus be invited to explore the Renaissance pictorial frame as interfacing both the retrospective projection of Charles's de-Christianized epiphany and the pre-Christian Druid myths. In this manner the phrase of the "universal parity of existence" is made to extend its spiritual or metaphysical dimension across the ages.

Admittedly, Charles's "natural Eucharist" is mixed with bitterness. The narrator points out that although Charles senses a "priority of [...] ecology over classification", he experiences this "profounder reality" rather like a "universal chaos, looming behind the fragile structure of human order" and feels 'excommunicated' (242). Perhaps this feeling signals that, unlike St. Hubert, Charles, though deeply awed by this over-determined experience of the natural environment, can no longer muster the religious faith that would make him fully belong to the world he witnesses; or it signals that he feels a gulf between the human and non-human, and incapable of shedding what, in ecocritical language, might be called his anthropocentric "speciism". This notwithstanding, there remains a mystical core to his experience that links widely different historical contexts.

So when Charles comes to understand "the universal parity of existence" here, we have to be clear about what this is supposed to imply. Does the passage suggest, only, that Charles moves from a "vertical" to a "horizontal" theory of evolution i.e. that he modifies his views about the laws governing the natural world? If this were all, then this cannot, without further premises, account in any way for the character's momentous change of attitude on a social plane (i.e. towards Sarah and his own future). If the passage suggests, however, that Charles's insight into the laws of evolution is tantamount to an insight, also, into a fundamental set of ethico-political values turning on the notion of "parity as recognition", then the text would appear to be concealing an important gap. No matter how skilfully the passage may orchestrate the shift from one to the other, knowledge of what *is* the case in the (natural) world does not and cannot, by itself alone, yield ethical or political knowledge of what *ought* to be the case.[9] What we see is the character and the narrator identifying the neutral laws of evolutionary parity (treated as fact) with an ethics of recognition (value); an ethics which, projected onto these laws, surreptitiously invests them with moral/ideological force.

And yet, as indicated in the beginning, this passage may also be considered from a very different angle. Today's scientific language, too, is a discursive construction which boasts of the historical achievement of excluding feelings and subjective responses from

[9]   In philosophical discourse, this move is called a "naturalistic fallacy"; for a brief discussion see Peter Schaber, "Naturalistischer Fehlschluss". *Handbuch Ethik*. Ed. Marcus Düwell, Christoph Hübenthal and Micha H. Werner. Stuttgart: Metzler, 2002. 437-40. From an ecocritical perspective Clark discusses the concept of the natural fallacy as the pivotal "site of a general struggle between differing conceptions of cultural authority" (*The Cambridge Introduction to Literature and the Environment* 145).

descriptions of natural phenomena. This scientific language contributes to what Latour considers to be a "fabrication of facts" precisely because this language completely abstracts from those natural phenomena's experiential qualities that generate, for instance, aesthetic pleasure and ethical awareness. So we may be right to insist that in terms of evolutionary theory (which the passage refers to) "universal parity" only means something like "'the parity of all living beings' exposure to generic randomness and contingency". Yet if we do this, then this concept of "parity" is constructed, within the context of the novel, by way of abstracting the notion of "parity" from the natural environment's experiential qualities so insistently staged in the text. To put it the other way round, the passage quoted massively enriches the abstract scientific notion of "parity" through a "thick" rendering of the objects' material qualities and the aesthetic and ethical responses they provoke. The novel could thus be seen to dexterously merge an advanced discourse of evolution with a neo-Romantic appreciation of natural history in the concept of "parity" which it thus textually creates as a metaphysical (or even mystical) secret of nature. The text could even be said to draw attention to this specific textualization of nature through the intertextual/medial references it foregrounds. As a result, the discursive object, "nature", rather than undergoing a radical historicization or scientific abstraction, is celebrated and posited through the text as universally valuable and accessible – in political, aesthetic and spiritual terms – in different cultural forms across widely differing historical periods. Thus perceived, this passage may count as an avant-garde instance of "Romantic retrieval" which

> is altogether more complex and politically perceptive than that of the many nature lovers and environmentalists who have more recently emphasized the dumb-striking and ineffable qualities of natural beauty [...], but who fail to acknowledge its dependency on subjective representation and articulation and the always aesthetically mediated quality of what we value in landscapes.
>
> (Soper, *Passing Glories and Romantic Retrievals* 22)

Investing "profound secrets" in nature as evolution nevertheless remains a highly ambivalent textual strategy. This can be seen in another controversial debate which I can only sketch here, i.e. Fowles's representation of gender relations and their feminist or patriarchal potential. Some critics appraise *The French Lieutenant's Woman* as challenging heteronormative assumptions or even as feminist[10], while others argue that the novel ties Sarah to an intuitive intelligence and, ultimately, nature, thus repeating the Pre-Raphaelite gender stereotypes the novel engages with on an intertextual level.[11] In this debate the description of the female protagonist as a "hopeful monster" would seem to belong to the second group as it bypasses acculturation altogether. However, Suzanne Ross's ecofeminist stance explicitly aligns the female protagonist with natural history. According to Ross, Sarah "strategically embraces the position of woman as more

---

[10] See William Stephenson, *Fowles's The French Lieutenant's Woman* 51 or Deborah Byrd, *The Evolution and Emancipation of Sarah Woodruff* 306.

[11] See Pamela Cooper, *The Fictions of John Fowles* 119-32 and Margaret Bozenna Goscilo, *John Fowles's Pre-Raphaelite Woman* 70-9.

closely connected to nature" (190). This "strategic" alignment notwithstanding, however, Ross maintains that the Undercliff offers "the potential for direct, unsublimated experience – sensual, sexual, emotional, physical" (188) which dislodges all binaries and leads towards self-liberation: Sarah accepts the "green chaos" within herself and helps Charles understand the Undercliff's significance as "a green and immediate place, resonant with the green chaos in all of us" (192).

This ecofeminist perspective on the natural history of the Undercliff as "an immediate place" recalls and perfectly fits Charles's epiphanic experience of this environment discussed above. However, this ecofeminist argument also has a high price attached to it, cementing as it does the analogy between Charles's insight into "nature's profoundest secret" and his attraction to a woman as deeply mysterious. However much the representation of Charles's experience of the mystery of woman – like his epiphany in the woods – may thrive on contradictory intertextual and interart echoes, his encounter with female mystery does have a universalizing, non-discursive core. Already in their first encounter, the focus is wholly on the look Sarah and Charles exchange (10-11), and will keep exchanging in the course of later meetings – a look more complex yet similar in many respects to the one Charles exchanges with the fox and the deer. In the case of Charles and the animals this look is momentous and telling, because this is the only language they appear to share. In the course of his meetings with Sarah, however, this look turns into a mystification because it ultimately replaces a discursiveness from which the female character is shown to withdraw. When given the line "I am not to be understood even by myself" (455), Sarah's position vis-à-vis Charles, reduced to a non-discursive parity, resembles – in a decidedly disturbing manner – that of the mute animals in their encounter with Charles.

I now move on to the second passage where the narrator, rather than the character, can be seen to deploy the discourse of the history of nature for a metaphysical account of human history and values. After Charles has lost the prospect of an inheritance, the pressure rises that he dedicate his life to the commercial empire headed by Ernestina Freeman's father. He suddenly senses that his own mode of life is doomed to disappear and that he and his status as a gentleman already belong to a 'saurian species' and will become a "victim of evolution" (293, 290). Yet even though he realizes that the future belongs to the Freemans he determinedly rejects the invitation to join Freeman's expanding business. This rejection of Freeman's offer affirms his own ideal of a life of self-determination and knowledge and produces an intense sense of freedom. At this point the narrator again extrapolates a more general significance from the character's experience. Waxing philosophical, he expounds his position:

> I hold no particular brief for the Gentleman [...]. But what dies is the form. The matter is immortal. There runs through this succession of superseded forms we call existence a certain kind of after-life. We can trace the Victorian gentleman's best qualities back to the parfit knights and *preux chevaliers* of the Middle Ages; and trace them forward into the modern gentleman, that breed we call scientists, since that is where the river has undoubtedly run. In other words, every culture, however undemocratic, or however egalitarian, needs a kind of self-questioning, ethical elite, and one that is bound by certain rules of conduct, some of which may be very unethical, and so account for the eventual death of the form, though their hidden purpose is good: to brace or act as structure for the

better effects of their function in history.

Perhaps you see very little link between the Charles of 1267 with all his newfangled French notions of chastity and chasing after Holy Grails, the Charles of 1867 with his loathing of trade, and the Charles of today, a computer scientist [...]. But there is a link: they all rejected or reject the notion of *possession* as the purpose of life, whether it be of a woman's body, or of high profit at all costs, or of the right to dictate the speed of progress. The scientist is but one more form; and will be superseded.

(Fowles, *The French Lieutenant's Woman* 297-98)

The sentence "what dies is the form, the matter is immortal" may not present such a strong statement when considered in the context of conceptions of the universe natural scientists advance today. In the context of the quoted passage, however, the announcement carries much more weight. "Immortal matter" here refers to a specific aspect of the social. Immortal matter signifies the sphere where a self-questioning elite acts as a motor of cultural achievement.

At a first glance the narrator appears to refer solely to the history of mankind, rather than natural history. Closer inspection suggests though, that the whole passage draws on an implicit analogy. The cultural history envisaged here is conceived in analogy to a natural history shaped by evolution. Cultural history produces social forms similar to species (knight, gentleman, computer scientist) that become stronger or weaker, the better (or worse) they fit their specific function in the history of a culture. This reading is supported by phrases like "that breed we call the scientist" or on a different plane "that is where the river has undoubtedly run". Thus, when considering Freeman and himself, Charles seems to move, again, from a hierarchical appreciation of social progress (the gentleman overtaken by the entrepreneurial class and on his way to extinction) to a consideration of parity in which the entrepreneurial species on the one hand and the self-reflecting species on the other, both looking back on a long ancestry of largely extinct forms, co-exist on a par.

Yet what kind of evolutionary theory lies at the core of this analogy which flags its twentieth-century credentials through a reference to the computer scientist? Jackson argues that Fowles "actually gives us a version of Darwin after the model of Stephen Jay Gould" (Jackson, *Hopeful Monster* 224-25) who suggests that "perhaps the actual reasons for survival do not support conventional ideas of cause as complexity, improvement, or anything moving at all humanward." (Jackson 225, qt. Gould, *Wonderful Life* 48). However, this reading hardly squares with the narrator's strong thesis concerning the *immortality* of cultural and ethical self-questioning. Without projecting a metaphysical telos – and thus, once again, enriching the scientific and impoverished idea of "their function in history" – what can we know about the ultimate evolutionary use or uselessness of this self-reflexive or "complex" practice?

In this passage, too, a textual strategy of implicit analogy invests the theory of evolution with specific values, and just as in the case of "a universal parity", the result remains perfectly reassuring. The narrator stipulates that collective self-questioning, following ethical standards, qualifies as an immortal cultural sphere or institution. His "evolutionist" philosophy of history promises, moreover, that this cultural practice of self-questioning shapes historical types that, taken together, produce some sort of functional continuity within the cultural sphere and allow for its increasingly perfect adaptation to that "function in history". So the individual existentialist struggling for the ethical attitude of authenticity does not simply face histories of nature and culture shaped by the contingent and absurd. Instead, he can believe himself to be part of a history which will integrate and immortalize his own self-questioning ethos within the eternal sphere of cultural self-questioning.

Natural History in *Waterland*: Geophysical Dynamics and Trauma

I will now turn to Graham Swift's novel *Waterland*, published more than a decade after Fowles's *The French Lieutenant's Woman* and also figuring as a paradigmatic case of British historiographic metafiction in the critical charts of this genre (Hutcheon, *A Poetics of Postmodernism* xi, and Nünning, *Where Historiographic Metafiction and Narratology Meet* 368). The novel's protagonist and autodiegetic narrator, Tom Crick, is a history teacher living in the British Fenlands. He faces a crisis in his private life that threatens to unhinge his life as a whole, because his wife Mary, formerly Mary Metcalf, has been committed to a psychiatric hospital for stealing a baby. His memories of the history leading up to this event preoccupy him and affect his teaching at school. During his history lessons on the French Revolution, Tom begins to respond to the challenging questions of one of his pupils by deviating from the official curriculum. From the storming of the Bastille, Robespierre and the guillotine, he swerves, over and again, to his own family history, branching out into that of the working-class Cricks, on his father's side, and the entrepreneurial Atkinsons, on his mother's. Significantly, this history also encompasses the deaths of a school friend and his older brother in which he himself and Mary Metcalf were implicated before their marriage.

Tom Crick's narratives skilfully interweave "universal" and "regional" historiography, official and counter-history, as well as family history and fictional autobiography. The narratives are marked by analeptic jumps crossing several generations, shifting analogies between different narrative strands, past and present, and they are interspersed with a number of dialogues, "real" or imagined, with pupils and the principal. The narrator raises a plethora of self-reflexive questions or comments which focus, among other things, on the structuring of material in constructing history (139-42), or on the blurry boundary between the historiographic textbook narrative proper for the classroom and mythologizing stories that include local legend, romances and fairytales (5-8, 62).[12] The novel thus both displays and scrutinizes the ways in which these different kinds of (his)stories construct selves and cultures alike, dwelling on the instability of these constructions, the therapeutic power of the telling of (his)stories as well as the limits of that power.

In this metafictional novel, too, the history of nature plays a principal role on several different levels of the text. Most obviously this history is associated with the region of the Fenlands where the story is set, a landscape characterized by a constant interaction between land and water. Unlike the Undercliff in Fowles's novel, the Fenlands in

---

[12] For a perspicacious discussion of these features see Heike Hartung, *Die Dezentrale Geschichte: Historisches Erzählen und literarische Geschichte(n) bei Peter Ackroyed, Graham Swift und Salman Rushdie* 177-194.

Swift's, do not, however, function within the binary opposition of town and countryside and its symbolic import of leisure and refuge from social strictures. Instead, the Fenlands provide the setting within which almost all of the plot unfolds. Nor is this landscape centrally related to the discourse of art history, which Fowles establishes through the Pisanello painting and, in a more mediated manner, through references to the Pre-Raphaelites. Rather, the Fens as setting are closely associated with the social history of agrarian capitalism and rural labour and their material moorings. This history encompasses the cultivation of land and the brewing of beer and is related in more than one way to the history of the British Empire (see Berlatsky 262-71). On a second level, the significance of natural history is foregrounded in chapters actually entitled "About the Fens" and "About the Ouse", "About the Eel" and "About Natural History". Yet whereas Fowles's narrator eventually associates the protagonist with the ethos of the scientist, Swifts narrator explicitly drops the term "biology" in favour of "natural history" (205), thus emphasizing as his frame of reference the vagaries of narrative rather than those of science.

The chapters on natural history provide factual information in a discursive manner and are complemented by references to natural history in other parts of the text. Heike Hartung points out that the novel here seems to be inspired by Fernand Braudel's *La Méditerranee et le monde méditerraneen à l'epoque de Phillippe II* (1949, trans. 1972), a milestone in the historiography of the *Annales* school which relates geological, social and individual levels of history in its encyclopaedic approach. In Hartung's reading, the novel's intertextual evocation of Braudel's text ultimately serves to deconstruct his claim to represent history in its totality (*Die Dezentrale Geschichte* 191-94). In Swift's novel, too, natural history turns into a point of reference that shapes models of temporality, inspires reflections on values and, as has been pointed out repeatedly, affects the novel's form (e.g. Cooper, Imperial *Typographies* 375-76 and Haefner, *Geschichte und Natur in Graham Swifts* Waterland 211-13).

The metafictional depiction of the history of nature in *Waterland* has attracted different readings; two of them, in particular, mark paradigmatically opposing positions. Pamela Cooper gives sustained attention to the setting of the Fenlands and their changing landscape. She reads *Waterland* as a postcolonial novel "ironically mimicking the realism of its forbears" and thus as a "hypertrophic postmodern object" (375). Stressing the importance of the setting, Cooper argues that the fluidity of the marshes turns into a "*mise-en-abyme*" of the "infinitely migrating binary" (371) of fiction and fact and, ultimately, of the novel itself. Her focus is on the infinite mobility of this textual binary as "the land itself becomes a sort of miniature simulacrum: a tense impersonation of the 'natural world' at a levitated remove from itself, a performance of a performance within a performance" (376). By contrast, Eric Berlatsky investigates how *Waterland*, especially in its depiction of the Fenlands, foregrounds the materiality of history which he relates to the representation of both labour and the human psyche. He expressly intends to "open up debates obscured by the hegemony of poststructuralist discourse" (259). Both perspectives will bear on my discussion.

Early in the text, Swift's novel introduces a distinction between the concepts of "history" and "reality" which, as Ernst van Alphen observes, runs counter to the usage of these terms in postmodern theories. There, historical reality "recedes and yields to the rhetorical and narrative working of our discourse" and the (discursive) reality it creates

(*The Performativity of Histories* 203). In Swift's *Waterland*, however, human history and historiography together are juxtaposed to "reality". In fact, the novel introduces the notion of "reality" as belonging, above all, to natural history:

To live in the Fens is to receive strong doses of reality. The great, flat monotony of reality; the wide, empty space of reality. Melancholia and self-murder are not unknown in the Fens. "[…] How do you surmount reality, children? How do you acquire, in a flat country, the tonic of elevated feelings?" (*Waterland* 17) The reality the natural environment communicates is located in a natural history emblematic of *non-history*. Natural history figures as a void, and as utterly de-void of secrets/values to be surmised and accessed. This is a natural history defined as non-progressive "monotony" and "empty space". Later in the novel the specific temporality of this history is spelt out explicitly: "Natural History. Which doesn't go anywhere. Which cleaves to itself. Which perpetually travels back to where it came from" (205). This depiction of natural history evokes the concept of "'deep time' – 'the great temporal limitation imposed by geology upon human importance" (Gould, *Time's Arrow, Time's Cycle* 2). For Gould, it is the ungraspable magnitude of geological time scales that decentres the history of mankind: "how threatening […] the notion of an almost incomprehensible immensity" (2). Rather than presenting this alternative time scale as stratographic depth, however, the novel tropes this immensity as sheer horizontal extension, and its dynamic as cyclical recurrence.

With a minimal change of context natural history in the Fenlands turns into a metonymy for something much more encompassing than landscape. It now seems that its description is tantamount to an existentialist statement about man's/woman's situation in the world. Yet whereas Fowles associates existentialism with the notion of contingent events, Swift pits it against a material temporality of uneventfulness:

> Reality is uneventfulness, vacancy, flatness. Reality is that nothing happens. How many of the events of history have occurred, ask yourselves, for this and for that reason, but for no other reason, fundamentally, than the desire to make things happen? I present to you History, the fabrication, the diversion, the reality-obscuring drama. History, and its near relative, Histrionics [...]
>
> (Swift, *Waterland* 40)

In his account, history-as-event on the one hand and historiography-as-storytelling on the other merely present different responses to reality as non-history. Faced with reality as vacancy "you can make things happen" – Atkinson founds a commercial enterprise, the British extend their Empire, and Napoleon conquers Europe.

> Or you can tell stories, whether as history teacher, family chronicler, and collector of myths, or as a nurse of war veterans. In their attempt to keep 'reality' at bay, both these strategies can count on a third, a fall-back option – or you drink and forget what sober minds tell you.
>
> (Swift, *Waterland* 6)

This representation of the natural history of the Fenlands seems to lend itself to ecocritical analyses that draw on a cultural memory approach, investigating places in literature "less as geographical realities than as symbolic entities" that shape the perception of natural environments (Goodbody, 'Sense of Place and Lie de Mémoire' 57). Swift's text does indeed insist that the symbolic and temporal structures envisaged here do not simply emerge from but are enacted vis-à-vis the geography of the Fenlands.

When the "reality" figured in the Fenlands cannot be kept at bay (by means of action, stories or drugs) this tends to prove shattering. Where Fowles imagines epiphanic insights transcending time, Swift focuses on spasms of time-arresting trauma. Such experiences are associated with dead bodies (the corpse of Freddy Parr), physical violation (the domestic violence suffered by Sarah Atkinson, the torturous abortion suffered by Mary Medcalf, the experiences of war veterans), and, sometimes, sexuality (the incestuous sexuality of Ernest Atkinson and his daughter Helen, the narrator's impotence as he fears the loss of his love). Berlatzky relates the traumatic aspect of these experiences to the Lacanian Real (277); for my argument it is significant that these experiences, bound up with corporeality and lack of articulation, are associated with non-linear time, whether in modes of repetition or in the slowing down or standstill of time, if only "for a brief while" (33).

Although the novel initially introduces a clear-cut juxtaposition between reality and different types of responses to it, the relation between these two poles soon becomes much more complex. If the Fens signify reality, they signify a reality in motion. The Fens are "reclaimed land" (8), and the process of reclaiming the land turns on the issue of "silt":

> Silt: The Fens were formed by silt. Silt: a word which when you utter it, letting the air slip thinly between your teeth, invokes a slow, sly, insinuating agency. Silt: which shapes and undermines continents; which demolishes as it builds; which is simultaneous accretion and erosion; neither progress nor decay.
>
> (Swift, *Waterland* 8)

The passage describes a geophysical motion, however monotonous, which creates land at one place only to flood land in another. The human reclamation and cultivation of land builds on this basic geophysical activity, which it attempts to use and give a direction to: "what silt began, man continued" (9). Drainage canals and pumping systems produce rich and peaty soil. This promising soil, however, is constantly endangered by flooding and precisely that motion of water and land to which the reclamation process owes its success – a motion always ready to flood canals and sluices, to make whole rivers disappear and create new ones. The novel offers precise historical dates – "1713" and "1874" – for these recurring disasters in "waterland" (*Waterland* 12, 100).

In this manner the people living in the novel's Fenlands have created a history which does not simply resist, in an existentialist sense, the reality signified by natural history. They have also entered this natural history in a material sense, attempting to tame its motions and render them productive. Berlatsky argues that the kind of history thus emerging is "non-narratable" in the traditional sense (272). It is characterized by an almost complete lack of progress and therefore "interest" – like the working-class history of the Cricks who partake in the day-to-day activity of dredging and keeping the locks. Berlatsky points out that this kind of history usually only surfaces as the non-narratable edge or residue of the narratable history. It must be added that in *Waterland* this history moves into visibility also because it is presented as materially bound and metonymically related to a strongly foregrounded natural environment. Berlatsky distinguishes this history from a history "consistent with traditional Western historical narrative" characterized by "progress" like the Atkinsons' capitalist and imperialist history (262). Yet this latter history, though at a remove from the natural environment, also finds itself affected, albeit intermittently, by the motions of natural history – e.g. through the destructive power of exceptional floods which, when peaking, become part of a "narratable" history of disaster and reconstruction.

In Swift's novel, the relationship between the history of nature and that of humans initially evolves from a highly specific geophysical context of considerable metonymical force. Yet, right from the beginning, the language intimates that the interrelation of natural and social history signifies symbolically in a wider context of history, too. Introducing the lock-keeper's work the narrator tells us "he would have to raise the sluice which cut across the far side of the stream like a giant guillotine" (3). A mechanical apparatus associated with the excesses of the French Revolution here cuts across land-as-body metaphorically. The text thus invests the landscape and its history, elsewhere presented as empty and void, with life and sentience.

The natural history originally bound up with the history of the English Fenlands continues to be likened to events in other parts of the world, especially with the revolutionary processes in France. The assimilation is brought about through a figurative language and through inconspicuous parallels in the vocabulary: While on the continent the millennium arrives, while the Bastille tumbles, Jacobins oust Girondins and there is widespread *draining away of blood*, Thomas Atkinson studies the principles of "*land drainage*, of river velocity and siltation. [...]" (69, emphasis UB).

What begins as a parallel inserted almost in passing, the mere contiguity of the terms "draining" and "drainage", and of their metaphorical and literal use, then swerves into more complex technicalities of land drainage that metaphorically evoke the abstract planning and totalitarian canalization of all social movement in France (see also Hartung, *Die Dezentrale Geschichte*, 190).[13]

These shifting figurations of the interrelation between the history of nature and that of humans also extend from the local present to other places and periods in world history. When the lock-keeper from the Fenlands finds himself in the trenches of the Great War, the problems there are immediately transparent to him: the water in the trenches, the sliding of mud and the issue of drainage. Again the material landscape is turned into a metonymy – here for a military tenaciously making ground in one place while loosing it in another, sacrificing large numbers of lives in years of a largely nonnarratable history. By thus associating the place of the Fenlands with events in other parts of Europe the text heightens the significance of a narrative that, at a first glance, appears to be closely bound up with regional history. Moreover, from an ecocritical perspective the novel could be said to display both a 'sense of place' and 'a sense of planet'. By placing industrialized agriculture and military manoeuvres in different countries side by side, the text suggests what Heise calls an overarching "allegory of

---

[13]   This comparison is strengthened through analogous emplotments – the rise and fall of an empire – and hagiographical portrayals of the protagonists – Atkinson and Napoleon.

connectedness" (Heise, *Sense of Self and Sense of Planet* 22)[14]. The fact that the novel figures materiality and physical labour in symbols of the body helps to reinforce this allegory of connectedness. The symbolic construction of the environment as body is deployed in a mode of resistance; the full-scale technological intervention into the land-scape is depicted as a massive violation of an organic, sentient environment-as-body; conversely the French *terreur* and its wider effects are presented as the weakening not so much of a nation, but of a continent-as-body. Nevertheless, on a larger discursive plane, the implications of thus investing the natural environment with corporeal attrib-utes remain ambivalent.

In critical discussions of the novel this ambivalence has surfaced especially in rela-tion to the representation of gender and of Mary Metcalf, in particular. As Cooper points out, the Fenlands mediate the contradictions of history in *Waterland* with meto-nymic reference to the maternal body as "ambiguous terrain"; for her, this forms part of "postmodernism's concern with women's historical agency" (372). "Stereotyped and essentialized as a kind of 'eternal feminine' Mary, […] becomes less a character than a placeholder or conduit for desire" (385). However, in view of Tom Crick's controlling and masculine voice and the palimpsestic depiction of Mary as Eve and Madonna or Mary's blending, in Crick's mind, with the other women of the Atkinson family, Cooper argues that her "'naturalness' is undermined by the very strategies which construct it" (385). Contradicting Cooper, Katrina Powell observes that the concern with female agency aims, on the contrary, to release female characters from being exclusively identified with femaleness and to provide, instead, more complex social positions for the female characters. Powell argues that in this respect the novel is not postmodern at all (62). She points out that the text does not offer any position for women outside the line of a patrilinear reproduction which is not essentialized or mythologized rather than historicized; all the female characters are either mothers or insane. Thus perceived Mary's case appears to clinch the matter since her insanity is presented as the delayed consequence of the loss of her reproductive organs in the course of an abortion. So even if, as Cooper argues, the text does dislodge the cyclical temporality apparently characterizing the Fenlands and female subjects alike, all the novel can possibly do here is point to its own limitations.

An analogous ambiguity emerges for the reading of Tom Crick's brother Dick, referred to as "potato head" (32), a character with a mental disability who commits suicide when he learns about his incestuous family history. The narrator closely associ-ates his brother's final dive into the water with natural history and the mysteries of the far-travelling eel. This narrative myth-making is prepared for on the level of the plot and through a long chapter on the natural history of the eel – a history which remained highly speculative up into the twentieth century. Dominic Head praises this textual move from an ecocritical perspective. He reads Dick as a "scape-goat figure" on whom society projects their "collective sins", and who helps to foster the reader's realization "that a disastrous banishing of the natural is the product of modern social and industrial history" (240). However, the metonymical association of Dick with the eel and the natu-ral in general also shifts the focus to his sexuality and physical strength, his

---

[14]   Heise dates the emergence of such allegories of connectedness (especially Gaia theories) in the nineteen sixties and seventies; *Sense of Place and Sense of Planet* 22-28.

"precivilized" or "ahistorical state of being" (Hartung, *Die Dezentrale Geschichte* 179, 181) and closes the novel on a questionable sense of poetic justice (Dick killed another boy). The symbolic power of the scape-goat figure praised by Dominic Head may well be derived from a reductive and stereotypical image of the subject-position of the disabled which, like that of the woman, the novel simply re-iterates rather than re-conceptualizes.

In a passage towards the end of the text, the relations between natural history, a history called, more specifically, "civilization", and the concept of "progress" are related in a manner that has complex philosophical and political overtones. This is brought about through a textual siltation, both thematic and performative, that revolves around the concept of "progress" and its redefinition:

> Children, there's this thing called civilization. It's built of hopes and dreams. It's only an idea. It's not real. It's artificial. No one ever said it was real. It's not natural. No one ever said it was natural. It's built by the learning process; by trial and error. It breaks easily. No one said it couldn't fall to bits. And no one said it would last for ever. [...] There's this thing called progress. But it doesn't progress, it doesn't go anywhere. Even as progress progresses the world can slip away. It's progress if you can stop the world slipping away. My humble model for progress is the reclamation of land. Which is repeatedly, never-endingly retrieving what is lost. A dogged, vigilant business. A dull yet valuable business. A hard, inglorious, business. But you shouldn't go mistaking the reclamation of land for the building of empires.
>
> (Swift, *Waterland* 336)

In the first part the passage once more configures the material void of the "real/natural" against which – or in the face of which – the existential resilience shown in human or "artificial" history appears fragile and potentially transitory. This history can rely neither on continuity nor on immortality – "no one said it would last forever". Thus embedded this concept of human/artificial history is then deployed to deconstruct a concept of "progress" that relies on a stable and linear temporal structure.

Within the meta-context of a natural history, Swift's narrator turns the specific temporality of this highly fragile "artificial" history into the source of an ethos of struggle. This existentialist ethos defends "hopes and dreams", but the temporal model suggested for this defence is the cyclical reclamation of land – "repeatedly, never-endingly retrieving what is lost" – a temporal structure that is proposed as an alternative, as a re-definition of "progress". Instead of "leaving behind" the past, the narrator envisions past, present and future in a constant process of being re-ordered and re-valued. Modelled on the gradualism of geophysical processes and emphasizing the past as a source of value, this model of history might appear to resemble a Burkean grand narrative, yet the similarities are deceptive. The unruly movement of silt, submerging and resurfacing, from which, in Swift's *Waterland*, the land of history has to be constantly retrieved, is a far cry from the teleological organicism permeating Burke's metaphors in *Reflections on the Revolution in France*, for instance. On a political plane, Swift's narrator strategically deploys a re-conceived notion of "progress" against hubristic imperialist pretensions and invests non-narratable history of life and work with enduring values ("inglorious" yet "valuable").

Last but not least, in the Swiftean universe self-reflection plays a principal role in shaping cultural history, too. Whereas Fowles's narrator considers "self-reflection" as the professional occupation of a cultural elite, Swift's Tom Crick argues that this self-reflection emerges whenever things go wrong, whether in individual lives or historical periods (106). For this reason he famously defines the human being *per se* as "the animal which asks Why" (106).

Natural Histories and Temporalities: Un/Reconstructed Naturalizations and the Re/Configuration of Values

As we have seen, on different structural levels and in different fields of discourse, the two historical novels by John Fowles and Graham Swift accord a central place to the history of nature. To begin with, it is the fictional world's spatial and temporal structures that are shaped by history. In Fowles's novel the environment of the Undercliff harbours a counter-culture with its own licentious social history; in Swift's novel the landscape of the Fenlands forms the central setting that changes with the social history of its inhabitants. Both novels highlight that the histories of these settings predate the social history taking place, associating the Undercliff with rare fossils and the Fenlands with age-old geophysical movement. The two fictional environments thus create a sense both of the embeddedness of the social in natural history, and of these environments' specific "givenness" that precedes yet "in-forms" their long-cultivated, present state and adds to their symbolic power.

The representations of these natural environments and histories imply specific temporal models. While the natural environments are presented as veritable embodiments of these particular models of temporality, the fact that the models still have to be 'read off' the physical manifestations is persistently and self-consciously referred to. On an ontological level, this could be seen to emphasize that the natural/historical environments the novels refer to – a stretch of coastline in the south and a marshy region in the east of Britain – might give rise to very different conceptions of temporality. And *within* each of the fictional worlds, these natural environments and their history do, indeed, give rise to more than one model of temporality. In both novels the depicted natural environment and its history are related, first, to linear and progressivist conceptions dominating the fictional worlds. These conceptions appear to be rooted in the nineteenth century, they are deployed by the narrators recounting the success stories of two nineteenth-century entrepreneurs, and they shape the characters' perspectives in many ways. More specifically, these temporal models are manifest in the narratives of both Freeman's (Fowles), and Atkinsons' (Swift) commercial empires, the former consisting of trade and warehouses in Victorian London, the latter of breweries and the ownership of land and waterways in the nineteenth-century Fenlands. When Fowles's narrator/focalizer initially reflects on Freeman's commercial empire, he does so in evolutionary terms that invite a teleological version of Victorian evolutionary discourse. And when Tom Crick recounts the Atkinsons' story, he presents it as an imperialist cultivation of land in a progressivist account of social history subordinating and exploiting natural history. In both cases, these temporal models are shown to support patriarchal social hierarchies and the acquisition of material wealth.

Second, and just as importantly, the narrators draw on natural history to figure alternative temporalities or to re-interpret the temporal patterns supporting the dominant accounts of Whig history. In Fowles's novel the protagonist experiences an epiphany in the countryside that opens up his mind for a particular aspect of evolution he calls "nature's profoundest mystery". This mystery takes the form of an aesthetico-ethical plenitude which, the narrator suggests, to be accessed experientially in historically specific forms all through human history – whether through magic (the Druids), through Christian revelation (St. Hubertus); or through an epiphany (Charles Smithson). Furthermore, Fowles's narrator posits the immortality of a self-reflecting cultural elite, thus offering, again on a transhistorical level, an alternative way of life to the possessive individualism also outlined in the novel. As these alternative conceptions of temporality counterbalance progressivist historiography, they come to destabilize also the opposition between natural and human history. Fowles's novel creates a transitory moment in which the protagonist consciously enters a world experienced both as his own and that of individualized animals whom he encounters with an evolutionary as well as ethico-political sense of parity/equality. While the implications of this momentous experience do not benefit the non-human species, they do change the protagonist's attitude in the social realm. At the same time this epiphanic moment's emphasis on a non-discursive selfhood corresponds to scenes highlighting the female protagonist's non-discursivity. Though embraced from an ecofeminist perspective, the consistent association of women, animals and an unmediated access to nature thus moves perilously close to familiar gender stereotypes.

In Swift's novel the narrator Tom Crick de-centres the Atkinsons' progressivist success story by re-considering it in the face of a natural history whose existential emptiness and dynamic non-progression are identified as the driving force for the very making and recounting of human history. The intense individual experience of the natural environment that Fowles's narrator relates to an epiphanic widening of the historical horizon is here associated, transhistorically, with materiality as subjection and non-progression. For the individual, these traumatic experiences of corporeality actually contract an open temporal horizon into a circular temporality of recurrence. The rudimentary existentialist philosophy of history which is here projected onto the geophysical dynamics of silt (rather than the narrative of evolution as in Fowles) is deployed both to render visible a temporality of everyday life and labour obscured by a historiography dependent on progression, and to warn of the hubris of totalitarian and imperialist projects. Immortality of whatever kind is explicitly ruled out, while self-reflection becomes *the* defining feature of all humans. In Swift's novel, too, the constant switching between a linear and progressive and a largely non-narratable and cyclical history contribute to weakening the opposition between human and natural history. The narrator's description renders the geophysical dynamics of the Fenlands through the metaphor of a sentient body and offers a long account of attempts to discover the life-cycle of the eel. At the same time the close figurative relation between the emptiness of the landscape and the description of woman as "an empty but fillable vessel" corresponds to the way that all the female characters are presented within a framework of motherhood. And the association of the mysterious life-cycle of the eel with the sexuality and suicide of the disabled brother Dick, though rich in connotations, also has a questionable ring to it.

The two novels' respective discourses of natural history open up even wider fields of literary negotiations. Deriving its models of temporality and history from an advanced and radical version of evolutionary theory, Fowles's novel ends up with a sustaining meta-narrative that grants collective immortality to a self-reflecting cultural elite. By contrast, Swift's novel, which derives its model of history from a comparatively conventional and empirically grounded natural history, opts for a much more precarious temporality of contingent duration and an inclusive practice of self-reflection.

In addition to providing fictional spaces and models of temporality, the histories of nature represented in the novels turn into forces that shape the plots, the narration and the texts' very textuality. In Fowles's novel the notion of a "hopeful monster" is recreated as a character in the plot, a notion that depends on the concept of contingency that informs the text's scientific discourse. Yet contingency also becomes the focus of a paradoxical construction witnessing a planning and devising narrator attempting to stage, in various ways, the contingencies of his own carefully built text (three endings, throwing coins etc.). In Swift's novel, the deep time of a natural history of shifting silt, lifting and submerging (un)cultivated land, acquires a kind of "agency" in the plot; an analogous motion characterizes the narrator's moves, revealing and concealing details as he retrieves and cultivates memories, whether as autobiographical memory, textbook historiography or myth. Lastly, the construction of natural history affects the novels' texture and links it to literary and art historical tradition. In the *French Lieutenant's Woman*, the discourse of natural history shapes many of the novel's descriptive passages, rendering the rich and colourful flora and fauna of the Undercliff in aestheticized and celebratory details that evoke an Arcadian pastoral. In contrast, *Waterland* stages its landscapes in a realist mode wielding expressionistic power, and enmeshes the natural and the social in a manner gesturing towards the georgic. The heterogeneous discourse of natural history, in other words, does not provide mere settings or topics; in both novels it also emerges as a central resource for self-reflexive and intertextual novelistic structures which inform texture, plot, and the conceptual figurations of temporality and which allow for constant reconceptions of the boundaries between the "natural" and the "cultural".

Finally, and perhaps most importantly, the metafictional representations of the history of nature become the site of conspicuous revaluations that exploit the discursive malleability of the natural and transcend the divide between fact and value in a decidedly political manner. Fowles's novel depicts, on the one hand, how mainstream Victorian discourse (including Charles in his unenlightened state) deploys Darwin's writings to naturalize social, gendered, and species-related hierarchies as well as teleological progression. Yet the text also draws on a different version of evolutionary discourse as it represents Charles's encounter with the natural world (in his enlightened state) and in so doing deftly "counter-naturalizes", through the concept of parity, a non-hierarchical politics of mutual recognition which the novel can be seen to extend to different genders, classes, and species alike. Hence the standard cultural critique which accuses Victorian progressivism of bolstering its political ideology through appropriating scientific theory/facts of evolution (in a teleological version), may in principle, also be levelled against a late twentieth-century politics of recognition that bolsters its ideology by interpretations of that same theory/facts of evolution (in a contemporary

version foregrounding contingency). A crucial difference between the two appropria-
tions of scientific theory/facts for political ends is simply this: the twentieth-century
attempt to draw on the theory of evolution to support the ethico-political values of
parity/equality and recognition happens to correspond to so-called "core values" of
Western Culture that have become very dear also to cultural critics.

In Swift's novel natural history is attributed the status of a challenge from a
markedly anthropocentric perspective: the Fenlands function as an empty stage calling
forth human history and histrionics. As already pointed out, on one level this accounts
for a progressivist conception of history following the values of agrarian capitalism. Yet
on another level the natural history of the Fenlands is also shown to acquire value
through the social history it has enabled, both as a huge storeroom of narratable *and*
non-narratable human labour and as the site of people's memories and their sense of
dwelling. And on a much more submerged level of language, the narrator tropes this
environment as a sentient body thus, arguably, infusing it with a form of neo-romantic
animation and sentience. If this figuration of corporeality seems familiar from organicist
nationalist and patriarchal rhetoric propelling and legitimating capitalists projects like
that of the Atkinsons, this rhetoric is – at least partly – being rewritten here. Swift's
metaphors highlight the violence produced by totalitarian politics and agrarian capitalist
technology through figuring a trans-species body, or rather a cosmic sentient body. So
even though the text does not formulate a politics of recognition, it can still be seen to
include natural history in its critique of imperialist politics and agrarian technologies,
and thus to gesture towards biocentric sensibilities.

Even though historiographic metafiction offers a generic format that lends itself to a
self-reflexive and paradoxical exploration of the discourse of natural history, the
revaluations undertaken in Fowles's and Swift's novels do not or cannot avoid discursive affiliations that remain deeply ambivalent in other respects, especially when
suggesting specific affinities between the natural and the female, focusing, e.g. on non-
discursivity and patrilinear reproduction. Yet even if scepticism must be allowed here, it
should be balanced against these novels' achievement in exploring natural history not
simply as a contextual framework, but in re-figuring it as a historical meta-context that
lends itself to pluralizations and revaluations on all levels of the text. In this perspective,
the two novels could be taken to critique both "unreconstructed" naturalizations *and* the
blindness towards natural history as a potential source of value that is worth fighting
for, *both* for its own sake and for the reconstructed naturalizations it makes
possible/brings forth. In other words, Fowles's and Swift's historical novels could even
be seen as advocating re-constructed naturalizations as a metafictional device for drawing attention to the history of nature as a valuable material/textual resource. Not least
through their metafictional strategies do the two novels foreground the history of nature
as a material and textual resource that engenders foundational experiences/represen-
tations from which a plurality of temporal models and ethico-political values have been
and will be constructed in human history and its historiographical or literary
textualizations.

Works Cited

Alphen, Ernst van. 'The Performativity of Histories: Graham Swift's *Waterland* as a Theory of History.' *The Point of Theory: Practices of Culture Analysis*. New York: Continuum, 1994. 202-10.

Aubrey, James R. 'Introduction.' *John Fowles and Nature: Fourteen Perspectives on Landscape*. Ed. James R. Aubrey. Madison NJ: Fairleigh Dickinson University Press, 1999.

Beatty, Patricia V. 'The Undercliff as Inverted Pastoral: The Fowlesian *Felix Culpa* in *The French Lieutenant's Woman*.' *John Fowles and Nature: Fourteen Perspectives on Landscape*. Ed. James R. Aubrey. Madison, NJ: Fairleigh Dickinson University Press, 1999. 169-80.

Berlatsky, Eric. '"The Swamps of Myth… and Empirical Fishing Lines": Historiography, Narrativity, and the "Here and Now" in Graham Swift's *Waterland*.' *Journal of Narrative Theory* 36-2 (Summer 2006): 254-92.

Blumenbach, Johann Friedrich. *Handbuch der Naturgeschichte*. Göttingen: Dieterich, 1779.

Buell, Lawrence. *The Environmental Imagination: Thoreau, Nature Writing, and the Formation of American Culture*. Cambridge, MA: The Belknap Press of Harvard University Press, 1995.

Buffon, Georges-Louis Leclerc Comte de. *Histoire Naturelle, Generale et Particulière*. Paris: L'Imprimerie Royale, 1749.

Burke, Edmund. *Reflections on the Revolution in France*. London: printed for J. Dodsley, In Pall Mall, 1790.

Byrd, Deborah. 'The Evolution and Emancipation of Sarah Woodruff: *The French Lieutenant's Woman* as a Feminist Novel.' *International Journal of Women's Studies* 7-4 (1984): 306-21.

Chakarbarty, Dipesh. 'Climate History: Four Theses.' *Critical Inquiry* 35-2 (2009): 197-222.

Clark, Timothy. *The Cambridge Introduction to Literature and the Environment*. Cambridge: Cambridge University Press, 2011.

Conradi, Peter. *John Fowles*. London: Methuen, 1983.

Cooper, Pamela. *The Fictions of John Fowles: Power, Creativity, Femininity*. Ottawa: University of Ottawa Press, 1991.

Cooper, Pamela. 'Imperial Topographies: The Spaces of History in *Waterland*.' *Modern Fiction Studies* 42-2 (1996): 371-96.

Dunkerton, Jill, et al. *Early Renaissance Painting in the National Gallery*. New Haven: Yale University Press, 1991.

Engelhardt, Dietrich von. 'Historical Consciousness in the German Romantic Naturforschung.' Trans. Christine Salazar. *Romanticism and the Sciences*. Eds. Andrew Cunningham and Nicholas Jardine. Cambridge & New York: Cambridge University Press, 1990. 55-68

Fludernik, Monika. 'History and Metafiction.' *Historiographic Metafiction in Modern American and Canadian Literature*. Ed. Bernd Engler. Paderborn: Schöningh, 1994. 81-101.

Fowles, John. *The French Lieutenant's Woman*. London: Vintage, 1996.

Fowles, John. 'Notes on an Unfinished Novel.' *Wormholes: Essays and Occasional Writings*. Ed. Jan Relf. London: Jonathan Cape, 1998. 13-26.

Goodbody, Axel. 'Sense of Place and Lie de Mémoire: A Cultural Memory Approach to Environmental Texts.' *Ecocritical Theory: New European Approaches*. Eds. Axel Goodbody and Kate Rigby. Charlottesville & London: University of Virginia Press, 2011. 55-70.

Goscilo, Margaret Bozenna. 'John Fowles's Pre-Raphaelite Woman: Interart Strategies and Gender Politics.' *Mosaic: A Journal for the Interdisciplinary Study of Literature* 26-2 (1993): 63-82.

Gould, Stephen Jay. *Time's Arrow, Time's Cycle: Myth and Metaphor in the Discovery of Geological Time*. London: Penguin, 1987.

Gould, Stephen Jay. *Wonderful Life: The Burgess Shale and the Nature of History*. New York: Norton, 1989.

Haefner, Gerhard. 'Geschichte und Natur in Graham Swifts *Waterland*.' *Das Natur/Kultur-Paradigma in der englischsprachigen Erzählliteratur des 19. und 20. Jahrhunderts*. Eds. Konrad Groß et al. Tübingen: Gunter Narr, 1994. 208-21.

Hartung, Heike. *Dezentrale Geschichte(n).: Historisches Erzählen und literarische Geschichte(n) bei Peter Ackroyd, Graham Swift und Salman Rushdie*. Trier: Wissenschftlicher Verlag Trier, 2002.

Heise, Ursula K. *Chronoschisms: Time, Narrative and Postmodernism*. Cambridge: Cambridge University Press, 1997.

Hutcheon, Linda. *A Poetics of Postmodernism: History, Theory, Fiction*. New York & London: Routledge, 1988.

Hutton, James. *Theory of the Earth*. Edinburgh: printed for Cadell et al, 1795.

Jackson, Tony E. 'Charles and the Hopeful Monster: Postmodern Evolutionary Theory in *The French Lieutenant's Woman*.' *Twentieth Century Literature* 43-2 (Summer 1997): 221-42.

Kerridge, Richard. 'Ecothrillers: Environmental Cliffhangers.' *The Green Studies Reader: From Romanticism to Ecocriticism*. Ed. Laurence Couper. London: Routledge, 2000. 242-9.

Latour, Bruno. *Politics of Nature: How to Bring the Sciences into Democracy*. Cambridge, MA, & London: Harvard University Press, 2004.

Lepenies, Wolf. *Das Ende der Naturgeschichte: Wandel kultureller Selbstverständlichkeiten in den Wissenschaften des 18. und 19. Jahrhunderts*. Frankfurt am Main: Suhrkamp, 1978.

Loveday, Simon. *The Romances of John Fowles*. London: Palgrave Macmillan, 1985.

Lynch, Richard P. 'Freedoms in "The French Lieutenant's Woman."' *Twentieth Century Literature* 48-1 (Spring 2002): 50-76.

Nünning, Ansgar. 'Where Historiographic Metafiction and Narratology Meet: Towards an Applied Cultural Narratology.' *Style* 38-3 (Fall 2004): 352-75.

Onega, Susana. 'British Historiographic Metafiction.' *Metafiction*. Ed. Mark Currie. London & New York: Longman, 1995. 92-103.

Pohler, Eva Mokry. 'Genetic and Cultural Selection in *The French Lieutenant's Woman*.' *Mosaic: A Journal for the Interdisciplinary Study of Literature* 35-2 (June 2002): 57-72.

Powell, Katrina M. 'Mary Metcalf's Attempt at Reclamation: Maternal Representation in Graham Swift's *Waterland.' Women's Studies* 32 (2003): 59-77.

Ross, Suzanne. '"Water out of a Woodland Spring": Sarah Woodruff and Nature in *The French Lieutenant's Woman.' John Fowles and Nature: Fourteen Perspectives on Landscape*. Ed. James R. Aubrey. Madison, NJ: Fairleigh Dickinson University Press, 1999. 181-94.

Schaber, Peter. 'Naturalistischer Fehlschluss.' *Handbuch Ethik*. Eds. Marcus Düwell, Christoph Hübenthal and Micha H. Werner. Stuttgart: Metzler, 2002. 437-40.

Soper, Kate. 'Passing Glories and Romantic Retrievals: Avant-Garde Nostalgia and Hedonist Renewal.' *Ecocritical Theory: New European Approaches*. Eds. Axel Goodbody and Kate Rigby. Charlottesville & London: University of Virginia Press, 2011. 17-29.

Soper, Kate. *What is Nature? Culture, Politics and the Non-Human*. Oxford: Blackwell, 1995.

Stephenson, William. *Fowles's The French Lieutenant's Woman*. London & New York: Continuum, 2008.

Swift, Graham. *Waterland*. Basingstoke: Picador, 1992.

Tarbox, Katherine. '*The French Lieutenant's Woman* and the Evolution of Narrative.' *Twentieth Century Literature* 42-1, John Fowles Issue (Spring 1996): 88-102.

White, Hayden. 'The Historical Text as Literary Artifact.' *Narrative Dynamics: Essays on Time, Plot, Closure, and Frames*. Ed. Brian Richardson. Columbus: The Ohio State University Press, 2002. 191-210.

RUSSELL WEST-PAVLOV

The Production of History:
M. G. Vassanji's Postcolonial Historical Novel on the Indian Ocean Rim

Saleem Sinai, the protagonist of Salman Rushdie's now classic *Midnight's Children* (1981), is famously "handcuffed to history", born as he is at the exact moment at which India gains its independence (Rushdie, *Midnight's Children* 9). Though Rushdie's hyperbolic parody of the historical novel has been a central figure in the postmodern recrafting of the genre built, according to Lukács, on the synecdoche of national and individual histories, it too has ossified into the lone representative of an atrophied post-colonial canon (Anderson, 'From Progress to Catastrophe' 27-8; Lazarus, 'The Politics of Postcolonial Modernism' 424). Rushdie's epic has become curiously 'handcuffed', in part because of its reception by Anglo-American critics ignorant of its local allusions, in part because its own display of intertextual allegiances to canonical European texts such as Sterne's *Tristram Shandy* (1759-67), to the very tradition whose yoke it seeks to buck. In this essay I seek to renew the gesture of the 'provincialization' of the European historical novel by reading a subsequent avatar of the genre from beyond the postcolo-nial pale, Tanzanian-Canadian M. J. Vassanji's début novel *The Gunny Sack* (1989) – a compendium of East African colonial and postcolonial history which traces the trajec-tory of an Indian diaspora family and its community via German and British imperial rule through to independence.[1]

Vassanji's East African historical novel appears, at first glance, to make numerous allusions to Rushdie's masterpiece: echoing Saleem Sinai, its protagonist-narrator is named Salim Juma; a bloodied muslin shirt is among the mnemonic objects mentioned in the opening paragraph (3), seemingly in imitation of the perforated sheet of Rushdie's first chapter; where Rushdie apostrophizes his parodic muse Padma, Vassanji addresses his even more parodic source of inspiration, the humble gunny sack of the novel's title, a jute bag containing the mementos of the narrator's family history; echo-ing Rushdie's evocation of Scheherazade in his prefatory comments, Vassanji inaugu-rates his narrative by naming the eponymous gunny sack 'Shehrbanboo', or 'Shehru' for short, as a derivation of Scheherazade (5-6). Yet the resemblances, so ostentatiously displayed in the novel's incipit, are taken no further. Perplexingly, Vassanji eagerly offers these all-too-obvious tokens of intertextual allegiance, only to abandon the link-ages as soon as they are suggested. The moorings that might harness Vassanji's text to

[1] Chakrabarty, *Provincializing Europe: Postcolonial Thought and Historical Difference*; M. J. Vassanji, *The Gunny Sack*. London: Heinemann, 1989, all subsequent references in the text.

Rushdie's are so slack as to be loosed almost immediately, allowing Vassanji's text to float away into its own limbo. Fully cognizant of this increasing gap, the narrator coyly notes, "Shehrbanoo, Schehrazade, how close in sound, yet worlds apart" (6).

The looseness of the fit, I suggest in this chapter, typifies Vassanji's strategy, which consists of constructing a historical novel which obstinately refuses to be chained to history. Not only that, the constantly puzzling tenuousness of its connections to history, I submit, are at the core of its historical project. In his defence of hybrid ethnic entanglements as a viable sociological model for the future of African polities, Vassanji rejects linear genealogies, and by the same token, comes to eschew all models of historiography which do not embrace fractured, zig-zag cartographies of past, present and future, and the ways they interact. In my exploration of Vassanji's project, I will dwell upon three main facets of his undertaking. I begin by pursuing the ongoing 'provincialization' of the European historical novel by reviewing successive relocations of the genre outside of Europe. I then continue by further dismantling the connection between national history and individual life-story that lies at the core of the European historical novel. I do this, on the one hand by questioning the notion of the self which constitutes one part of this nexus; and on the other by noting a dispersal of the nation, the other part of the nexus, into a transnational and then a natural context. In this way, this essay seeks to recalibrate the notion of the historical novel, breaking it out of its generic connection to the European nation and its meta-narratives. The essay does this by suggesting there can be a historical novel which responds to historical trajectories outside of the national framework, and without an individual subject as its principal synecdoche.

National History and Historical Novel

Lukács's historical novel is a European genre. It arises according to his thesis out of the nexus between the European nation-state and its citizens. The novel is that genre par excellence which operates metonymically and allows the unique experience of the citizen to appear as a synecdoche of the historical experience of the nation. Indeed, the operation of synecdoche allows the life of the individual to be experienced as historical *per se* (Lukács, *The Historical Novel* 20,22). Conversely, however, the nation needs the life of its individuals to be experienced as historical material in order to endow the nation with an organic temporal existence and make it accessible for those citizens who in this way will swear allegiance to it. The object of allegiance is no longer a person, but rather an abstract entity, and without a 'life' of its own it cannot become the object of allegiance and thus runs the risk of suffering a lack of legitimacy. For this reason that nation too is dependent upon its subjects' experience of historical time as the medium which stabilizes the 'imagined community' to which they henceforth belong (Anderson, *Imagined Communities* 6-7). Whence the doubly over-determined 'nationalist pedagogy' which is both underpinned and undermined by the constant imperative of the 'performative' (Bhabha, *The Location of Culture* 142, 145-6). One of the salient narrative performances of the nation has been the historical novel, a genre whose 'pedagogical' function has become increasingly ambivalent following its mid-nineteenth-century 'decline' (Lukács, *The Historical Novel* 204-17). The genre has manifested more and more the 'performative' underpinning/undermining ambivalence at the core of national identity as the nation has experienced repeated crises of legitimacy under late capitalism.[2]

In questioning this paradigm, however, it is not enough merely to relocate the historical novel from a European into a non-European context. The example of Rushdie's *Midnight's Children* shows how even the hyperbolic nexus of self and nation may merely finish by reinscribing that which it seeks to unsettle. Further less obviously iconoclastic, but perhaps ultimately more subversive, gestures may be necessary to complete this deconstructive work. In the context of Vassanji's *The Gunny Sack*, another geographical shift, from India towards Africa, exemplified concretely in nineteenth-century immigration from the Gujarati port of Porbander to Zanzibar and then coastal Kilwa which opens the novel (8-9), may be salutary. Such a shift of focus, faithful to historical patterns of migration as it is, might appear methodologically fairly tame, but in fact conceals some paradigmatic adjustments to the contours of the post-colonial canon, and this for several reasons.

First, India has not by chance always been the privileged domain of British-based postcolonial studies, in part because India as the 'jewel in the crown' enjoyed a particular status within the imperial-colonial configuration, and as an object of literary-historical study continued to focus post-colonial nostalgias well beyond the point of independence.[3] Indian literature has continued thus within the domain of postcolonial studies to incorporate shadowy residues of late-colonial retrogression. The study of Indian literature within the postcolonial syllabus of the metropolitan universities has thus never been entirely free of traces of neoimperialism in disguised form. By the same token, recastings of traditional genres within the Indian tradition may in some cases, and this is arguably so for some of Rushdie's fiction, potentially play into an ongoing neo-colonial cringe.

Second, India as a locus of postcolonial rewriting is itself not free of the effects of a powerful system of cultural hierarchies which do not merely arrange 'the West' and 'the Rest' on a ladder of cultural value, but also set up hierarchies among 'the Rest'. One of these hierarchies, which will become particularly relevant in a number of ways to my subsequent discussion of the Indian Ocean World novel, sets Africa at the very bottom of the cultural ladder, well below Asia. In one context where Asia and Africa frequently size up against each other, the emergent field of Indian Ocean studies, this hierarchy is frequently visible, with Pearson claiming that "the inhabitants of [the Indian Ocean's] littoral ranged from primitive East Africans to notoriously skilful Gujarati merchants and courtly sophisticated rulers and governors" ('Introduction I: The State of the Subject' 12), or Chaudhuri justifying "[t]he exclusion of East Africa from our civilizational identities" by claiming that "the indigenous African communities appear to have

2 See Habermas, *Legitimationsprobleme im Spätkapitalismus*, and more recently, Streeck, *Die gekaufte Zeit: Die vertagte Krise des demokratischen Kapitalismus* .
3 This tendency is exemplified, for instance, in the fact that of the five volumes that have appeared to date in the OUP series 'Oxford Studies in Postcolonial Literatures', only Priyamvada Gopal's *The Indian English Novel: Nation, History, and Narration* has been a commercial success; this is a clear (commercial) index of institutional hierarchies of value among the respective areas of academic postcolonial studies and the attendant (textbook-buying) audiences they command.

been structured by a historical logic separate and independent from the rest of the Indian Ocean" (*Asia Before Europe* 36). Implicit in this claim is that African polities, lacking the centralized political and social structures necessary to allow them to enter Modernity in the manner that, say, emergent Indian polities have done, cannot make claims to represent even 'alternative' modernities (see Campbell, 'The Role of Africa'). Thus the postcolonial historical novel, if we can refer generically to a trend epitomized by Rushdie's *Midnight's Children*, is caught up in a set of hierarchies in which the ostensible subaltern is constituted no less by its own sub-subalterns.

Precisely for this reason, however, there would seem to be a particular need to explore recalibrations of the historical novel which are set in Africa so as to begin to sketch an alternative theory of the 'subaltern' historical novel *within* postcolonial subaltern studies itself. For, if it is true that contemporary Africa continues to labour under a burden of stereoptypes of embodied negativity and historical void, then there may be call for the re-working of the European historical novel on just that terrain which, since Hegel, has been constructed as the constitutive outside of European historicity.[4] In Vassanji's fiction, this task is typically undertaken by relocating his fictionalized histories to the East African littoral of the Indian Ocean, which thus becomes the privileged site of more complex historical imbrications between historical actors and their nation. In his narrative, both of these players will be fissured and thereby transformed into something which far exceeds the purview of the historical novel in its existing guises.

Trade, Migration, Indian Ocean

Though Vassanji's fictions have been described as postmodern, they are not postmodern in the sense imagined by Perry Anderson in his sustained historical sketch of the transformations of the historical novel; that is, they do little in the way of mixing myth and fact, magic and realism, or juggling historical planes (Ojwang, 'Memory, Migrancy and Modernity' 141; Anderson, 'From Progress to Catastrophe' 28). Vassanji's novel is strikingly conventional in its mode of narration, and even the fantastical device of a speaking gunny sack as muse becomes the site for the curt dismissal of the sort of magical-realist effects the Rushdiesque opening pages might have led the reader to expect: "And so much for mythology, says Shehru. Now for some history" (7). It is hardly surprising, then, that at first glance, *The Gunny Sack* appears to offer a chronologically coherent historical macrocosm for its social microcosm. Beginning with late-nineteenth-century Indian immigration to Africa (1885 is given as a bench-mark date [10]), and moving via the Maji Maji uprising against colonial German rule (15-17), the First and Second World Wars (45, 65), it then passes via the Mau Mau emergency in Kenya from 1952 (74ff), and subsequent Independence in Kenya (156, 161). Shifting its geographical focus slightly, it records the bloodshed in Zanzibar in 1963, with the concomitant expulsions of Arabs and Asians (173ff), the subsequent Federation of Tanzania and

---

4   See Ferguson, *Global Shadows: Africa in the Neoliberal World Order*; Mbembe, *On the Postcolony*; Hegel famously claimed that Africa "forms no historical part of the World; it exhibits no movement or development" (Hegel, *The Philosophy of History* 91).

Zanzibar (185), the Arusha declaration 1967 and Tanzanian *Ujamaa* socialism (241), through to the rise of Idi Amin and the Ugandan Asian exodus (240, 246-7), which signals the demise of the East African hybrid world Vassanji is committed to memorializing.

Yet, for all the density of these historical references, there is a strong sense that they remain largely tangential to the main events of the characters' lives. When the account of the early twentieth-century Maji Maji uprising, in itself curiously uneventful, concludes with the words, "Thus the [...] revolt, which spread like a bush fire in the night across more than a quarter of the country, bypassed Matamu" (17), we have a succinct summary of the entire historical narrative in its apparent tendency to 'bypass' the lived trajectories of its main protagonists.

One primary reason for the failure of this history to genuinely overlap with the narrative of the characters' lives is that these histories are in the main histories of nations, or of their conflicts, or of their postcolonial avatars. By contrast, Vassanji's narrative concerns the immigrant traders of the Shamsi sect, whose identities are largely cut loose from that of the nation: "Among trading peoples, loyalty to a land or a government, always loudly professed, is a trait one can normally look for in vain. Governments may come and go, but the immigrants' only concern is the security of their family, their trade and savings" (52). Trade as the historically stereotypical characteristic of East African Asian populations becomes the crowbar which levers them out of national allegiances. Certainly in the eyes of the postcolonial polities, their erstwhile proximity to the institutions of colonial power made them collaborators in the eyes of the new post-independence power-holders, despite their enthusiastically "renounc[ing] the Queen's rule for a new [postcolonial] future" (249) (Vassanji notes that many of his generation gave up their British passports at Independence, embracing the cause of the new nation, only to find themselves second-class citizens under nativist ideology).[5] Any link with the polity appears tenuous at best, with the inherent connections between trade and hybridity rendering Vassanji's characters constitutionally unfit for an easy allegiance to the nation as a restrictive category of subjecthood, if not citizenship. Vassanji's narrative thus resolutely eschews categorization as a third-world national allegory (*pace* Jameson).[6]

Trade creates the geographies sketched in the novel, rather like the emblematic bush village of Rukanga, "put there by Swahili, Arab, and Indian foreigners from the coast for the mere purposes of trading" (50). Vassanji's historical novel roams over the globe, beginning in India, shifting to Zanzibar, then to Dar es Salaam in erstwhile German East Africa, then to Nairobi in British Kenya Colony, and then on to pre- and post-independence Tanganyika/Tanzania, finishing apparently somewhere in an unspecified exilic Canada. In fact, what is sketched here is not the history of a nation, but rather, the

---

[5]   In an interview with Susheila Nasta, Vassanji has said, "the Asians always thought – at least the Asians that I was in touch with in my community – that we were there to stay and these were very conscious decisions. British citizenships were renounced, we sent back our British passports and it was a wholehearted embrace of the new political situation." (Vassanji, 'Moyez Vassanji with Susheila Nasta (1991)' [Interview], 73)

[6]   Fredric Jameson, 'Third-World Literature in the Era of Multinational Capitalism', *Social Text* 15 (Autumn 1986): 65-88 (here 69).

history of what has come to be called, in recent scholarship, the Indian Ocean World. It is the diasporic trajectory of an offshore-Indian religious trading community, the Shamsis, as they move around the Indian Ocean and around various loci on the East African littoral and its interior, that creates the historical geographies explored by the fiction. Thus this historical novel is clearly not one which emerges at the interface between an historical subject and its national community. The narrator's brother Sona leaves Tanzania to become a researcher in the USA, declaring that he wants to study "History – of our community" (234). This brief, which ostentatiously narrows its focus well below the threshold of the nation-state, subsequently expands to a scale well above that of the nation: "Sona's later interest [became] Coastal East Africa" (234). Restricted initially to the Shamsi community and its vicissitudes, Sona's research area later embraces the entire region. Enter, thus, the historical novel in which the life of a community (not an individual) is the synecdoche of the life of a region (not a nation).

Vassanji's narrative approximates, but perhaps even going beyond what Jameson has described as "the novel of the anonymous masses, the movements of the peoples, the historical period itself (whose events are little more than its symptoms)" (*The Antinomies of Realism* 307). For this last shift of focus is however, not the novel's conceptual terminus. For it reveals in fact a further actant in Vassanji's version of the historical novel which differentiates it even more significantly from the European template for the genre. The force underpinning this trade-driven diasporic history of a coastal religious minority is the Indian Ocean itself. At the opening of the narrative we are shown Dhanji Govindji "feeling the cool salty air from the ocean" (28), at the close we see him "listening to the ocean" (268). It is the Indian Ocean itself, with its patterns of trade, enabled by the monsoon winds, that frames the narrative, and creates its contours according to a form of history that Braudel, in his *magnum opus* on the Mediterranean, characterized as 'longue durée' (*The Mediterranean and the Mediterranean World* 1947). This form of history, which he opposed to the short-term history of human events and the middle-term history of economic cycles, is that of the natural world itself, with patterns of geographical formation and climate change lasting millennia. 'Longue durée' history underpins and enables historical action. It is its very condition of possibility of, and for most of history, the ultimate determinant of human destinies. And indeed, the human interaction with the system of Indian Ocean winds and currents has constituted an environment whose history goes back at least five millennia (Pearson, *The Indian Ocean* 3).[7]

Trade, carried by the currents and driven by the winds of the Indian Ocean, has been the main motor of cross-cultural interaction, not only in this novel but within world history in general (Curtin, *Cros-Cultural Trade in World History*). In tracing the history of the hybridity which Vassanji is at pains to stress in his East African littoral historical novel, the text has no qualms about short-circuiting the copula trade-hybridity to reveal the foundations of that nexus in the natural world. Upon arriving as a trader in the coastal town of Matamu, Dhanji Govindji enters a common-law marriage with the slave girl Bibi Taratibu, following the advice of the local Mukhi or religious leader: "'it can

---

[7]   See also Bose, *A Hundred Horizons: The Indian Ocean in the Age of Global Empire*; Kearney, *The Indian Ocean in World History*; McPherson, *The Indian Ocean: A History of People and The Sea*.

get quite cold at night. The ocean, you know'" (11). This partnership, initiated in the last analysis by the natural elements themselves, results in the birth of the mixed-race Huseni, the narrator's grandfather. Though that common-law marriage subsequently collapses under the pressure of Dhanji Govindji's second marriage to a Zanzibari Indian woman, the mixed-race partnership inaugurates the hybrid identity which, despite much resistance (11), becomes the *basso continuo* of Salim's family history, and the burden of Vassanji's project in all of his fictions: "Tell me, Shehrbanoo, would the world be different if that trend had continued, if there had been more Husenis, and if these chocolate Husenis with curly hair had grown up unhindered, playing barefoot in kanzus and kofias, clutching Arabic readers" (11). At the origin of this family history is not cultural cohesion, but the intersection of cultural difference, driven in the last analysis by the imperatives of the natural world as they re-emerge into the epistemological purview of later generations: "'The ocean, you know'" (11). In the words of Ghosh and Muecke, "The ocean, no longer simply the object of our enquiring gaze, is now treated respectfully as an actor in this network" (Ghosh and Muecke, 'Natural Logics of the Indian Ocean' 153).

Vassanji's historical novel thus registers a series of dislocations from the historical novel as national synecdoche, via a narrative of diaspora and cultural hybridity and that of a trade-based region, arriving finally at a form of the historical novel that one might tentatively, and catachrestically, name 'natural history'.[8] This is the first aspect of its dual reconfiguration of the European historical novel. The second recalibration, which of course cannot be entirely separated from the first, is located at the site of the other element of the nation-individual nexus consecrated by the historical novel, namely, the protagonist as historical subject.

Loose Connections

Critics generally classify the novel as thinly-disguised autobiography, thus taxing it, somewhat in the manner of T. S. Eliot, with an inadequate artistic 'transmutation' of individual experience.[9] The novel is often compared unfavourably to the better-crafted successors such as *The Book of Secrets* (1994) or *The In-Between World of Vikram Lall* (2003). And indeed, the protagonist Salim Juma does indeed appear to be poorly motivated, at times even shoddily crafted. As a character, he is curiously bland, and never quite attains the 'complexity' that a traditional form of evaluative criticism once demanded of so-called 'round characters'. He has a curiously sparse personal history, marked only by a few salient events, in themselves oddly anomalous within the plot: the death of his father triggers the family's removal to Dar es Salaam, but the superstitious

---

[8] In a manner not entirely foreign to the underlying impulse of Gilbert White's *Natural History of Selborne*, nor to the radically different, but no less related (given the conflict-ridden twentieth-century history of the Indian Ocean region) notion of a 'natural history of destruction': see Sebald, *On the Natural History of Destruction*.

[9] Bardolph, 'Identité et frontières d'un domain de recherche: l'exemple de la littérature d'Afrique anglophone' 731-2; Nazareth, 'The First Tanz/Asian Novel'; Ojwang, 'Memory, Migrancy and Modernity in M. J. Vassanji's *The Gunny Sack* and *The Book of Secrets*' 141; Eliot, 'Tradition and the Individual Talent' 26-7.

attribution of fault to Salim himself ("How I killed my father" [67]) weakens the causal linkage in a generally realist plot; the affair with the African co-student Amina, which embodies the vitiated hybrid relationships that Vassanji offers as a model for a more tolerant postcolonial polity ("we started carrying the burdens of our races [...] our world was pulling us apart" [228]), fizzles out inconsequentially. As a fictional 'subject of history', Salim's self-constitution in narrative is uneven. Some segments of the narra-tive, such as the colourful account of growing up in straitened circumstances in Dar es Salaam (83-125), appear inordinately long and eventually become a little tedious. Others are telescoped to the point of incomprehensibility: we never know quite what triggers the narrator's hasty departure from post-independence Tanzania, except for the vagaries of political repression, and a less-than-convincing marital crisis; nor does the text ever explain why the narrator is confined in a cellar in Canada, which becomes the setting for the process of narrating his life. Vassanji is conscious of these anomalies: "Not all the mysteries of the past are resolved in the book (Kanagana-yakam,"'Broadening the Substrata'..." 22)." At times, one has the impression of reading a contingently motivated picaresque narrative rather than the sure trajectory of a *Bildungsroman*.

Yet the appropriateness of the concept of the 'picaresque', which has experienced a recent renewal in novels such as Aravind Adiga's *The White Tiger* (2008) (see Elze, *The Picaresque*), suggests that there is postcolonial method in this putative mediocrity. Rather than ascribing these seeming flaws in the narration to an early, apprenticeship-like phase of authorial artistic development, I would argue that these apparent faults of construction should be understood as indices of a lacunary relationship between fictional selfhood and fictional history. If the historical novel works to focalize histori-cal trends through the experiences of an individual self, thus making them accessible within the framework of a national narrative, then this mediating subjective instance is only imperfectly present in Vassanji's novel. The text's relationship to national narra-tives is uncertain, fragmented as they are through the various conflicting modes of trade-driven expatriation, shifting colonial sovereignties, transitions from one colonial domain to another, discrimination under the new postcolonial regime, and serial exile. Under these circumstances of contingency, there is no secure framework that the self can attach itself to or identify with; likewise, there is no 'collective national subject' to provide the individual subject with a template of historical development for which it, in turn, can become the locally instantiated synecdoche.

If the reciprocal, mutually reinforcing relationships between self and nation consti-tute the historical novel in its ideal form, this symbiosis collapses, if not completely then at least partially, in Vassanji's narrative. This in turn generates incoherencies in the model of history which is being presented. These incoherencies are not located in the pattern of historical events itself, as a more postmodern appropriation of the historical novel might tend to do. Thus, Vassanji's dislocation of the structures of the historical novel are not worked by the sorts of historiographical fallacies that Rushdie for instance employs (typically, Saleem's manipulation of the date of Mahatma Gandhi's death) (Rushdie, *Midnight's Children* 166). Rather, Vassanji's strategies of subversion appear more discretely, as anomalies within the narrative structure of the story itself.

From the outset, incomplete narratives litter the novel. Some of these are at the level of stories within the story. The half-caste son born to the narrator's great-grandfather

Dhanji Govindji and Bibi Taratibu his African slave mistress, Huseni "walked out. He never returned, he was never heard from again" (22). Likewise, his mother, Bibi Taratibu, suffers the same fate: "One day she too left Matamu and was never heard from again" (25). These broken-off filiations within the novel's genealogies may simply be indices of the repressive ideologies which enforce ethnic purity and impose the severance of hybrid connections. However, such loose ends are embedded in the narrative structure itself and continue to proliferate as an aporia at the level of the narrative discourse. When part of the narrator's family founds its own mystical sufi sect, only to see one of its leaders leave, "This left Fatu Aunti and Mad Mitha. What future for this fledgling sect? That remains to be seen" (256). Yet the sect is never mentioned again, and the implicit promise of a continuation of this narrateme remains unfulfilled. Similarly, when the narrator's school friend Shivji Shame makes his last appearance, still pursuing a career as a lone Asian in the African-dominated Tanzanian army, he whispers "'You watch me, I'll make it yet. I've been to Uganda.' Out he stomped into the dark night" (257). But watch as we may, there is no further mention of him, except the passing hint that an 'Asian' has been detained for sedition (261). The lacunary character of historical narrative and of the narrative of history respectively are not to be seen as a weakness within the novel's logic. Rather, they open up spaces of possibility which widen its purview.

The historical novel in its classic form forecloses on the individual subject as the point at which modern national history and modern experience are welded to each other. The 'seams' in the pre-colonial Indian ethnic edifice (7) which trigger Vassanji's Shamsi community's exile already foreshadow the fissures which later will be reflected in the body of Rushdie's Saleem Sinai after Independence (see Brennan *Salman Rushdie and the Third World* 94). Yet that isomorphism of fractured nation and fractured narrator, absent in Vassanji's fiction by virtue of his refusal to insert his fiction into a national narrative, has as its equivalent in *The Gunny Sack* a different sort of fracture, located elsewhere, endowed with a valency entirely positive.

The Textual Production of History

The defining moment in Salim's own personal history is the death of his father. Because this death is superstitiously ascribed by the family to Salim's spilling of milk (79-80), the episode comes to epitomize not only the family's geographical peregrinations, but also the causal inconsistencies in the narrative chain. The father's demise causes the family's subsequent relocation from prosperous colonial Nairobi to Dar es Salaam's tawdry Kariakoo quarter, under the sign of narrative and existential fragmentation: "The image of quiet, leafy suburbia impressed on the mind, of Nairobi's Desai Road, cracked in the heart of Dar into a myriad of refracting fragments, each a world unto its own" (86). The experience of exile and social demotion is simultaneously traumatic and salutary, as it describes the two facets of Vassanji's narrative and ethnic project, in which the twinned phenomena of lacunae and fragments become the key to a relegitimized and revitalized narrative aesthetics of hybridity.

One central episode is crucial in working this paradigm shift from physical loss to narrative restoration. Burdened by the guilt of his putative "crime [of] murder" (79),

Salim, together with his siblings, surreptitiously seeks out a medium to bring back the spirit of the father (131-3). They fail in their mission: "the djinns say the man was a big soul. He cannot be called" (133). Yet the absence of the father and the ongoing frag-mentation of the boy's world inaugurate a larger narrative project which, ultimately, becomes that of *The Gunny Sack* itself: on the way home from the medium, the children pass a mattress shop where, unbeknown to them, their great aunt Ji Bai, born of Dhanji Govinji's second marriage, is now living in Dar. Ji Bai is the owner of the gunny sack which will be later bequeathed to Salim, and is a curator of family stories, which she passes on to him: "Well, listen [Salim] son of Juma, you listen to me and I shall give you your father Juma and his father Huseni and his father [Dhanji Govinji]" (134). The 'absence of the body' is the motor of narrative (Marin, 'Du corps au text: Propositions métaphysiques sur l'origine du récit'), and this narrative, founded as it is on a constitu-tive experiential schism or chasm, in turn reinscribes family and community history with an ongoing element of cultural heterogeneity.

In much the same manner, an earlier narrative in which a father loses a son (rather than a son losing a father), the departure of the mixed-race Huseni vitiates neither the family lineage, albeit this is present as a series of absences and displacements (it is Huseni's son Juma who will be 'killed' by his son Salim) nor narrative. For Dhanji Govimndji's efforts to trace his son send him on long journeys which in turn generate extraordinary stories that open up the East African littoral in narrative (29-32). They evoke a continent whose character is that of infinite extension: "Africa was not as small as he had confidently thought [...] One could go deeper and deeper into it and never return. Perhaps that was what had happened to his son Huseni" (32). These stories are told to Ji Bai, who in turn passes on the legacy of story-telling, to Salim, and via the gunny sack as mnemonic metonymy, to the readers.

This history of heterogeneity is in danger of being repressed by those in the Shamsi community "for whom history was a contemptible record of a shameful past" (134), and its retrieval is one of the main impulses behind Vassanji's work:

> the life that we lived [...] has never been written about. It's slowly been wiped out [...] I think all people should have a sense of themselves, a sense of where they come from, and it just happens that people in East Africa – I think Indians as well as Africans in Tanzania – don't have that sense, a historical sense, of where they come from.
>
> (Vassanji, 'Moyez Vassanji with Susheila Nasta (1991)' 70)

But the undertaking is not merely part of a larger project of "salvaging a consciousness of the Indian Ocean rim, its littoral worlds" (Jamal, 'Telling and Selling on the Indian Ocean Rim' 414). It is far more a proactive enterprise founded upon the principle of creative extension over the horizon of what is known, familiar, mapped. Crucial to this notion of historical writing are metaphors of windows, openings, doors:

> Ji Bai opened a small window into that dark past for me. She took me past the overgrowth into that other jungle. And a whole world flew in, a world of my great-grandfather who left India and my great-grandmother who was African, the world of Matamu where India

and Africa met and the mixture exploded in the person of my half-caste grandfather Huseni who disappeared into the forest one day and never returned [...].

(Vassanji, *The Gunny Sack* 35)

The lacunary nature of historical narrative, figured in the roadside manholes with 'Cape Town' inscribed upon them, thus leads into another world (113), and the fragments that mirror those lacunae, are always indices of potential rather than of lack: "Why this fragment, Shehru, this frayed remnant of a memory? A tribute, she says, to an unknown woman, a woman with her own memories and her own world" (110). This theory of historical narrative is one in which lacunary fissures or narrative gaps become routes into reaches of history which lie beyond the horizons of the particular collective memory to which the subject has access at a specific point in time and space. This model of memory is not absolutely linear to the extent that it imagines, beyond the serial sequence of dates, linkages which may lead to other sequences with other tempos (see Lévi-Strauss, *La Pensée Sauvage* 310-11; Althusser and Balibar, *Reading Capital* 99). It imagines these linkages as apparently loose threads which may branch off into other historical strands with their own logic. In Vassanji's own words: "I did not see, nor wanted to give the impression of a simple, linear, historical truth emerging" (Kanaganayakam, '"Broadening the Substrata": An Interview with M.G.Vassanji' 22).

To that extent, the patent contingency of this mode of historical fiction is merely the flip side of the partial character of all historical writing. Thus, in a moment of hubristic desire, the narrator addresses his eponymous muse with the apostrophe, "Tell me, you who would know all. [...] She demurs, my gunny sack" (23). This refusal is as much a strength as a weakness, however. The capacity of historical writing is not exhaustive, but rather, extensive, in that it opens up possibilities of memory, retrieval, witnessing, which are performative and creative, not reproductive. The narrator substantiates this by sketching, albeit in a somewhat jocular manner, two theories of temporality which describe the mode of historical writing to which Vassanji subscribes, and one which he rejects, perhaps related to the historical novel in its classic European manifestation:

> Wisps of memory [...] each a window to a world [...] Asynchronous images projected on multiple cinema screens [...] Time here is not the continuous coordinate of Mr Kabir (who knew all the theorems by heart and could tell you the page numbers in the maths book on which you could find them) but a collection of blots like Uncle Jim drew in the *Sunday Herald* for the children, except that Uncle Jim numbered the blots for you so you traced the picture of a dog or a horse when you followed them with a pencil [...] here you number your own dots and there is no end to them, and each lies in wait for you like a black hole from which you could never return – .
>
> (Vassanji, *The Gunny Sack* 112)

This is first and foremost a theory of memory which is combinatory, not cumulative (or 'additive' in Benjamin's terms (*Illuminaions* 254). The fragments must be combined in an order which is not preordained and which is constitutive of memory itself. Rather than points, the fragments of memory are described as blots. They are blurred domains with uncertain boundaries, bespeaking contingency rather than the necessity assumed by backward-looking constructions of historicism (see Ferguson, *Virtual History*). This is a description of the historical novel as a "spongy, disconnected, often incoherent accretion of stories" (66). Because Vassanji's two models here are not merely models of time, but also of space, as befits an author cognisant of post-Einsteinian physics, these theories of the historical novel as an exemplification of an historical autopoesis rather than of a postdated linearity; in this way, they also become indices of the Indian Ocean diasporic world as a networked global domain conceived as the matrix for autopoietic historical narration. Sugata Bose, looking back across the long history of the Indian Ocean world, states that "there is no question that the history of the Indian Ocean World is enmeshed with its poetry and in some ways propelled by it" (Bose, *A Hundred Horizons* 5). Stephen Muecke, looking forward, suggests a more exploratory mode of (auto)poietic creation: "If a contemporary Indian Ocean literature is 'missing' in that [Deleuzian sense of 'the people who are missing'], it remains to be invented". This "kind of storytelling [...] takes off on a flight of becoming rather than repeating the available discourses and genres" (Muecke, 'Fabulation: Flying Carpets and Artful Politics in the Indian Ocean' 33, 41).

By way of conclusion it may be worth returning to the novel's *incipit*, where the narrator presents the eponymous metaphor of memorial narration, the gunny sack: "Memory, Ji Bai would say, is this old sack here" (3). A gunny sack is a bag made out of rough fabric such as jute; the name is a British imperial corruption of the Sanskrit *gōni*, meaning fibre. Thus the very denomination of this rough fabric bag is mediated through an Indian Ocean history – for much of which Gujarati cloths and cotton garments were dominant around the Indian Ocean until the British sidelined the Indian textile economy to the advantage of their own manufacturing and exports (see for instance Machado, 'Awash in a Sea of Cloth'). The gunny sack is a receptacle, empty in itself (it is "a gaping hole" [25]) but susceptible of housing memory-objects (it is "a brown pouch" [25]) collected by their curator Ji Bai and brought to 'speech' through the gunny's 'mouth' (3) by Salim the narrator. The selection of any one object from the gunny as a material support for memorialization causes all the other objects to reconfigure their interrelationships: "you bring out this naughty little nut and everything else rearranges itself" (3). Just as the gunny provides a space for historical narration which does not predetermine the nature of its contents, so too the mnemonic triggers have purely positional, relational value. The gunny thus serves as a concrete figure of the model of historical narration favoured by Vassanji's text, namely, relational rather than linear, community-based rather than individualist. The gunny, "a dumpy [...] sack enclosing a broken world, the debris of lives lived" (135), also figures the space of the Indian Ocean itself: a geographical receptacle traversed by relational vectors of trade and exchange, and bordered by an arc of intertwined fabric of hinterland-littoral-foreland interconnections. Beyond the caesura of Ji Bai's death (3) and against the family's desire to 'bury' a past tainted by a cross-cultural marriage between an Indian trader and an African slave (5, 134-5), Salim Juma, "one-eighth African" (227) and perhaps his brother Sona (268) preserve the gunny sack and its contents, tying, untying and retying the "sisal twine" (135) which opens its mouth, thereby weaving not only the past but also the future. Adopting such a humble object of Indian Ocean everyday material culture as its muse, Vassanji's historical novel does not merely cut itself free from European models in its endeavour to recreate the past, it seeks much more to create the future for a non-European world.

Works Cited

Althusser, Louis and Etienne Balibar. *Reading Capital.* Trans. Ben Brewster. New York: Monthly Review Press, 1970.

Anderson, Benedict. *Imagined Communities: Reflections on the Origins and Spread of Nationalism*. Rev. ed. London: Verso, 1991.

Anderson, Perry. 'From Progress to Catastrophe: Perry Anderson on the Historical Novel.' *London Review of Books* 33-15 (2011). 6 June 2012. <http://www.lrb.co.uk/v33/n15/perry-anderson/from-progress-to-catastrophe>.

Bardolph, Jacqueline. 'Identité et frontières d'un domain de recherche: l'exemple de la littérature d'Afrique anglophone.' *Cahiers d'études africaines* 35-140 (1995): 725-38.

Benjamin, Walter. *Illuminations*. Trans. Harry Zohn. London: Pimlico, 1999.

Bhabha, Homi K. *The Location of Culture*. London: Routledge, 1994.

Braudel, Fernand. *The Mediterranean and the Mediterranean World in the Age of Philip II*. Trans. Siân Reynolds. New York: Harper & Row, 1977 [1947].

Campbell, Gwyn. 'The Role of Africa in the Emergence of the "Indian Ocean World" Global Economy.' *Eyes Across the Water: Navigating the Indian Ocean*. Eds. Pamila Gupta, Isabel Hofmeyr and Michael Pearson. Pretoria: UNISA Press, 2010. 170-196.

Chakrabarty, Dipesh. *Provincializing Europe: Postcolonial Thought and Historical Difference.* Princeton: Princeton University Press, 2000.

Chaudhuri, K.N. *Asia Before Europe: Economy and Civilization of the Indian Ocean from the Rise of Islam to 1750.* Cambridge: Cambridge University Press, 1990.

Curtin, Philip. *Cross-Cultural Trade in World History*. Cambridge: Cambridge University Press, 1984.

Eliot, T.S. 'Tradition and the Individual Talent.' *Selected Prose*. Ed. John Hayward. Harmondsworth: Penguin, 1963. 26-7.

Ghosh, Devlaana, and Stephen Muecke. 'Natural Logics of the Indian Ocean.' *Cultures of Trade: Indian Ocean Exchanges*. Eds. Devlaana Ghosh and Stephen Muecke. Newcastle-upon-Tyne: Cambridge Scholars Press, 2007. 150-63.

Jamal, Ashraf. 'Telling and Selling on the Indian Ocean Rim.' *Indian Ocean Studies: Cultural, Social and Political Perspectives*. Eds. Shanti Moorthy and Ashraf Jamal. London: Routledge, 2010. 403-17.

Jameson, Fredric. *The Antinomies of Realism.* London: Verso, 2013.

Jameson, Fredric. 'Third-World Literature in the Era of Multinational Capitalism.' *Social Text* 15 (Autumn 1986): 65-88.

Kanaganayakam, C. '"Broadening the Substrata": An Interview with M. G. Vassanji.' *World Literature Written in English* 31-2 (1991): 19-35.

Kearney, Milo. *The Indian Ocean in World History.* New York: Routledge, 2004.

Lazarus, Neil. 'The Politics of Postcolonial Modernism.' *Postcolonial Studies and Beyond*. Eds. Ania Loomba et.al. Durham, NC: Duke University Press, 2005. 423-38.

Lukács, George. *The Historical Novel.* Trans. Hannah and Stanley Mitchell. Harmondsworth: Penguin, 1981 [1937].

Marin, Louis. 'Du corps au text: Propositions métaphysiques sur l'origine du récit.' *Le Récit évangélique*. Eds. Claude Chabrol and Louis Marin. Paris: Aubier Montaigne/Cerf/Delachaux & Niestlé/Desclée De Brower, 1974. 75-90.

McPherson, Kenneth. *The Indian Ocean: A History of People and The Sea*. Delhi: Oxford University Press, 1993.

Muecke, Stephan. 'Fabulation: Flying Carpets and Artful Politics in the Indian Ocean.' *Indian Ocean Studies: Cultural, Social and Political Perspectives*. Eds. Shanti Moorthy and Ashraf Jamal. London: Routledge, 2010. 32-44.

Nazareth, Peter. 'The First Tanz/Asian Novel.' *Research in African Literatures* 21-4 (1990): 129-33.

Ojwang, Dan. 'Memory, Migrancy and Modernity in M. J. Vassanji's *The Gunny Sack* and *The Book of Secrets.*' *Eyes Across the Water: Navigating the Indian Ocean*. Eds. Pamila Gupta, Isabel Hofmeyr and Michael Pearson. Pretoria: UNISA Press, 2010. 140-54.

Pearson, Michael. 'Introduction I: The State of the Subject.' *India and the Indian Ocean 1500-1800*. Eds. Ashin Das Gupta and Michael N. Pearson. Delhi: Oxford University Press, 1987. 1-24.

------------------. *The Indian Ocean*. London: Routledge, 2003.

Rushdie, Salman. *Midnight's Children*. London: Vintage, 1995 [1981].

Vassanji, M.J. *The Gunny Sack*. London: Heinemann, 1989.

------------------. *The Indian Ocean*. London: Routledge, 2003.

------------------. *The Book of Secrets*. London: Cannongate, 2006 [1994].

------------------. *The In-Between World of Vikram Lall*. London: Cannongate, 2004 [2003].

------------------. 'Moyez Vassanji with Susheila Nasta (1991)' [Interview]. *Writing Across Worlds: Contemporary Writers Talk*. Ed. Susheila Nasta. London: Routledge, 2004. 69-79.

Kai Wiegandt

History as Struggle of Generations:
J. M. Coetzee's *The Master of Petersburg*

"October, 1869. A droshky passes slowly down a street in the Haymarket district of St Petersburg" (*MP*[1] 1). In its very first sentence, naming both a past century and an antiquated means of transport, J. M. Coetzee's *The Master of Petersburg* (1994) stresses the historicity of its setting. The man in the droshky has come from Dresden where he lives with his wife and child and travels under the name Isaev, for he has debts in Russia and does not want to be recognized. The cause of his journey is the death of his stepson Pavel, the son of his deceased first wife, whom he has supported financially. The circumstances of Pavel's death are unclear. The man rents Pavel's room and begins looking for traces of Pavel. He meets the anarchist Sergei Nechaev of whom, it turns out, Pavel was a follower, and begins an affair with his stepson's host, Anna Sergeyevna. It becomes clear that the man from Dresden is Fyodor Dostoevsky. He is under the spell of the traces left by Pavel and of what he believes is Pavel's spirit surrounding him. He tries to conjure this spirit, but when it materializes and gradually takes possession of him, he attempts to exorcize it.[2] In the meantime, the angry youth of St Petersburg riot against the tsarist regime and there seems to be an uncanny relationship between Pavel's spirit and the spirit of the times that becomes visible in the pre-revolutionary riots and tensions between the generations. The manner in which historical processes here seem to be reflected by individual fates recalls György Lukács's demand that the historical novel must show individuals who are in the middle of and influenced by the clash of opposing "social trends and historical forces" (Lukács, *The Historical Novel* 33) rather than personify these forces in great leaders or enact them in momentous, well-known events. The protagonist must have individual features while being typical of the times, and must be an observer, not an agent, of historical events; only such a character can perceive history impartially. The "specifically historical" of the historical novel is for Lukács the "derivation of the individuality of characters from the historical peculiarity of their age" (Lukács, *The Historical Novel* 19). It is through empathizing with the protagonist that the reader becomes aware of his own historical specificity. Coetzee's Dostoevsky seems to fulfil these requirements. He stands on the margin of the historical events around him instead of taking part, while as a canonical

---

[1]   Henceforth *The Master of Petersburg* will be abbreviated as *MP*.
[2]   The novel's title possibly alludes to Bulgakov's *The Master and Margarita* in which the character Voland conjures spirits and tries to raise the dead (see Adelman, 'Stalking Stavrogin' 354).

Russian author of the nineteenth century he embodies the spirit of his time. He makes a fitting test subject for an unusual historical novel, which finds generational struggle over inheritance and independence at the heart of history, and explores how that struggle informs the notion of humanity.

The historical novel has been a hybrid genre since its creation, a quality which also features in Coetzee's novel. As in numerous historical novels of the gothic tradition, with the 'dead' past haunting and even attacking the present (see de Groot, *The Historical Novel* 16), the events are shrouded in an uncanny atmosphere. The stepson's spirit, for example, seems to appear in the most common objects, and the smile of Matryona, the host's daughter, suddenly metamorphoses into a bat's grin: "As he peers, holding his breath, the corners of her mouth seem to curve faintly upward in a victori- ous, bat-like grin. And the arm too, extended loosely over her mother, is like a wing" (*MP* 58). The historical Dostoevsky liked to employ uncanny motifs of the gothic genre such as inanimate things returning in animate form or humans returning as animals (see Frank, "*Demons*" 63), and Dostoevsky's growing desperation to exorcize Pavel's spirit in *The Master of Petersburg* is such a motif.[3]

At the same time, *The Master of Petersburg* is a detective novel in which the crime – if there is one – was committed before the plot develops and in which the protagonist is looking for traces. While the suspicion that Pavel committed suicide presides at first, the traces left by him make it seem possible that he was murdered. We encounter a detective who asks himself whether the omnipresent security police or Pavel's idol Nechaev caused his death, and who has to admit to himself that his reconstruction of traces rather resembles a construction of motives and events. In this respect Coetzee's historical detective novel is reminiscent of postmodern historical novels like Umberto Eco's *The Name of the Rose* which demonstrate that it is *a priori* impossible that they should be able to achieve their self-set task of reconstructing the past. Elements of the detective novel and gothic, historiographic metafiction and motifs of the *Künstlerroman* (Dostoevsky can be said to sign a pact with the 'devil' Nechaev to write *Demons*) com- bine in this novel which, in its treatment of Dostoevsky, seems painstakingly to avoid clashes with the known facts of the historical writer's life.

In 1869, the writer notoriously burdened by debt did indeed live in Dresden and would have had to use an alias in order to travel to Russia. The existence of a stepson is undoubted, as is Dostoevsky's support for the young man living in Petersburg. The historical Sergei Nechaev, author of the *Revolutionary's Catechism* from 1869, was a founding figure of modern terrorism and promoted terrorist attacks on Russian state institutions.[4] According to Nechaev, everything was allowed as long as it served the revolution – except compassion. It is not known whether Dostoevsky and Nechaev met, but both frequented the Russian quarter of Geneva in September 1869 when Dostoevsky

---

[3]   Dostoevsky was the only author of his stature to do so, "and he was severely rapped over the knuckles for the 'vulgarity' of doing so (a sniffish and snobbish critical tradition that has been regrettably carried into our own day by Vladimir Nabokov)." (Frank, "*Demons*" 63)

[4]   Karl Marx and Friedrich Engels commented at length on Nechaev in a tract addressing the anarchist scene led by Bakunin. Marx and Engels disparage Nechaev as a cretin whose deeds are not in the spirit of true revolution but its disfiguration (see Gerigk, *Dostojewskijs Entwicklung* 155-6).

attended a congress at which Bakunin and Garibaldi spoke to the crowd. Nechaev was already back in Russia by that time, but when news of his alleged murder of a Petersburg student named Ivanov was reported, with Ivanov having belonged to Nechaev's revolutionary cell, Nechaev came to embody the very devil of terrorism for Dostoevsky. He used Nechaev as a model for his character Verkhovensky in his novel *Demons*, begun in December 1869 (see Frank, *Dostoevsky* 626-49; Attridge, *J. M. Coetzee* 117; Scanlan, 'Incriminating Documents' 463-70). The novel underpins these historical facts with apparently insignificant sensual details creating reality effects and making the protagonist seem individual and authentic as demanded by Lukács. When Dostoevsky sniffs at the pillow in Pavel's former bed, he smells only soap and sun (see *MP* 3). Instead of only thinking about his epilepsy that is well-known to have plagued the historical Dostoevsky, Coetzee's protagonist wishes he had fresh underwear and suffers from indigestion.[5]

The novel thus appears to attempt a reconstruction of the outer and inner events of Dostoevsky's life in October and November 1869, and that it describes the conception of *Demons* – except for the fact that Pavel outlived Dostoevsky instead of dying before him. The alienating effect created by this clash with historical facts is all the more glaring as it disrupts a text that otherwise seems at pains to preserve truthfulness to history. Dostoevsky's biographer Joseph Frank criticized Coetzee for failing to include a warning to his readers who might take fiction for fact (see Frank, 'J. M. Coetzee' 197). However, if one presupposes a knowledgeable reader – a reader every literary work has a right to address and whom modernist texts in particular choose to address[6] – then the clash with historical fact can therefore only be understood as a signal *not* to equate the protagonist with the historical Dostoevsky. In this light, the choice of protagonist appears odd for a historical novel. The impartial and ordinary bystander promoted by Lukács has become a writer interested and unwillingly involved in history, a shift by which the novel draws attention to its being an artefact and attacks the idea that history can be experienced and represented impartially.

The novel seems to fall into a category that it does not quite fit. It inscribes itself in the tradition of the historical novel but keeps the genre at arm's length at the same time. We could understand this as a gesture by which the novel asserts its autonomy. In his programmatic essay 'The Novel Today', Coetzee argues that the novel can either be a mere supplement to history or history's rival, and demands that it not merely depict history but offer an alternative to it; not in the form of an alternative and previously repressed historiography like in many postcolonial novels, but as an alternative to history proper (see Coetzee, 'The Novel Today'). But *The Master of Petersburg* does not follow that call, for it renders an epoch of the past in detail and without extensive

---

[5]   Hence the following sentences: "[H]e is keenly aware that his clothes have begun to smell, that his skin is dry and flaky, that the dental plates he wears click when he talks. His haemmorrhoids, too, cause him endless discomfort." (*MP* 66)

[6]   As not only his most prominent intertexts, Coetzee is a late modernist, placing himself in a tradition comprising Eliot's *The Waste Land*, Pound's *Cantos* and Joyce's *Ulysses*, to name some works presupposing near omniscient readers. This is not to criticize Frank for naivety, who has given much thought to the complicated relationship between Dostoevsky's novel and history (see Frank, '*The Devils* and the Nechaev Affair').

use of alienation; in fact, it is the only one of Coetzee's novels that can be called historical in a narrow sense.[7] The fact that in Coetzee's novel Pavel dies before Dostoevsky and thereby breaks the illusion of historiography does not mean that it is not concerned with history. Quite to the contrary, the anachronism underlines this interest, for it is like a piece in a puzzle that will not fit and which thereby helps in revealing the problematic nature of what we call history.

My thesis is that Coetzee's novel, based on another novel, is not just concerned with the embattled genealogies of *literary* history but also with the anthropological preconditions of historicity, and that it tests the pre-revolutionary Russian discourse regarding these preconditions. The novel's concern with guilt and the struggle of generations is deeply informed by the violent death of Coetzee's own son, Nicholas, who died in similarly obscure circumstances as those of Pavel (see Kannemeyer, *J. M. Coetzee* 452-70). Coetzee's vision of history is marked by this highly personal concern even as the novel's manuscript undergoes a process of depersonalization and abstraction in the course of Coetzee's working it.[8] He employs the genre of the historical novel to show how traces are left, followed and erased, particularly between parents and children who bequeath, inherit and are shaped by one another.[9] Human beings, the novel suggests, rely on their descent for constructing their identity and at the same time deny this descent in order to be truly human. The popular reception of Darwinism shows that even as humans trace their descent to apes they simultaneously deny the ape within themselves. Coetzee looks at the interaction between father and son as a moment in the loving struggle between the generations, a struggle taking place between the fictional Dostoevsky and Pavel and, as a mirroring in terms of literary history, between Dostoevsky and Coetzee. It is this fundamental contradiction that constitutes history in *The Master of Petersburg.* Already with the traces left by one generation and rejected or followed by the next, the definition of the human is at stake, for every new generation defines itself as 'the human'. The recurring motifs of parricide and of the father who devours his child have their historical equivalents in the rioting Petersburg students and the clamping down on the riots by the tsarist police. Together they are the most extreme symptoms of a dynamic of history whose front line runs vertically, between older and

[7]   See the definition of the historical novel in Cuddon's *A Dictionary of Literary Terms and Literary Theory*: "A form of fictional narrative which reconstructs history and re-creates it imaginatively. Both historical and fictional characters may appear." (Cuddon, *A Dictionary* 383)

[8]   Of course, it is possible to still read the novel principally as Coetzee's elegy for his early-departed son Nicholas, or as a commentary on the political turmoil in South Africa before the first free elections in 1994. Monica Popescu, for example, argues that Coetzee chooses *Demons* as a model for his novel because Dostoevsky poses questions about authority and political authenticity that were central to South Africa in years of transition; drawing on *Demons, The Master of Petersburg* shows that politicians cannot be authentic when they want to achieve their political goals (see Popescu, *South African Literature* 94-5).

[9]   The topic of rivalry between parents and children is present already in *Dusklands* and reappears in the later novels. The magistrate in *Waiting for the Barbarians*, David Lurie in *Disgrace* or Elizabeth Costello in the novel of the same name appear antiquated or describe themselves as such (in *Disgrace*, for example, Lurie calls himself a "moral dinosaur", 89). Only in *The Master of Petersburg* does the topic take centre stage, however.

younger generations. Marx's theory of a horizontal class struggle characterizing history will become crucial some decades later.

Natural History of Parents and Children

Initially the novel conceals this dynamic almost completely behind the veil of Dostoevsky's mourning. He speaks Pavel's name, tries to revive memories and, together with Anna Sergeyevna and Matryona, visits his stepson's grave. He begins his affair with Anna Sergeyevna and feels drawn to Matryona who was close to Pavel. It is as though he were able to touch Pavel through them, and the night with Anna Sergeyevna seems a communion with his ghost to him (see *MP* 56). Dostoevsky wishes he were dead instead of Pavel. Once he even dons Pavel's suit, a gesture into which affection as well as the wish to replace Pavel can be read.

When Dostoevsky visits Pavel's grave on Yelagin Island, ambivalences in the stepfather's behaviour and thoughts become apparent. Dostoevsky lies down on Pavel's grave and, back home, on Pavel's bed to be close to the boy. Bed and grave signify conception and death and serve as memorial sites of natural history, but as authentic as Dostoevsky's mourning may be, his triumph in usurping the bed is just as real: "Poor child! The festival of the senses that would have been his inheritance stolen away from him! Lying in Pavel's bed, he cannot refrain from a quiver of dark triumph." (*MP* 135) The father triumphs over the law according to which sons become heirs to their fathers and themselves father sons. He becomes heir to his son.

Only much later does the novel mirror this perversion, i.e. this twisting of genealogies, by Dostoevsky's reactionary political stance that prompts him to oppose the revolutionary riots instigated by Nechaev. Before this happens, history as the strife in which one generation displaces the other appears in the form of *natural* history, namely in the characters' bodies and their traces. Dostoevsky's thoughts demonstrate this when they meander from Anna Sergeyevna, with whom he has been speaking, to her daughter Matryona:

> [Anna Sergeyevna's] tongue like a bird fluttering in her mouth: soft feathers, soft wing-beats. In the daughter he detects none of the mother's soft dryness. On the contrary, there is something liquid about her, something of the young doe, trusting yet nervous, stretching its neck to sniff the stranger's hand, tensed to leap away. How can this dark woman have mothered this fair child? Yet the telltale signs are all there: the fingers small, almost unformed; the dark eyes, lustrous as those of Byzantine saints; the fine, sculpted line of the brow; even the moody air. Strange how in a child the feature can take its perfect form while in the parent it seems a copy!
>
> (Coetzee, *MP* 13)

Ageing is a process of drying up, and the imagery of the hunt illustrates Dostoevsky's awakening desire. Less conventional is the fact that the idea of inheriting traits is turned upside down: Anna Sergeyevna's daughter is not the trace ("copy") of her mother but the mother appears to be the trace of the daughter insofar as their shared traits have reached perfection only in the daughter.[10] Matryona comes after her mother but is at the same time ahead of her because of her supposedly more developed nature. The topic of likeness and the animal imagery that Dostoevsky applies to mother and daughter are reminiscent of Genesis, in which God creates the animals before man only to give man more perfect, godlike features, and to order him to rule over the animals.[11] The provocation of the mother/daughter comparison is the suggestion that the mother has not reached fully developed humanity which is only achieved by Matryona who leaves her mother behind as an earlier developmental stage.

In order to understand what is happening here it is useful to consider Giorgio Agamben's claim that since Aristotle, the human has been defined through a distinction of human and animal in the human body itself. Some parts of the human body, for example the digestive system, are attributed to the realm of animal or bare life whereas others are considered to constitute an exclusively human form of life. Agamben has also shown that the attribution of particular organs and bodily functions to the realm of animal life or, respectively, exclusively to that of human life has changed considerably in the course of history (see Agamben, *The Open* 13-6, 33-8, 79-80). In Dostoevsky's thoughts, Anna Sergeyevna and Matryona have both human and animal attributes. The dividing line between animal and human runs through both human bodies, but the border seems drawn slightly differently in Matryona. *The Master of Petersburg* considers the time frame in which the parents' generation interacts with the children's and suggests that every new generation revises the definition of what makes the human human. Coetzee adds a bio-historical dimension to his previous explorations of the human by suggesting that the struggle over the attribution of human and animal parts is not only acted out in political conflicts, between dominant and oppressed civilizations and ethnicities as in his novels *Waiting for the Barbarians* and *Life & Times of Michael K*, but necessarily between parents and children. The novel's most disturbing insight into this subject is that the outcome of this struggle is open: the young do not simply replace the old; they can die before their parents, sometimes at their hands. Children can be corrupted, and history, of which we like to think as linear and progressive – a history of the children – can be rolled backwards by the fathers, including the novel's Dostoevsky, or into a collective parricide at the hands of children, like Nechaev, who for that or other reasons want to do away with all fathers. The title of Dostoevsky's *Demons* refers to Jesus's exorcism of devils into swine (see Matthew 8:28-33), and Coetzee's radical insight is likewise old Biblical prophecy: "And the brother shall deliver up the brother to death, and the father the child: and the children shall rise up against their parent, and cause them to be put to death" (Matthew 10:21). One can read this as an acknowledgement that not even eschatological time is exempt from generational struggle; that eschatological time coincides with secular time in consisting of generational struggle. A Christian reading would stress the hope that a redeemer will ultimately break the repetitive cycles of generational struggle of which the political strife between tsarists and anarchists will not be the last.

---

[10] Dostoewsky thinks similarly about Pavel and himself: "The father, faded copy of the son." (*MP* 67)

[11] For Derrida, this constitutes man's true fall from grace (see Derrida, *The Animal* 15-7).

Dostoevsky understands that he and Anna Sergeyevna belong to an older generation of the human than Pavel, Matryona and his young wife in Dresden:

> [H]e feels what he can only call kinship with her. He and she are of the same kind, the same generation. And all of a sudden the generations fall into place: Pavel and Matryona and his wife Anna ranked on the one side, he and Anna Sergeyevna on the other. The children against those who are not children.
>
> (Coetzee, *MP* 63)

In most cases Dostoevsky conceives of the strife between the generations as a struggle of sons against fathers, suggesting that the government official Maximov might be right when he says that he is a happy man nowadays who is a father of daughters instead of sons (see *MP* 45, 206-207). In the quote, however, Dostoevsky abandons this cliché and thinks of a conflict that is fought between the generations of the children and of the parents, regardless of sex. The assumption is supported by the fact that Nechaev's followers are predominantly female. A Finnish girl serves as his messenger and Matryona supports him, too, while Pavel is the only male supporter and dead by now. By disguising as a woman, Nechaev takes advantage of the fact that Russian society associates the youth riots with young men only (see *MP* 154-56). Thus Nechaev appears unconspicious enough to evade capture until the novel's end.

Cultural History as History of Spirit: The Generation

Expressing what it means to belong to a generation, the quoted passage complements the perspective of natural history on heredity and introduces the perspective of cultural history. The words "kinship" and "kind" refer to a kindredness that does not rely on blood relations but on date of birth, and therefore on the spirit of the times which is so clearly in the grip of the young and consequently inaccessible to the old. Anna Sergeyevna suggests this when she tells Dostoevsky he will not find Pavel in his old room; instead, he is told he should speak to Matryona: "She and your son were very close. If he has left a mark behind, it is on her." Dostoevsky asks whether he also left a mark on Anna Sergeyevna herself, and she answers that her ability to communicate with him was limited: "But I am not of his generation. He could not speak to me as he could to Matryona" (*MP* 142). The abyss between the generations seems as deep as that between humans and animals. This idea seems particularly astonishing because it is uttered by an otherwise pragmatic woman, but it was in fact a widespread view in Europe and Russia in the middle of the nineteenth century, when biology established itself as a scientific discipline and when questions of heredity were at the centre of biology's interest. Even in public opinion the theory of epigenesis replaced the theory of preformation which had still argued that all future generations and every future child were fully preformed in the fathers' semen (or what we today call genes). Already in the eighteenth century Caspar Friedrich Wolff and Johann Friedrich Blumenbach had postulated a drive or instinct which makes the organism reach its fully developed state after birth. Development is separated from conception and the fully developed human being is no longer considered preformed in the parents. Darwin's *On the Origin of Species by*

Means of Natural Selection from 1859, in which the author defines adaptation to the environment as the decisive criterion for the survival and reproduction of species, brings the irreversible victory of the epigenesis paradigm (see Weigel, *Genea-Logik* 131-34), but there are earlier and more popular variants of the epigenesis theory which belong to the movement of scientific materialism and whose arguments are more radical than Darwin's. One of the most influential books of this kind was Ludwig Büchner's *Kraft und Stoff* (*Force and Matter*) in which Büchner argued that under the influence of an utterly different environment a seed could produce a human being who is completely different from his or her progenitor (see Parnes et al., *Das Konzept* 211-12), a view reminiscent of the radical discontinuity of generations claimed by Anna Sergeyevna.

Ivan Turgenev's novel *Fathers and Children* (1861), which is concerned with questions of generations and of generational change, is a literary model for the idea of radical discontinuity of generations in *The Master of Petersburg*, and a model Dostoevsky himself had drawn on in *Demons* (see Frank, "*Demons*" 50). Having grown old and now belonging to the generation of the fathers, the brothers Nikolai and Pavel (!) acknowledge that they cannot evade the power of generational relations – like Matryona, whose features may be more perfect than her mother's but who still bears her features – and that this relation will never change. One brother tells the other: "I once had a dispute with our poor mother; she stormed, and wouldn't listen to me. At last I said to her, 'Of course you can't understand me; we belong', I said, 'to different generations.'" (Turgenev, *The Novels* 93) The young Nihilist Basarow – a trained scientist – claims something different: that he has no forebear and that his parents have no significance for him. Using arguments reminiscent of Büchner's *Kraft und Stoff*, he belittles the idea of heredity and thereby qualifies as a possible forerunner of Coetzee's Nechaev. However, *Fathers and Children* does not only deal with the discontinuity of generations but also with the rivalry between them, and contains a duel between Pavel and Basarow. The fathers do not willingly cede the arena to the sons but try to survive them. The decisive aspect of this discourse on the discontinuity of generations encouraged by materialists like Ludwig Büchner is that it is controlled by the youth. The generation of the fathers still conceives of the relation between the generations as an inescapable continuity, and Coetzee's Dostoevsky conceives of the relation between Matryona and her mother in precisely that way. The discourse of discontinuity fulfils the function of a meta-discourse according to which the discourses of the fathers and of the sons do not overlap, the two generations follow different language games and cannot understand each other – a transposition of the thesis of the discontinuity of generations from natural history to communication. This discursive constellation also informs *The Master of Petersburg* in which Pavel and Nechev utilize the discourse of scientific materialism to position themselves as utterly other *vis à vis* the fathers. In this way the young generation controls what one could call the spirit of the times or *zeitgeist*. The novel's concern with the historical dimension of being human is poignant as it becomes clear that cultural inheritances infringe on human autonomy even if they force the children into a conflict rather than identity with the fathers, and even if the children proclaim radical bodily difference from the fathers. Genealogy and cultural history force humans to act out the roles of parents and children, even if acting the role of the child entails the claim of *not* depending on the parents. The generations are embedded into one another in the sense that they rely on their descent for constructing their identity and at the same time deny this descent in order to preserve the illusion of their autonomy.

Zeitgeist, Spirit and Madness

It is the spirit of the times or *zeitgeist* that links Pavel's spirit, or Dostoevsky's search for his dead son by whom he is haunted, with the historical events in Petersburg. When Dostoevsky appears before the government official Maximov and asks for Pavel's letters and belongings, he learns that Pavel was a follower of Sergei Nechaev. Even worse, Pavel had elected Nechaev to be his father, which implies that the relation between father and son was merely an elective affinity after the death of Pavel's biological father. Dostoevsky calls it a "sickness of this age of ours" (*MP* 137) that the youth turn from their parents and become spiritual sons and daughters of Bakunin and Stenka Razin. Maximov mentions a list with names of people who were to be eliminated but remains silent on whether Dostoevsky was on it. Among the documents there are stories written by Pavel, and Maximov reads one of them out loud. It is about a young man who one day kills his detested master on whose farm he works. The government official is sure that Pavel's story which will later serve Dostoevsky as seed of his novel *The Brothers Karamazov* is inspired by the virulent *zeitgeist*, namely by an unusually obsessive spirit of vengefulness possessing the youth and targeting the generation of the parents: "It is in their blood, so to speak, to wish us ill, our generation. Something they are born with. Not easy to be a father, is it? [...] Perhaps it is just the old matter of fathers and sons after all, such as we have always had, only deadlier in this particular generation, more unforgiving." (*MP* 45) Sons against fathers against sons: that would be the usual way of history, and since all fathers are sons, Dostoevsky can understand his stepson's fascination with Nechaev, thinks Maximov. The situation on Petersburg's streets seems to verify his interpretation of the *zeitgeist*. Anna Sergeyevna has to close the shop in which she works because the university students engage in street fights with the police all day long. She tells Dostoevsky that the old shop-owner's nephew was hit by a cobblestone and had his wrist injured when he returned from the market in his horse cart. Matryona overhears the conversation and is drawn to the rioting crowd. The fact that she, the youngest of the young generation, is also infected by Nechaev's spirit of vengefulness becomes obvious when she delivers a flask of poison for him to one of his followers who wants to evade cross-examination by the police, and when she hangs the flag of the 'People's Vengeance', as Nechaev's group calls itself, in Dostoevsky's room (see *MP* 173, 229).

When Maximov interprets Pavel's fantasies of parricide and his commitment to Nechaev's cause in terms of the old story of sons rebelling against fathers, however, he ignores that it is Pavel who is dead, not his stepfather. Pavel's case constitutes a perversion of the historiography outlined by Maximov and Dostoevsky. Haunting Dostoevsky, Pavel's spirit forces the stepfather to revise his model of history which must now take the reciprocity of the strife between fathers and sons into account. There are not only sons who commit parricide but also those fathers whom Nechaev accuses of doing away with their sons out of envy of youth and greed for life. In some sense, that category of fathers could apply to Pavel's elected father and possible murderer Nechaev as well as to his stepfather Dostoevsky who, instead of Pavel, occupies Anna Sergeyevna's bed and who in her household occupies the father's position in the family scheme father-mother-child (see *MP* 187-88).

By taking into account the embeddedness of generations in one another, Coetzee revises the ideological bent of Dostoevsky's novel *Demons* to which *The Master of Petersburg* constantly refers. When, in Dostoevsky's conservative novel, the youth agitate against their parents who represent tried and tested wisdom, they are possessed by 'demons' and suffer from delusions. In Coetzee, this simplistic conservatism is echoed in the words of the government official Maximov: "[T]hese child conspirators [...] believe they are immortal. In that sense it is indeed like fighting demons" (*MP* 45). The demons soon threaten to take possession not only of the youth but also of those who oppose them like Dostoevsky and Maximov. As in Dostoevsky's novel, the demons haunting Coetzee's characters refer to the Biblical story in which Jesus drives unclean spirits out of a madman. The spirits enter into a herd of swine that then drown themselves in the sea. However, Coetzee applies the biblical story not only to Russia and the nihilism of the young revolutionaries but also to his protagonist Dostoevsky. As a Russian subject, as subject of Russia's history and as the father of a deceased stepson who joined the radical movement, he, too, is infected by the madness of vengefulness, and the border between himself and his environment becomes porous when he refers to his epilepsy as the "emblematic sickness of the age" (*MP* 235, see Marais, *Secretary of the Invisible* 131-36). Vice versa, Russia, which is referred to as the motherland (see *MP* 15), is not extraneous but relates to him organically and even in a motherly fashion: "I am not here in Russia in this time of ours to live a life free of pain. I am required to live – what shall I call it? – a Russian life: a life inside Russia, or with Russia inside me, and whatever Russia means. It is not a fate I can evade." (*MP* 221)

The reciprocal infection and influence of fathers or of mothers and sons should make it clear that Coetzee's novel does not primarily deal with influences in literary history in the manner of Harold Bloom's *The Anxiety of Influence*, according to which the driving force behind literary history is the rebellion of any young generation of authors against the influence of their forefathers. Coetzee constantly refers to Dostoevsky, Kafka, Beckett and other authors in his works, blending and rearranging their heritage. Writings of the past influence Coetzee and call for his creative response, but it is T. S. Eliot's idea of such a creative response's ability to change past works, rather than Bloom's model of unilateral rivalry, that informs Coetzee's fictional discourse. In *The Master of Petersburg*, this idea becomes the subject of discourse. In 'Tradition and the Individual Talent' Eliot points out that by modifying the order of pre-existing canonical works, a new work that consciously adds to tradition does not change the words of the canonical authors; but it changes the spirit in which these words are read, and thus the works themselves (see Eliot, *Selected Prose* 38-40). *The Master of Petersburg* demonstrates that this holds for the rivalry over the idea of the human as expressed by past authors as well as past generation. Literary history and history as portrayed in the novel function alike, because in both realms the struggle of generations over the idea of the human does not end with the death of fathers. Neither does it end with the death of the sons whose spirit can become alive by being embodied in the living. Pavel's spirit, for example, has a devilishly energetic representative among the living: Nechaev.

In *The Master of Petersburg*, then, parents and children are linked by their need to drive out each other's spirits – a radical reinterpretation of the Christian Trinity where the Father, the Son and the Holy Spirit are united in God. In the novel, parents and children are unable to separate precisely because they need to drive out each other's spirits. In this respect, the relations between the generations reminds one of Beckett's *Endgame* in which Hamm keeps his senile parents in garbage cans. He assures their survival but beyond this does not want to have anything to do with them, which is conversely true of the parents, as a dialogue between Hamm and his father Nagg illustrates:

> Hamm: Scoundrel! Why did you engender me?
> Nagg: I didn't know.
> Hamm: What? What didn't you know?
> Nagg: That it'd be you.

(Beckett, Dramatic Works 126)

Beckett has been an important influence on Coetzee as a literary forefather – he even was the topic of Coetzee's doctoral thesis – and one can read *The Master of Petersburg* as a blending of Beckett's cruel parable on history with Hegel's philosophy of history trimmed down to family size, in which ever new generations of children oppose the parents and mimic the relationship between servant and master. Indeed, Coetzee and Beckett have both quite overtly drawn on Hegel's *Phenomenology of Spirit* and its dialectic of master and servant before, Coetzee in his novel *In the Heart of the Country* (1977) and Beckett in *Waiting for Godot* and *Endgame*. *The Master of Petersburg* plays off the view of history as natural history favoured by the fathers and their belief in genetic influence against its antithesis, namely the interpretation of history as history of ideas or spirit which allows the young generation to define itself as radically different. The youth embrace Büchner's discourse of radical discontinuity so fervently precisely because to them it is a means of beating the fathers on their preferred terrain of natural history; instead of guaranteeing continuity by genetic influence, nature now incessantly produces the radically new.

The Spirit of the Fathers: Epilepsy

Whereas in Beckett Hegel's spirit is only parodically evoked as the character Vladimir's bad breath (for *Endgame* in this context, see Adorno, 'Trying to Understand' 281-321), Coetzee identifies it as *zeitgeist* or madness, where madness does not necessarily mean something bad but is the discourse that is inaccessible to reason because reason must speak reasonably about madness when it wants to give madness a voice, as Coetzee has shown in his essay on Erasmus's *Praise of Folly* (see Coetzee, 'Erasmus' 84-9). The relationship between madness and reason thus resembles that between the incompatible discourses of discontinuous generations. In contrast to Beckett, Coetzee localizes spirit – regardless of whether it comes in the form of reason or madness – in the concrete historical milieu of Petersburg, and with Nechaev finds a character who hosts this spirit and embodies it for the sake of literary realism. While Nechaev represents the spirit of the times or *zeitgeist*, a spirit which is controlled by the revolutionary youth, the epileptic fits haunting Dostoevsky represent the spirit of the fathers, an inherited curse that strikes the novelist episodically. Since Dostoevsky's epilepsy is portrayed as a curse, the fits are not revelations of some divine truth in an ecstatic state, as Christianity was prone to interpret epilepsy. Dostoevsky is possessed in the sense of pagan antiquity which conceived of the epileptic fit as a demon sent by higher forces, wrestling with the afflicted person's body but bringing no enlightenment (see Porter, *Madness* 15-18), and it is inheritance as the higher biological force that sends this curse onto him:

> The attacks are the burden he carries with him through the world. [...] Why am I accursed? he cries to himself. [...] Nor do the trances themselves provide illumination. They are not visitations. Far from it: they are nothing – mouthfuls of his life sucked out of him as if by a whirlwind that leaves behind not even a memory of darkness.
>
> (Coetzee, *MP* 69)

In terms of natural history, the fits are his parents' heritage; in terms of cultural history, of mother Russia. The fits show that Pavel's father, too, is still the son of his biological and spiritual parents.[12] The only promise lying in Dostoevsky's epilepsy is to be "tugged out of time" (*MP* 20), i.e., for a moment to be neither victim nor perpetrator in the dialectic of history. In this way, Dostoevsky's fits also repeat Pavel's fall without being able to undo it.

Only Nechaev believes that there is a place outside history and that this place is neither death nor unconsciousness. He says that Pavel had told him that Dostoevsky's father was a tyrant and that everybody hated him until his own servants murdered him. He claims that the only reason Dostoevsky conceives of history as strife between fathers and sons is that he and his father hated each other. Nechaev sounds like Turgenev's Basarow when he argues that the revolution will do away with fathers and sons, dynasties and successors, because each generation will start the old revolution anew and make history begin afresh (see *MP* 188-89). But the naivety of Nechaev's belief in revolution as a remedy to heredity indirectly confirms Dostoevsky's view of history as a struggle between generations. Through his incredible statement that the idea of an eternal strife between fathers and sons is Dostoevsky's private neurosis he undermines the credibility

---

[12]   Franklyn A. Hyde draws attention to Freud's "Dostoevsky and Parricide" as an intertext of the novel. Freud sees the relation between father and son in Dostoevsky's novels, his epilepsy, his political and religious views, his gambling, and his obsession with crime and moral responsibility as inseparable from each other. He argues that an unresolved Oedipus complex gives rise to Dostoevsky's epileptic fits: Dostoevsky desired his father's death, but when his father actually died, the son's wish and lighter attacks turned into severe non-organic attacks followed by gnawing guilt. The fits also shaped Dostoevsky's deeply ambivalent attitude to authority in general (political, religious). According to Hyde, *The Master of Petersburg* incorporates this linkage of the private and the public and contests it at the same time. Whereas Freud's Dostoevsky is locked in the position of the son, Coetzee's rather occupies that of the father, or of the radical who has turned conservative in his later days (see Hyde, "Rage against the rule of fathers"). I would argue that Coetzee's Dostoevsky occupies both positions. He is at the same time subject and object of parricidal fantasy. As shown above, markers of his wish to kill the son are visibly embedded in the novel.

of his claim: "'The day I'm thirty-five, I'll put a bullet through my brains, I swear!' [...] 'I will never be a father'" (*MP* 188).

Nechaev's claim that Pavel did not kill himself but was pushed off the tower by the police is to be taken more seriously. But the better Dostoevsky gets to know the young revolutionary, the more he despises his nihilism and the stronger his conviction becomes that Nechaev killed Pavel in order to lure him, Dostoevsky, to Petersburg to use him for his ends. Nechaev wants to force Dostoevsky to write a pamphlet for the anarchists, in which he accuses the police of Pavel's murder and calls for resistance against the state. Nechaev believes that Dostoevsky's high profile with the university students will increase their commitment to the revolutionary cause – a calculation that paradoxically testifies to the dependence of the young upon the old that they are about to attack (see *MP* 179-82).

Nechaev's attempted blackmail does not work out, however, just as Dostoevsky's hope to find the truth about Pavel is frustrated. The novel ends with Dostoevsky taking first steps towards turning his recent experiences into fiction when, on the blank pages of his stepson's diary, he drafts two stories about Pavel, stories that throw an unfavourable light on Pavel. These drafts will later serve as the seeds of the novel *Demons*.[13] As though it were not enough that Dostoevsky survives Pavel, his stepson's death provides Dostoevsky with the material allowing him to write one of the novels by which he will be best remembered. Dostoevsky makes Pavel's trace his own. The fact that Dostoevsky's trace overwrites Pavel's life in such an irritating manner makes it necessary to contemplate the idea of the trace itself and to relate it to the meaning of the historical in Coetzee's novel.

Trace, Confession, Autobiography

One of the central insights of hermeneutics is that while historical events differ from all previous events, we make use of concepts derived from experience and therefore from previous events to perceive an event as an event. Future events, too, are intelligible only as repetitions of events already experienced. Perception of the present and anticipation of the future therefore depend on remembrance and expectation that in turn depend on iterability, which means that the singularity and the iterability of an event can only be thought in interdependence. The trace is the iterability inherent in every experience. It is the absence of a presence; it is there, but only to show that what it refers to is absent. This makes the trace – be it the trace of a horse, of a thief or of a dead person – the embodiment of 'archi-writing' (Derrida) because in writing every sign refers to something absent while simulating its presence (see, for example, Derrida, *Writing and Difference* 246-91).

The Master of Petersburg, I argue, shows that, in principle, a spirit is no different from a trace, and thus the novel reminds one of Derrida who, in his early writings, analyzes the concept of the trace by taking a close look at writing whilst in his later works tends to replace the concept of the trace by that of the spirit. Like the trace, the

---

[13]   The novel incorporates characters and themes from *Demons*, *The Brothers Karamazov* and other novels and stories by Dostoevsky, amongst them *Crime and Punishment* and *The Idiot*.

spirit is a presence that refers to something absent, but its presence is not limited to writing but can be any kind of trace. *The Master of Petersburg* repeats this movement from the particular (writing) to the general (spirit as any trace) in an uncanny way when it adopts the concept of the trace from writing and applies it to the heritage conflict between fathers and sons and to the *zeitgeist* which haunts the father in the form of Pavel's spirit.

When the connection between Nechaev and Pavel is still unknown to Dostoevsky, and when Dostoevsky has not yet been pulled into the whirl of historical events, Pavel's most obvious trace are his diaries. Only much later in his inquiries does Dostoevsky dare to read them. What immediately mesmerizes him is not their content, however, but the fact that he is looking at a physical trace of Pavel: "[H]is attention keeps wandering from the sense of the words to the words themselves, to the letters on the paper, to the trace in ink of the hand's movements, the shadings left by the pressure of the fingers" (*MP* 216). Dostoevsky's last desire will be to continue his trace in Pavel's name, but in his, Dostoevsky's, spirit. The example shows, in a particularly disturbing manner, that a trace left becomes the trace of whoever follows and uses it, as every repetition of a trace changes the trace. Furthermore, traces can be constructed – even traces attributed to natural history, as demonstrated by Pavel's choice of Nechaev as father, Dostoevsky's choice of Pavel as his 'real' son and Dostoevsky's travelling to Russia under the name of the deceased Isaev. Two options for someone trying to control his or her trace – to immunize it against manipulation by others – are confession and, still more radically, autobiography. Whatever someone says in confession wants to be taken as the definite trace of a life episode, and the confessor claims this authority because he subjects himself to sincerity conditions.

Coetzee is aware of the limitations of confession in a secular context, as it is impossible even for the confessor – and even if his or her contrition is sincere – to rule out that the confession is influenced by unconscious ulterior motives. Nevertheless, truth-intention is inherent to the genre of confession, and it is also inherent to autobiography. Any autobiography that does not acknowledge or gesture towards the futility of the claim to authoritatively narrate one's entire life's trace – any autobiography of this kind generically entails such a claim and bases it on the authority of an I which claims to be transparent to itself; for the genre entails an implicit contract between author and reader concerning authenticity, no matter how problematic the relationship between authenticity, truth and truth-telling may be (see Lejeune, "The Autobiographical Contract" 219-20). Dostoevsky's *Demons* will become a chapter of his unwritten autobiography, and Nechaev, too, makes an attempt at autobiography when he tells Dostoevsky the story of how he broke free from his father and became his own master. The cross-examination at the novel's beginning between Maximov and Dostoevsky testifies to Dostoevsky's wish to immunize his life's trace against manipulation – not least against the most natural of manipulations, i.e. the continuation of his trace by his son. What Coetzee's novel demonstrates, however, is that the confession or the autobiography of an 'I' possessed by the spirit of another will necessarily be an ascription by someone else: "He knows the word *I*, but as he stares at it it becomes as enigmatic as a rock in the desert" (*MP* 71).

The beginning and end of the novel, then, are framed by Pavel's (and ultimately Dostoevsky's) trace in the form of writing, metafictionally stressing the relation between Coetzee and the historical Dostoevsky. In between, however, it is Pavel's spirit, not writing, that is the presence of an absence and that fulfils the function of the trace. The link between Pavel's writing and his spirit is his name, on which *The Master of Petersburg* comments: "When death cuts all other links, there remains still the name" (*MP* 5). The name has a ghostly quality because it simulates the presence of its bearer after the bearer's death, and because, according to Derrida, it foreshadows the bearer's death during his lifetime (see Derrida, *The Animal* 19-20). Already in *Dusklands* the act of naming was an act of conjuring for Coetzee, because naming makes things exist in the first place (see Clarkson, *J. M. Coetzee* 143-44). Dostoevsky conjures up the presence of Pavel's spirit by repeating his name. However, since writing relies on names that are used and have been used by others a long time ago, it amounts to a constant awakening of unsuspected spirits of history. In an interview, Coetzee says about writing that it involves "an awareness, as you put pen to paper, that you are setting in train a certain play of signifiers with their own ghostly history of past interplay" (*DP* 63). The signs of language are historically charged and therefore ghostly. Thus Dostoevsky's calls for Pavel are particularly personal conjurations of a professional conjuror about whom Anna Sergeyevna says: "You are an artist, a master […] It is for you, not for me, to bring him back to life" (*MP* 141).

Being a writer, Dostoevsky is used to externalizing and even to driving out his thoughts and his spirit with the help of language. It is a process for which Hegel, in *The Phenomenology of Spirit*, invents the term self-estrangement, which Marx will later use to describe the worker's loss of identification with the product he has created. In Hegel, however, the term refers to the spirit being objectified in the spoken word that originates from the speaker but no longer belongs to him, now having its own objectivity and materiality (see Hegel, *Phänomenologie des Geistes* 359-98). Experiencing this verbal phenomenon every day as a writer, Dostoevsky is rather upset by Pavel's non-verbal presences as an ungraspable spirit that cannot be objectified. This spirit appears in the form of a hatred of children. Seeing them makes Pavel's loss even more unbearable, and Dostoevsky discovers himself to be possessed by the spirit of vengefulness: "A terrible malice streams out of him toward the living, and most of all toward living children. If there were a newborn babe here at this moment, he would pluck it from its mother's arms and dash it against a rock. Herod, he thinks: now I understand Herod! Let breeding come to an end!" (*MP* 9-10, see also 16) There is also Dostoevsky's bad conscience (see *MP* 64-65), the nights with Anna Sergeyevna become uncanny encounters with his stepson, and Pavel follows Dostoevsky even into his dreams. In Dostoevsky's conscience, Pavel's ghostly appearances finally condense into an image:

> He shakes his head as if to rid it of a plague of devils. What is it that is corrupting the integrity of his grieving, that insists it is nothing but a lugubrious disguise? Somewhere inside him truth has lost its way. As if in the labyrinth of his brain, but also in the labyrinth of his body – veins, bones, intestines, organs – a tiny child is wandering, searching for the light, searching to emerge. How can he find the child lost within himself, allow him a voice to sing a sad song?
>
> *Piping on a bone.* An old story comes back to him of a youth killed, mutilated, scattered, whose thigh-bone, when the wind blows, pipes a lament and names his murderers. One by one, in fact, the old stories are coming back, stories he heard from his

grandmother and did not know the meaning of, but stored up unwittingly like bones for the future. A great ossuary of stories before history began, built up and tended by the people. Let Pavel find his way to my thigh-bone and pipe to me from there! *Father, why have you left me in the dark forest? Father, when will you come to save me?*

(Coetzee, *MP* 125-26; italics in original)

Like an alchemist, Dostoevsky's imagination thickens the novel's layers of meaning into a handful of sentences. There is first the biblical story of the demons possessing a man ("a plague of devils"), then, with the evocation of "disguise", "truth" and "light" in short succession, Plato's parable of the cave: the cave in which ideas appear in different forms and degrees of truth is Dostoevsky's "head" in which mourning appears as a shadow over truth; it shadows truth instead of putting it into the light – but not forever. For in the figure of Pavel truth persists in Dostoevsky, who is opaque or a "labyrinth" to himself. Like Orpheus, Pavel wants to return from the realm of death to life and is looking for an exit. In Plato's parable light – the idea of truth itself – streams from the exit into the cave.[14] The skull of the passage cited also has connotations of death and evokes natural history. The second paragraph deals with natural history more explicitly by adding bones to the skull as evidence of past human lives ("thigh-bone", "ossuary"). Again, natural history is perverted, for the bones do not belong to the ancestors but to their youngest successor. Only the unperverted traces of natural history reach back to before history where mythology seems located ("A great ossuary of stories before history began, built up and tended by the people"). These traces are "stored up unwittingly" from generation to generation to serve as vessels or, to speak with Coetzee, as "veins" of truth in some unforeseeable future when spirit drives into the old traces, as the wind blowing on the bone suggests. The "sad song" of the wandering Pavel/Orpheus suggests that the passage develops a theory of art and defines the inspiration or source of art as "grieving". In practical terms, art is a reworking of myths, the following and manipulation of traces left a long time ago, as the novel itself demonstrates by rewriting Dostoevsky's *Demons*. The purpose of art is a bringing of truth to the light in a future that cannot yet be foreseen and in which a tale kept like an old bone suddenly matches the present like key and lock. When Dostoevsky will have written *Demons*, Pavel's story will indeed have become a key to the times in which the young rebel against the old and the old clutch their possessions. The Bible's demons drive into the herd of swine; Pavel's spirit drives into the novel.

The image of bones illustrates the past's reaching into the present and the ways available to humans of dealing with history's traces: stemming from the past and kept for the future, the bones are traces haunting the present as Pavel haunts Dostoevsky; the present can follow and change these traces like Dostoevsky when he writes *Demons*; the present can also deny these traces as Nechaev denies his father, the very idea of heredity and, in an extended sense, of authority and authorship. The bones are human signs – and signs of the human – beyond language, signifying a struggle for survival against time and against each other, and regardless of whether they haunt someone, are followed,

---

[14]   The image of the skull is again reminiscent of Beckett's *Endgame* whose protagonists are caught in a room with two windows. In contrast to Coetzee, however, the image seems to suggest the solipsism of the characters.

used or manipulated, they are the traces of a history into which the human is necessarily embedded. In this way they are emblems of how the novel conceptualizes the historicity of the human. Its concern with writing, spirit and bones as forms of the trace shows that the present consists of traces of the past and is full of spirits which the living cannot avoid inheriting: regardless of whether they are sons or fathers, even when they attempt to evade this heritage by confessing or by writing an autobiography, and even when in an autobiography the spirit of parents and ancestors is defined as not-yet-human or fundamentally other. This and only this merges the detective novel in which Dostoevsky looks for traces, the gothic novel with the uncanny return of the past, and the historiographic metafiction about historicity and its narratability into Coetzee's unusual historical novel.

Works Cited

Adorno, Theodor W. 'Trying to Understand Endgame.' Trans. Michael T. Jones. *New German Critique* 26 (1982): 119-150.

Agamben, Giorgio. *The Open: Man and Animal*. Trans. Kevin Attell. Stanford: Stanford University Press, 2004.

Attridge, Derek, and Peter McDonald, eds. "J. M. Coetzee's 'Disgrace'." Special issue of *Interventions: International Journal of Postcolonial Studies* 4-3 (2002): 315-468.

Beckett, Samuel. *Dramatic Works. The Grove Centenary Edition*. New York: Grove, 2006.

Clarkson, Carrol. *J. M. Coetzee: Countervoices*. Basingstoke: Palgrave, 2009.

Coetzee, J. M. 'Erasmus: Madness and Rivalry.' *Giving Offense: Essays on Censorship*. Chicago: University of Chicago Press, 1996. 83-103.

Coetzee, J. M. 'The Novel Today.' *Upstream* 6-1 (1988): 2-5.

Coetzee, J. M. *Disgrace*. London: Secker & Warburg, 1999.

Coetzee, J. M. *Doubling the Point: Essays and Interviews*. Ed. David Attwell. Cambridge, Mass.: Harvard University Press, 1992.

Coetzee, J. M. *Dusklands*. London: Secker & Warburg: 1982.

Coetzee, J. M. *In the Heart of the Country*. London: Secker & Warburg, 1977.

Coetzee, J. M. *Life & Times of Michael K*. London: Secker & Warburg, 1983.

Coetzee, J. M. *The Master of Petersburg*. London: Secker & Warburg, 1994.

Coetzee, J. M. *Waiting for the Barbarians*. London: Secker & Warburg, 1980.

Derrida, Jacques. *The Animal That Therefore I Am*. New York: Fordham University Press, 2008.

Derrida, Jacques. *Writing and Difference*. London, New York: Routledge, 2002.

Eliot, T. S. *Selected Prose*. Ed. Frank Kermode. New York: Farrar, Straus & Giroux, 1975.

Frank, Joseph. "*Demons*". *Between Religion and Rationality: Essays in Russian Literature and Culture*. Princeton, Oxford: Princeton University Press, 2010.

Frank, Joseph. '*The Devils* and the Nechaev Affair.' *Through the Russian Prism: Essays on Literature and Culture*. Princeton: Princeton University Press, 1990. 137-152.

Frank, Joseph. *Dostoevsky: A Writer in His Time*. Ed. Mary Petrusewicz. Princeton, Oxford: Princeton University Press, 2010.

Gerigk, Horst-Jürgen. *Dostojewskijs Entwicklung als Schriftsteller: Vom ,Toten Haus'
zu den ,Brüdern Karamasow'*. Frankfurt: S. Fischer, 2013.

Groot, Jerome de. *The Historical Novel*. London: Routledge, 2010.

Hegel, Georg Friedrich. *Phänomenologie des Geistes. Werke 3*. Frankfurt: Suhrkamp,
1986.

Hyde, Franklin A. "'Rage against the rule of Fathers': Freud's 'Dostoevsky and
Parricide' in J. M. Coetzee's *The Master of Petersburg*." *Ariel* 41:3-4 (2011):
207-29.

Kannemeyer, John C. *J. M. Coetzee: A Life in Writing*. Trans. Michiel Heyns.
Johannesburg, Cape Town: Jonathan Ball, 2012.

Lejeune, Philippe. 'The Autobiographical Contract.' *French Literary Theory Today: A
Reader*. Ed. Tzvetan Todorov. Trans. R. Carter. Cambridge: Cambridge University
Press, 1982. 192-222.

Lukács, György. *The Historical Novel*. Lincoln: University of Nebraska Press, 1983.

Marais, Mike. *Secretary of the Invisible: The Idea of Hospitality in the Fiction of J. M.
Coetzee*. Amsterdam, New York: Rodopi, 2009.

Parnes, Ohad, Ulrike Vedder, and Stefan Willer, eds. *Das Konzept der Generation: Eine
Wissens- und Kulturgeschichte*. Frankfurt: Suhrkamp, 2008.

Popescu, Monica. *South African Literature Beyond the Cold War*. New York: Palgrave
Macmillan, 2010.

Porter, Roy. *Madness: A Brief History*. Oxford: Oxford University Press, 2003.

Scanlan, Margaret. "Incriminating Documents: Nechaev and Dostoevsky in J. M.
Coetzee's 'The Master of Petersburg' (Sergei Nechaev, Fyodor Dostoevsky)."
Philological Quarterly 76-4 (1997), 463+. *Literature Resource Center*. Web. 11 Jan.
2011.

Turgenev, Ivan. *The Novels of Ivan Turgenev: Fathers and Children*. Trans. Constance
Garrett. New York: Macmillan, 1916.

Weigel, Sigrid. *Genea-Logik: Generation, Tradition und Evolution zwischen Kultur-
und Naturwissenschaften*. Munich: Fink, 2006.

H ELGA S CHWALM

Figurations of Authorship in Postmodern Historical Fiction

This chapter aims to explore figurations of authorship in postmodern fiction, focussing on a special subgenre that might be labelled – for want of a more elegant term – *postmodern historiographic bio-metafiction*. This monstrous concatenation, merging various seminal concepts,[1] comprises historical novels that do not merely make the writing of history their subject but do so by means of historical biography. As such, they negotiate the possibilities and epistemological frames of historiography as much as those of life writing and its endeavour to capture the life of another person (long since dead). Such texts operate as historical novels insofar as they fictionalize "real" events or persons of the past; they operate as biographical novels or *biofiction* insofar as they fictionalize the lives of "real" persons; and they operate as metafiction insofar as they call attention to their own status as text or fiction.

It is a commonplace of literary criticism that metafictional novels are characteristic of, although not exclusive to, postmodernism. Although self-consciousness has notoriously been the novel's hallmark from its very beginning, the postmodern novel has undoubtedly displayed a particular affinity to metafiction. More specifically, historiographic metafiction tends to stage a Lyotardian doubt of the validity of *grands récits*, calling attention to the "emplotment", i.e. the narrative and rhetorical constructedness of history. These bits of theoretical insight in the wake of the linguistic turn have – at least in a tamed version – entered the canon of literary criticism and self-conscious literature alike. In particular, metafictional historical novels question the possibility of historical truth, reflecting these doubts by aesthetic means, and thus epitomize postmodern fiction as such.[2]

With respect to the issue of biography and authorship in metafiction, a further recounting of postmodern critical commonplaces is called for. In the wake of 'Theory' (with a capital T), the notions of subjectivity and of the author as authorial subject were discarded or qualified as transitory historical phenomena. In either case, a shift of focus occurred from the subject to the text (rather than work) as a 'subjectless', highly unstable, structure. "What does it matter who's speaking?" is the phrase Foucault

---

[1]   See Nünning, *Von historischer Fiktion zu historiographischer Metafiktion*; Hutcheon, *A Poetics of Postmodernism*; Huber & Middeke, *Biofictions: The Rewriting of Romantic Lives in Contemporary Fiction and Drama*.

[2]   Under the impact of French philosophy and the noveau roman, John Fowles was the first to initiate this trend in British fiction with *The French Lieutenant's Woman* (1969). Offering a highly detached and self-conscious narration of a Victorian love story, the novel famously ends with providing three alternative endings, thus refusing narrative closure.

('What is an author' 141) aptly borrowed from Beckett's *Unnamable*, leaving the reader in command of the 'writerly' (Roland Barthes) text. Even though the epistemological status of the diagnosed 'death of the author' (Barthes) varied, it certainly spread contagiously to literary biography, generally dissolving the biographical subject into the text.[3]

Literary theory, however, had far earlier dispensed with a focus on the author as originator of meaning. What – for want of a better word – might be called 'Biographism' notoriously came to an end with Wimsatt's/Beardsley's 'Intentional Fallacy'. The history of German theory is somewhat different, but in any case the term 'Biographismus' or 'Biographism' indicates the low esteem in which biography as a critical source has been held ever since the New Critics' verdict – in contrast to the immense popularity of biography on British bookshelves. The New Criticism discarded the tradition of linking a literary work to the life, personality and the intentions of its author. The generic paradigm of the traditional 'life and works' approach would seem to be the genre of literary biography, or *Dichterbiographie*, which goes back to Johnson's *Lives of the Poets* (published 1779-81) and Boswell's *Life of Johnson* (1791). Wordsworth, in his 'A letter to a friend of Robert Burns' (1816), attacked the contemporary obsession with biographical facts; yet at the same time, his *Prelude* does construct a connection between poetic consciousness and the poet's life. In spite of the critical overtones, then, and in spite of the genre's inherent positivism, biography evolved into an essentially Romantic (and hermeneutic) project, staging the poet as 'hero' in a Diltheyian mode of historical understanding (see Schwalm, 'Das eigene und das fremde Leben' 73-2). Even today, critical reflections of and theoretical approaches to the genre continue to define the objective of biography as tracing the 'naked self' or 'inner myth' of its biographical subject by means of a kind of informed empathy or, in more hermeneutic terms, *Einfühlung*[4] and thus to uncover the 'essential spirit' of the author or poet.

In Britain, the 'New Biography' of the Bloomsbury Circle revised the epistemology, methodology and objective of biography, but retained its fascination with it. It is in this context, too, that the deliberate and self-conscious fictionalizing of biography materializes – Woolf's *Orlando* is a case in point. Indeed, Woolf explicitly and paradoxically places biography between scholarship and art: "Truth of fact and truth of fiction are incompatible; yet he [the biographer, H.S.] is now more than ever urged to combine them". The reason is to be found in the subject of biography, for according to Woolf it "dwells in the personality rather than in the act" (Woolf, 'The New Biography' 234). As it seeks to grasp the personality of its subject, biography needs to resort to fictional or aesthetic means. The new biography does so consciously, the more traditional biography perhaps unwittingly. In any case, the biographer's vision of and empathy with his subject necessarily involves some degree of conjecture, construction, and, as Iris Nadel has emphasized in her study of the genre, 'emplotment'. No matter what the literary pretensions, a degree of emplotment and constructedness imposing coherence

---

3   However, the battlefield and test case has been autobiography rather than heterobiography. – From the perspective of cultural and media history, it needs to be added that collective forms of authorship have increasingly come to replace the individual author (see Woodmannsee, 'On the Author Effect: Recovering Collectivity').

4   Thus, e.g., Kaplan, 'The Naked Self' 46-8 and 55.

and aiming at an essence will always be there. Also, it will involve two subjects, or subjectivities: the biographer as constructing agent and his subject.

The New Critics' objection to biography, to conclude my critical analepsis, was, of course, not to the literariness or fictionality of biography. The New Critics denied its part in literary understanding: they denied that literary meaning and authorial intention and thus literary meaning and biography belong together. This is certainly the point where literary theory since Deconstruction has found itself in accordance with New Critical thought. In their campaign for the 'return of the author', the opponents of Deconstruction/Poststructuralism have in turn resorted to biography as a safe haven of "agency, personhood, cause, and effect" (Fish, 'Biography and Intention' 15).

The debate surrounding biography also marks a significant point where the concerns of critical theory and fiction overlapped. Since the 1980s, novels concerned with biography have regularly won critical acclaim. In various different ways, such biofictions explore biography as the 'secondary discourse of life par excellence', negotiating its precarious status between radical intertextuality and "fundamentally … conservative" (Schläger, 'Biography: Cult as Culture' 62-3) bastion of the self as author and agent.

Reinventing the past as fiction, this chapter argues, these texts still insist on the inevitability of historical and biographical narration. They do so by different strategies of rehabilitating the figure of the Romantic author – either clad in postmodern fashion as is the case in Peter Ackroyd's *Chatterton*, reinventing the author as collective and authentic subject, as in both Ackroyd and Alan Massie's *The Ragged Lion,* or revealed as precarious centre behind a seemingly conventional double plot as in Julian Barnes's *Arthur & George.*

I will begin with the least metabiographical of the texts selected, Allan Massie's *The Ragged Lion,* first published in 1994, a novel which has undeservedly received little critical acclaim outside Scotland. In this piece of biofiction, the typical metafictional motifs of quest and lost documents are confined to a framing narrative. More precisely, it is a double frame. In a pseudo-nonfictional preface, the author-narrator signing with the initials 'AM' claims to have inherited a copy of a lost manuscript from an Italian Countess whose great grandmother had been given it by Sir Walter Scott's son after Scott's death. This manuscript is said to be a memoir of Scott's, written during his stay in Rome shortly before his death. "We have to consider an Italian copyist, with perhaps an uncertain command of English, transcribing a manuscript which Charles Scott who knew his father's hand well had difficulty in reading" (Massie, *The Ragged Lion* XVII). The authenticity of the supposed memoir is thus both questioned and asserted, fiction and history are blurred. The afterword (the second narrative frame), which the purported editor refers us to for further confirmation, adds more: It identifies the main biographical intertexts and obliquely formulates Massie's biofictional objective. The purported author of this afterword is Charles Scott, Walter's younger son, who gives his account of how he came to be in the possession of the memoir, thus asserting the preface. More importantly, it is by this afterword that the reader is presented with a dual key to the narrative. Firstly, Charles explains his plans concerning the manuscript. According to this afterword, he will leave a copy with John Lockhart (Scott's authorized biographer and son-in-law) who will disregard much here; but he may find some things of value to him. Then I suspect he will – out of a wish to protect my father's good name of which he is a very jealous guardian – a wish that, in my view, would be quite mistaken – destroy the copy I send him.

(Massie, *The Ragged Lion* 295)

Hence the difference between Massie's memoir and Lockhart's real portrait. Secondly, Charles remarks on his sense of astonishment and incomprehension when confronted with this memoir, for it presents a dark side of its subject hitherto unknown to him, and to Lockhart's readers: "one thing has been made clear to me by my reading of this, his last work and perhaps testament: that my father was a stranger, more uncanny being than I had supposed" (Massie, *The Ragged Lion* 286; 294). The afterword thus helps the reader ignorant of the biographical novelties in Massie's version.

The fictional memoir itself, framed by preface and afterword, does indeed present a different Scott from the Scott of the 'real' journals and the Scott of Lockhart's biography. It covers a longer span of time than the real *Journal*, but above all, it shows a deeply melancholy, torn and guilt-ridden man beneath the public appearance of a rational, aloof gentleman. A dual Scott emerges, a 'ragged lion' increasingly losing command of himself, finding himself "thrown about like branches in a big wind [...] wild, changeable, and erratic as Lear" (Massie, *The Ragged Lion* 261).

The gist of the fictionalizing techniques involved in constructing this image is as follows: Consisting of autobiographical recollections alternating with reflections in the present, the memoir enlarges upon themes not fully pursued in the real memoirs, such as the psychological effect of Scott's bankruptcy, but it also imagines dimensions of Scott's inner life which neither the real *Journal* nor the real biography (Lockhart's *Life*) cover. To give an example: Scott's journal entry on his grandson's death in 1832, is:

> Another piece of intelligence was certainly to be expected but now it has come afflicts us much – poor Johnny Lockhart. The boy is gone whom we have made so much of. It could not have been latter better and might have been much worse
>
> (*The Journal of Sir Walter Scott* 781),

which is followed immediately by an account of his visit to the opera. Massie's novel offers a different version:

> Then there was the grief occasioned by the news of my beloved grandson, little Johnny Lockhart, a pain too deep for words. The night we heard of his passing, when in Naples, I attended the opera, and I believe poor Anne was a little shocked and dismayed, as she loved the boy as if he had been her own [...] She did not understand that I attended the opera to staunch my wound. I could not have borne to sit at home and mope; it was that or the oblivion of the bottle, the refuge of Prince Charles in his long years of exile here.
>
> (Massie, *The Ragged Lion* 274)

In his fictional memoir, then, Massie's Scott reveals a melancholy, suffering, hidden Scott, torn between his public image as rational, enlightened, politically conservative and someone deeply afraid of losing his sense, suffering from the loss of memory (258) and from the loss of his literary powers, from physical deterioration and above all, a fear of madness. Indeed, next to King Lear, it is the figure of Samuel Johnson who crops up again and again in the text: "that noble, struggling soul", embodying conservative reason, common sense (and Jacobitism, of course) and at the same time a man with a terrible fear of the 'dangers of the imagination' and of death.

Within the represented events of the memoir, the theme of loss of reason and looming death is triggered off by several instances of hallucination afflicting Scott in the Edinburgh underworld of Cowgate (the dark, low-level parallel to the High St or Royal Mile). A fiddler and a dancer appear to him on more than one occasion, singing:

> And will ye come wi' me, cuddy,
> Beyond the land and sea,
> And will ye tak the road, cuddy,
> The road you ken, wi' me?"

For a moment Scott awakes from this dream-like state, but then, as he is speaking to his son-in-law and future biographer, Lockhart, the scene continues:

> I heard the cackle of an old woman from the crowd:
>   Take up your bonnie bridegroom while ye may, Ailsie, for his time is but short. [...]
> Then the brandy commenced its recuperative work, and I felt myself steady. My head cloudy as the Eildon hills [...], I muttered. [...] What was that, Sir Walter? he enquired [...].
>   Did you not hear her, Scott asks him, Did you not hear her, John?– Sir Walter, is Lockhart's answer, I must tell you I heard no woman speak [...] these words you have recited, though in a broken and quavering voice that it pains me to hear, these words I recognize. They are your own, Sir Walter, taken with some modification and a change of person from *The Bride of Lammermoor*.
>
> (Massie, *The Ragged Lion* 270-2)

It seems, then, that Scott, unaware of what they are, is haunted by lines from his own work – his work has re-entered, as it were, his life. Not only does Massie link certain events or episodes in Scott's life to specific poems (35), but in the life itself Scott's literary creations have returned to be part of his self on an unconscious, irrational and disturbing level. "The works that have proceeded from my imagination", to use the fictional Scott's phrase, which he has "ever shrunk from talking" about, these works, as they have slipped from him, are becoming part of his life, of himself again. This mode of inverse connection of life/self and literary work belies Scott's self-fashioning as the educated, 'robust' and 'sceptical' (25) Scott of Abbortsford (his country home) who published his novels anonymously, believing, as biographers have explained, that his authorship of the Waverley novels could do his social identity no credit, that his life achievement was to be aristocratic master of Abbotsford, not his literary work. Thoughts of authorship "occupied but a small part of my mind", he says, his labours committed instead to his life as 'country gentleman' (60). It is this denial of authorship as an integral part of himself which – according to Massie's version – Scott has finally come to regret, and his son's reading of the memoir confirms this: Charles believes that his father had come to see his low esteem of his authorship as a failure to "the gifts bestowed on him" (289). In severing authorship from his self image, Scott has betrayed himself, his 'richer self', as it were. He only comes to realize his own need for literature at a moment in life when his literary powers are failing him – and when he is on the verge of financial ruin (227). "Only to Lockhart, I think, could I ever have offered the confession that I could never have brought myself to abandon literature for ten times my income" (170). But the "wand is broken", as his recurrent phrase goes (66 and passim).

In other instances, however, authorship is not as exclusive. Some snippets of poetry in Massie's novel are indeed taken from the *Border Minstrelsy*, i.e. Scott's collection of ballads with some his own contributions, while some are of Massie's own hand (in imitation of Scott) (see Rubenstein, 'Auld Acquaintance'). In either case, authorship would be dual and diffused: it involves either Scott transcribing and imitating folk song, or Massie 're-inscribing' Scott. Be it Massie or be it Scott himself, poetic authorship re-enters Scott's biography as a key issue, as the suppressed and lost dimension of his life. Authorship is reclaimed. Yet it is one involving more than one subject pointing to its dual and intertextual, interauthorial, nature: Massie obliquely reveals himself as vacillating between the roles of biographer and author of biofiction, as both empathizing with and inventing, or even 'usurping', his subject.

The reclaiming of a decentred and interauthorial authorship is also, on a different level and with different techniques and objectives, at the centre of Peter Ackroyd's *Chatterton* (first published in 1987). Unlike Massie, Ackroyd incorporates metabiographical reflections into the plot itself. Again, the reader is confronted with different temporal planes: the present, the Victorian age, and the time of Chatterton's death, i.e. 1770. However, these temporal levels do not form a diegetic hierarchy, and there is no extradiegetic narrator visibly or audibly claiming authority over the text as a whole. Rather, the alternating diegetic planes are simply juxtaposed. In the present, Charles, an unemployed, unsuccessful and impoverished poet, acquires a painting which he soon believes to be a portrait of the Romantic poet Chatterton in middle age. Given that Chatterton, the famous forger of mediaeval poems, is said to have died of his own hand at the age of 18, Charles's find would mean he has discovered an incredible forgery: Chatterton, he comes to believe, must have faked his own death. Chatterton lived on and, having vanished as a person, is probably the true voice behind Blake and others. "'You know'", Charles explains to his friend and assistant detective Philip, "'half the poetry of the eighteenth century is probably written by him'". "'He's the greatest forger in history'", Philip responds, but Charles is not happy with this superlative, nor with 'The greatest plagiarist'. "In his enthusiasm Charles looked triumphantly at him. 'He was the greatest poet in history!'" (Ackroyd, *Chatterton* 94).

This conviction, apparently confirmed by a confessional Chatterton manuscript also obtained by him, triggers off Charles's detective quest for Chatterton.

Charles, however, has fallen victim to the forgery of a forgery. As it turns out, the manuscript confessing the forgery is a fake, and Chatterton perished young after all, as does Charles, who dies of a brain tumour half way through the novel. As his physical symptoms get worse, Charles's curiosity turns into an obsession and finally an identification with Chatterton who lived on in others and who now increasingly invades Charles's disease-ridden imagination (47). The 'anxiety of influence', or Eliot's individual talent engulfed in the poetic tradition, is staged as a pathological symptom and at the same time serves as a metafictional point of reference. Outside Charles' consciousness (or semi-consciousness towards the latter stages), Charles is constructed to resemble Chatterton, too – his death pose imitates Chatterton's, etc. In short, Charles and Chatterton merge. As Charles had projected his ideal of the poet's creative imagination onto the figure of an eternal Chatterton, rewriting Chatterton's biography, as it were, as a transgression of authorial self, Chatterton has invaded and taken possession of Charles's self.

What is at stake in this novel, then, is literary authenticity and authorship. This issue is taken up (and altered in its connotations) in the subplot revolving around the issue of forgery and plagiarism in modern art. And it is taken up on the second temporal plane: As George Meredith, the novelist, poses as model for Henry Wallis's portrait of Chatterton (completed in 1856), they discuss the indistinguishability between the real and its (aesthetic) representation: To his model's objection, "'You want My face, but not myself. I am to be Thomas Chatterton, not George Meredith'", Wallis responds: "'But it will be you. After all, I can only paint what I see'" (Ackroyd, *Chatterton* 133).

On the third temporal plane presenting the last days of Chatterton himself in a stream-of-consciousness-like narrative, the issue of forgery, of course, returns, as Chatterton locates his poetic genius precisely in the ability to forge others. This is the crucial paradox: Forgery is the perfect Romantic sympathy. "A great genius can affect anything" (92-3), Chatterton comments on his forgeries. Poetic genius proves itself in the transgression of self; biography turns into literary history.

Two metafictional and metabiographical conclusions, then, seem on offer in Ackroyd's construction of the biographical quest: Firstly, authorial identity is necessarily plural. Secondly, reality and art, authentic and fake cannot and, more importantly, need not be distinguished. But this not the end of authorship in the sense of authorial subjectivity, for the text insists on the superior quality of the poet's imagination over reality.

Ackroyd grants his semi-protagonist a surprisingly emotional final speech:

> And why is it he confronts a friend, a popular novelist that some people try all their lives to become writers or poets, even though they are too ashamed to show their works to anyone? Why do they keep on trying? [...] Where does *their* dream come from? [...] It is a dream of wholeness, and of beauty. All the yearning and all the unhappiness and all the sickness can be taken away by that vision. And the vision is real. I know. I've seen it, and I am sick.
>
> (Ackroyd, *Chatterton* 152)

This is the poet who has no qualms about being a ghost writer, who is not concerned about plagiarism. Authorship as a legal category is a dispensable instrument, but the author as subject is at the heart of literature. Accordingly, intertextuality is not the end of the subject but the means of reinventing the past and the locus of a reinstated authorial subjectivity.

Ackroyd's novel confirms this poetological tenet through its own narrative performance. The invisible extradiegetic narrator inserts his version of the author's end into the text by means of an interior monologue spoken by Chatterton: Chatterton has contracted a venereal disease; the mixture of arsenic and opium he is recommended as a cure causes an accidental death. This is Ackroyd's final word, suspended however, in the realm of representations, for anachronistic details of Wallis's portrait re-enter the original biographical scene.[5] The text thus offers his version of death as an accident and at the same time invalidates his construction as yet another representation.

There is a twist of irony in it, for after all, Charles's sickness remains only too real and fatal. Yet while historical reality and fiction are blurred, forger and genius are one, authorship is reformulated as inevitable plagiarism, the plot strongly maintains a notion of authorship as originating in the authentic expression of experience. Charles himself does not find out the truth before his death, but it is his pale and plain friend, the librarian Philip, who continues to pursue his quest, solves the mystery and reverses the fusion of past and present, forgery and reality, Chatterton and Charles. The biographical quest he has inherited from Charles turns into the story of his self-authorization: Not only does he emerge as both detective hero of the latter part of the narrative and Charles's successor as father and lover, but also, possibly, as the concealed narrative agent of the entire text. Crucially, he echoes Charles's deathbed speech on poetic vision when explaining how he found his own literary voice:

> [H]e told her [Charles's widow] how he, too, was bewildered by a world in which no significant pattern could be found. Everything just seemed to *take place*. […] there's no real *origin* for anything. […] And you remember, he was saying now, I told you how I used to read novelists, to see if any of them had felt the mystery, too? But none of them had […] So I tried writing my own novel but it didn't work, you know. I kept on imitating other people. I had no real story, either, but now, […] with Charles' theory – I might be able to – […] Of course, he added, grave again, I must tell it in my own way. How Chatterton might have lived on. […] And you know […] I might discover that I had a style of my own, after all.
>
> (Ackroyd, *Chatterton* 232)

The contingency of experience and history is transformed into the deeply emotional poetics of authentic expression. And thus the reader is presented with the suggestion of a perfectly closed narrative – that of Chatterton's continuity in Charles's reception and Charles's continuity in Philip. Philip is thus able to write a triple biography: of Chatterton, Wallis's portrait, and of Charles's discovery of Chatterton as his own poet father, and of Philip becoming himself in this process. (In contrast, the plagiarist Scrope is incapable of writing her own autobiography.) Equally, there is a clear priority of authenticity on the level of interpersonal relations – what may be a necessity of plagiarism on the literary level is betrayal on an interpersonal level. In spite of the deconstruction of the Romantic cult of originality, the author is resurrected in a paradoxical notion of intertextual authenticity.

Similar to Ackroyd, Julian Barnes's early novels like *Flaubert's Parrot* (1984) are driven by a broken and yet emphatic commitment to the author as subject and origin of literary speech, and/or insist on the necessity of historical or biographical narration – to the point of an "obsession with the past" (Henke, *Vergangenheitsobsessionen*). In his more recent historical novel, *Arthur & George* (2005), the engagement with history and biography is significantly de-metafictionalized. Historical distance or self-

---

[5]   See the rose plant 132 and 137.

consciousness is signalled only through authorial prolepses referring to the outcome of the historical events and – at least in an oblique way – through the alternation of narrative time: the text oscillates between episodes narrated in the past tense and in the present tense. The effect is one of temporal instability and uncertainty both with regard to the time of narration and the temporal relation between the plot lines. Apart from this, the novel displays an astounding lack of historiographic self-consciousness, while historical authorship slips into it from the periphery of the narrated events only.

Barnes's novel is based on authentic facts, telling the story of the wrongful conviction of a young man for a crime that he did not commit. The famous author of *Sherlock Holmes*, Sir Arthur Conan Doyle, middle-aged and in the midst of a personal crisis, is called upon to help out as detective in order to prove the young man's innocence. The story of this miscarriage of justice goes as follows: George Eldalji, the son of an Indian vicar and an English mother, grows up in a small Midlands village, continuing to live with his family as a young man, sleeping in his father's study locked from the outside at night, commuting to work in Birmingham. With virtually no social life of his own, he spends his leisure time going for solitary strolls in the countryside and pursuing juridical questions related to railway transport. For years, his half Indian family is pestered with anonymous letters, threatening and slandering them. All attempts at getting help from the police are frustrated by disinterest and latent, at times even explicit, racism. After an interim period of calm, the attacks on George's family are renewed, culminating in a mysterious series of cruel butchering of farm animals. George is quickly suspected, eventually convicted of the crime and sentenced to prison – wrongfully and on the basis of a hardly tangible chain of evidence. All attempts to prove his innocence are doomed to failure. Although he is eventually granted early release, his conviction is upheld. Only once Conan Doyle has become involved in support of his case is the young man's innocence proven. However, while the famous author manages to free George from blame, he does not establish the true culprit, who only reveals himself towards the end.

Obviously, Julian Barnes has researched the famous case of miscarriage of justice carefully, just as he obviously makes use of Conan Doyle's autobiographical writings. Fraught with binary oppositions, his story focuses on a number of themes: Scotland/England, Britain/Orient, precariously linked through the Empire, centre/periphery, private/public person, art (fiction)/reality, the material/spiritual.

In fact, however, Sir Arthur enters the narrative no earlier than on page 206. The novel as a whole delivers a historical double, or parallel, biography, hence rewriting a classical form of ancient historiography. Unlike the ancient model, Barnes's version sets the two lives in relation to one another from the beginning, yet calling the respective protagonists by first name only and thus initially leaving the reader in the dark as to their identity. The two biographical strands are alternated between throughout the entire narrative, highlighting the difference between the two characters – imaginative, storytelling and athletic Arthur, full of contempt for his drunkard father and full of admiration for his strong and dominating mother on the one hand; shy and obedient George, lacking all imagination, on the other. One seems born to be an author, the other destined to live a modest provincial life, oppressed by his family situation and discriminated against for his paternal background, stubborn and ambitious as an aspiring solicitor, and finally, fascinated with the epitome of modernity – the railway. While George remains a bachelor, women playing no role in his life, three classic women characters –

mother, wife and mistress (second wife subsequently) – drive Arthur's life. Women constitute the motor of the author's creative energy.

Authorship thus mainly enters the text via the plot, more precisely via the protagonist's personal relationships with women. Although the historical novel's (implied) author does indeed occasionally and subtly call attention to the purpose of his narrative manoeuvres (such as the condensation of Arthur's experience of the Boer war into merely a few sentences), Barnes's fiction leaves authorship to the plot, and plotting to its intradiegetic author in turn: Arthur Conan Doyle, the brilliant author of detective stories, turns detective himself. And indeed, Conan Doyle was asked for help by the public on a number of occasions. Just as he adhered to his audience's wishes and resurrected his hero, he was prepared to accept George Edalji's request to intervene and solve the crime, copying his hero in terms of his method of detection. As he manages to establish his protégée's innocence, however, he falls victim to his precarious chain of evidence, blaming another. His 'client' George does not fail to notice the ironic inversion of fiction and reality: "This was where Sir Arthur's excess of enthusiasm had led him. [...] Sir Arthur had been too influenced by his own creation" (Barnes, *Arthur & George* 305).

Sir Arthur's plotting imitates his own fictional art, allowing the historical events to follow the laws of the detective novel. Still, the ironic inversion of fiction and reality typical of historiographic metafiction is endowed with a psychological motivation and thus causality: as detective, Sir Arthur can only operate along the lines of his fictional hero because Sherlock Holmes's rationalist strategy is the only one at his author's command. Apart from his medical knowledge, the Holmesian forensic logic corresponds to both Doyle's mental disposition and professional competence.

This is the point where self-reflexivity does after all enter the novel, bringing in the author as plotter in a twofold sense. First, on the level of narrative design, the intersection of alternating life stories qua alternating narrative is made to appear as both historically contingent and yet consequential, inevitable. In other words: the parallel biography of Barnes's historical novel stages the logic of historiography and biography alike, which is to turn contingent events into a necessary causal sequence by the act of retrospective narration. Thus, the inspector is portrayed to be committed to the new school of sexual psychology, which inevitably leads him to develop his entirely plausible, yet erroneous hypothesis of George's suppressed sexuality in the face of his locked bed room door, making him a prime suspect for the atrocious crimes against animals. At the same time, the narration brings another discursive causality into play: the power of imperial racism, always at work when the Indian vicar's family is concerned. It is the community's perception of them as other, as alien that again almost inevitably targets young George as suspect of the Great Wyrley Outrages. Barnes's historical fiction exhibits precisely this multiple logic in both its ideological and rationalist versions – after all, Conan Doyle also falls into the trap of speculating along the lines of a convincing but misleading chain of causality, only to be detected as fallible in narrative retrospect.

The precarious interplay of the narrative logic of inevitability/necessity on the one hand and the fallibility of authorial command and plotting on the other returns on a second level of the novel, as it is shown to determine Sir Arthur's professional and private life, too. By means of establishing an isotopy of robust efficiency, Conan

Doyle's biographical plotline provides his literary career with a psychological motive, attributing his strength of purpose to young Arthur's experience of paternal sluggishness and failure:

> Arthur had not visited his father in years, and did not attend the funeral; none of the family did. Charles Doyle had let down the Mam and condemned the children to genteel poverty. He had been weak and unmanly, incapable of winning his fight against liquor. Fight? He had barely raised his gloves at the demon. Excuses were occasionally made for him, but Arthur did not find the claim of an artistic temperament persuasive. That was just self-indulgence and self-exculpation. It was perfectly possible to be an artist, yet also to be robust and responsible.
>
> (Barnes, *Arthur & George* 61)

His efficient, pragmatic and responsible professionalism thus becomes Arthur's prime feature.

> Then there is Conan Doyle's life, which is also in fine fettle. He is too professional and too energetic ever to suffer from writer's block for more than a day or two. He identifies a story, researches and plans it to be intelligible, secondly, to be interesting, and thirdly, to be clever. He knows his own abilities, and he also knows that in the end the reader is king. That is why Sherlock Holmes was brought back to life, allowed to have escaped the Reichenbach Falls […].
>
> (Barnes, *Arthur & George* 198)

Doyle's authorial self-fashioning in terms of creative efficiency – beyond any Romanticism–, compensated for at best and in another corner of life by his spiritualism, does not escape a certain irony, though. Not only does Doyle as detective overshoot the mark, but his plotting with regard to women also ultimately eludes his control. Just as his mother does not require his protection, his self-division into the loyal husband of a terminally ill wife on the one hand and the platonic lover of a mistress on the other does not work. The shield of protection and silence that he has erected in order to spare his wife turns out to have been cracked all along. The novel closes with the following sentences:

> Mary Conan Doyle, Arthur's first child, died in 1976. She had always kept one secret from her father. Touie, on her deathbed, had not only warned her daughter that Arthur would marry again; she had also named his future bride as Miss Jean Leckie. J.B. January 2005.
>
> (Barnes, *Arthur & George* 360)

The fictional double biography *Arthur & George* thus reveals Arthur Conan Doyle's self-fashioning as efficient professional and private man to be motivated biographically, psychologically plausible, and yet an illusion. At the same time, it closes with an act of temporal self-positioning ('January 2005') that both underlines the detached historical view of its subject and metaleptically transgresses the narrative frame to identify 'J.B.' as author.

Conclusion

On the one hand, I have pursued a conventional postmodern line, reading *Chatterton* and *The Ragged Lion* as examples of postmodern *historiographic biofiction* collapsing historical biographies and authorial practices into a web of intertextuality. On the other hand, a counter-movement has come to light. Almost to the point of nostalgia, these novels strive to save (or resurrect) the figure of the Romantic author, along with its pertinent connection of life and work. Despite their intense intertextual engagement, these texts – by way of plot or autodiegetic voice – emphatically locate the origin of literature in the author's life, his subjectivity.

In a more disguised, undercover fashion, Barnes's fictional parallel/double biography *Arthur & George* undertakes to explore on various intersecting levels the operations of narrative in terms of authorial command, or invention, of causality overwriting contingency and its fallibility. Again, the novel chooses a canonical author (reminiscent of Sir Walter Scott) who strove to create for himself a public persona as professional author, separate from his private self; to be ultimately returned, however, to the contingency of life.

Works Cited

Ackroyd, Peter. *Chatterton*. London: Hamish Hamilton, 1987.

Barnes, Julian. *Arthur & George*. London: Cape, 2005.

Barnes, Julian. *Flaubert's Parrot*. London: Cape, 1984.

Barthes, Roland. 'The Death of the Author.' *The Rustle of Language*. Trans. Richard Howard. Berkeley: University of California Press, 1989. 49-55.

Beardsley, M. C., and W. K. Wimsatt. 'The Intentional Fallacy.' *The Verbal Icon*. Lexington: University of Kentucky Press, 1954. 3-20.

Bloom, Harold. *The Anxiety of Influence. A Theory of Poetry*. Oxford: Oxford University Press, 1973.

Boswell, James. *Life of Johnson*. Ed. R. W. Chapman. Oxford: Oxford University Press, 1998.

Fish, Stanley. 'Biography and Intention.' *Contesting the Subject. Essays in the Postmodern Theory and Practice of Biography and Biographical Criticism*. Ed. William H. Epstein. West Lafayette: Purdue University Press, 1991. 9-16.

Foucault, Michel. 'What is an Author?' *Textual Strategies: Perspectives in Post Structuralist Criticism*. Ed. Josué V. Harari. London: Methuen, 1980. 141-160.

Fowles, John. *The French Lieutenant's Woman*. London: Random House, 1969.

Henke, Christoph. *Vergangenheitsobsessionen: Geschichte und Gedächtnis im Erzählwerk von Julian Barnes*. Trier: WVT, 2001.

Huber, Werner, and Martin Middeke, eds. *Biofictions: The Rewriting of Romantic Lives in Contemporary Fiction and Drama*. Rochester: Camden House, 1999.

Hutcheon, Linda. *A Poetics of Postmodernism. History, Theory, Fiction*. New York, London: Routledge, 1989.

Kaplan, Justin. 'The Naked Self and Other Problems.' *Telling Lives: The Bio-grapher's Art*. Ed. Marc Pachter. Washington: New Republic Books, 1979. 36-55.

Massie, Allan. *The Ragged Lion*. London: Hodder and Stoughton, 1995.

Nadel, Iris. *Biography. Fiction, Fact and Form*. London, Basingstoke: Macmillan, 1984.

Nünning, Ansgar. 'An Intertextual Quest for Thomas Chatterton: The Deconstruction of the Romantic Cult of Originality and the Paradoxes of Life-Writing in Peter Ackroyd's Fictional Metabiography Chatterton.' *Biofictions: The Rewriting of Romantic Lives in Contemporary Fiction and Drama*. Eds. Werner Huber and Martin Middeke. Rochester: Camden House, 1999. 27-49.

Nünning, Ansgar. *Von historischer Fiktion zu historiographischer Metafiktion*. 2 vols. Trier: Wissenschaftlicher Verlag Trier, 1995.

Rubenstein, Jill. 'Auld Acquaintance: New Lives of Scott and Hogg.' *Biofictions: The Rewriting of Romantic Lives in Contemporary Fiction and Drama*. Eds. Werner Huber and Martin Middeke. Rochester: Camden House, 1999. 64-76.

Schabert, Ina. 'Fictional Biography, Factual Biography, and Their Contaminations.' *Biography* 5-1 (Winter 1982): 1-16.

Schabert, Ina. *In Quest of the Other Person: Fiction as Biography*. Tübingen: Francke, 1990.

Schläger, Jürgen. 'Biography: Cult as Culture.' *The Art of Literary Biography*. Ed. John Batchelor. Oxford: Clarendon Press, 1995. 57-72.

Schwalm, Helga. 'The Lake Poets/Authors: Topography, Authorship and Romantic Subjectivities.' *Gender and Creation. Surveying Gendered Myths of Creativity, Authority and Authorship*. Ed. Anne-Julia Zwierlein. Heidelberg: Winter 2010. 131-48.

Scott, Walter. *The Journal of Sir Walter Scott*. Ed. W. E. K. Anderson. Edinburgh: Canongate, 1998.

Woodmansee, Martha. 'On the Author Effect: Recovering Collectivity.' *The Construction of Authorship. Textual Appropriation in Law and Literature*. Eds. id. and Peter Jaszi. Durham & London: Duke University Press, 1994. 14-28.

Woolf, Virginia. 'The New Biography.' *Collected Essays*. Vol. 4. London: Hogarth Press, 1967. 229-235.

Wordsworth, William. 'A Letter to a Friend of Robert Burns (1816).' *The Major Works*. Ed. Stephen Gill. Oxford: Oxford University Press, 1984. 663-675.

Wordsworth, William. 'Prelude.' *The Major Works*. Ed. Stephen Gill. Oxford: Oxford University Press, 1984. 375-590.

HEIKE HARTUNG

History, the Contemporary, and Life in Time: Timescapes in Ian McEwan's and Julian Barnes's Novels

Writing the literary history of the contemporary novel is a provisional endeavour that is beset by uncertainties. Bearing in mind the speculative nature of this kind of criticism, we can claim, nevertheless, that Ian McEwan and Julian Barnes range securely among the most significant British writers of the generation who started their careers during the mid-1970s.[1] The work of both authors has also been situated firmly within the contemporary literary scene with particular critical emphasis on Barnes's "commitment to capturing, and ability to penetrate, the contemporary" (Groes, *Barnes* 5) and on McEwan's engagement with major social and political changes – an engagement making him, in the words of one critic, "the foremost cartographer of our time" (Groes, *McEwan* 1).

Julian Barnes's concern in his early texts, especially in his novels *Flaubert's Parrot* (1984) and *A History of the World in 10 1/2 Chapters* (1989), with the problems of representing the past has been read within the critical framework of 'historiographic metafiction', defined by Linda Hutcheon as self-reflexive fiction that problematizes the construction of historical knowledge (105).[2] Just as the latter novel dismisses 'world history' as a series of cruelties mainly inflicted on the dispossessed, Barnes himself has remained sceptical of the neatness of the 'grand narratives' of history. While the historical remains an interest also of his later writings, the formal challenges of his more recent work focus more pointedly, I argue, on the interplay between an individual's

---

[1] Among recent monographs and edited collections substantiating this claim see Head, *McEwan*, Groes (ed.), *McEwan* and Roberts (ed.) on Ian McEwan, Guignery and Roberts (eds.), Groes (ed.) *Barnes* and Childs for Julian Barnes.

[2] Linda Hutcheon defined this feature broadly as a characteristic of a postmodern aesthetic. Her term 'historiographic metafiction' was complemented by Brian McHale's "postmodernist revisionist historical novel" to signify a reinterpretation and rewriting of "the historical record" (90). Elisabeth Wesseling, furthermore, distinguished a "self-reflexive" mode of historical fiction that highlights the search for the past from "uchronian fiction" that emphasizes the feature of the contrafactual in critical fictional rewritings of an alternative history (90, 102). The most detailed typology of the 'new' historical novel in England was provided by Ansgar Nünning, who distinguished five types of historical fiction on a scale from the documentary to the metafictional (*Von historischer Fiktion*, Vol. 1, 256-291). Nünning reads *Flaubert's Parrot* as foregrounding "the paradoxical relation between history and writing", claiming that *A History of the World in 10 1/2 Chapters* represents "a paradigm example of postmodern historical fiction" ('Crossing Borders' 229, 234).

lifetime and historical time as represented in Barnes's continuous concern with the endings of life, with old age and death. This can be illustrated most comprehensively in his short novel *The Sense of an Ending* (2011).

If Barnes's early texts have highlighted problems of representing the past from the perspective of marginalized subjects, McEwan's early texts have focused on disturbing aspects of the human psyche. This early work has been termed a "literature of shock", the effects of which have been conceptualized as a "strategy for awakening the collective conscience" (Head, *McEwan* 2). McEwan's shift from the eccentric, even abnormal protagonists of the early fiction to a focus on the exceptional event in ordinary lives in the later texts has also been read as an aspect of his exploring the ethical dimension of literature (Nicklas, *Ian McEwan*; Puschmann-Nalenz, 'Ethics in Ian McEwan's Twenty-First Century Novels' 190). While his novel *Atonement* (2001) makes use of the techniques of historiographic metafiction (Alden, 'Words of War, War of Words' 59-60), McEwan employs these specific devices mainly in order to dismiss them as part of a high modernist and postmodernist aesthetics he has pointedly been distancing himself from both in his fiction and non-fictional works of the last decade. As I will show with reference to *On Chesil Beach* (2007), McEwan's continuous return to the periods of childhood and early adulthood can be related also to his shifting approach to the issues of a life's temporality vs. the historical.

Since both Barnes and McEwan are perceived as writers who engage critically with the contemporary and the historical in their novels, I will present the difference of their approaches with reference to the particular life stages their work appears to be most fascinated with: a dramatization of childhood and the beginnings of life in McEwan's case, old age and life's ending in Barnes's. In what follows I will first explore the relationship between the historical and the contemporary as it has been theorized in recent literary criticism, revisiting conceptions of history in their relevance to these two writers. Before turning to a comparative reading of the two short novels mentioned above, I will contextualize these more recent texts in some of the authors' earlier writings. By following the different timescapes both writers develop throughout their work, I will show how they move from postmodern metafictional approaches to history and the novel to a strongly asserted narrative authority. While both writers approach questions of life in time from different directions, I will argue that they produce in their work, nevertheless, the effect of a displacement of history.

Time between History and the Contemporary

Friedrich Nietzsche theorized the relationship between history and the contemporary in his second *Unzeitgemäße Betrachtung (Untimely Meditations: On the Use and Abuse of History for Life)* by distinguishing three perspectives on the historical he identified as different approaches taken toward contemporary life, namely the monumental, the antiquarian and the critical approach. His text anticipates the shift in historical knowledge from the nineteenth to the twentieth century. As Hayden White has pointed out, this shift turned historiography from a positivist science into a metahistorical construction whose epistemological status and cultural function have been subjected to critical scrutiny (2). By depicting the 'use' and 'abuse' of history as a balance between memory and forgetting, Nietzsche, furthermore, insisted on the necessity of combining historical inquiry with an ideological interest, a subjective perspective and an individual question for it to remain relevant to life and the 'real' (253).

The focus on the discursive and narrative constructedness of history in twentieth-century historical and literary theory distinguishes the "*realistic effect*" from the place of the 'real' in historical discourse, which, according to Roland Barthes, "does not follow the real, it can do no more than signify the real, constantly repeating that *it happened*, without this assertion amounting to anything but the signified 'other side' of the whole process of historical narration" ('The Discourse of History' 17; 17-18; emphasis in the text). Furthermore, Barthes draws attention to the paradox that narrative structure, originating in the realm of the fictional, "becomes at once the sign and the proof of reality" (18).

If the reinvention of the historical novel in postmodernism can be seen as "one of the most astonishing transformations in literary history", as the British historian Perry Anderson has argued in a recent survey of the genre (n. p.), one of the historical novel's defining features, I argue, is its problematic relationship to time. In his broad global perspective on the historical novel, Anderson follows the genre from its classical origins in Walter Scott's *Waverley* (1814), theorized by George Lukács as an affirmation of human progress, through its nineteenth-century diffusions into European nation-building and modernist allegories of the past, to depict the new forms of the genre associated with the postmodern, which he identifies principally with Latin American magical realism, as "the antipodes of its classical forms. Not the emergence of the nation, but the ravages of empire; not progress as emancipation, but impending or consummated catastrophe" (n. p.).

My focus on the interplay of the historical and the contemporary in the writings of Julian Barnes and Ian McEwan, especially concerning their treatment of time, however, is at odds with this grand narrative of the historical novel, which follows it, as the title indicates, "[f]rom [p]rogress to [c]atastrophe". The postmodern reinvention of the historical represents time frequently as an interplay of different layers in tension with each other. This encompasses also the incorporation of conjectures, anachronisms and other forms of temporal displacement into the narration. The attempt to make the past present in fictional story-telling can be represented as a depiction of time in parallel layers of narrative suggesting the possibility of an exchange or interaction between them for different ideological and political purposes.[3]

Historical fiction has also been influenced by the way that temporal concepts were interrogated by French historians linked to the Annales school in the early twentieth century. By shifting their focus from the relatively short-lived history of the individual at the center of political history to the longer durations of social history, *Annales* historians drew attention to the different time levels into which history can be divided.

---

[3]   As I have argued elsewhere, the specific relationship of a writer to history is at evidence in this treatment of time, for instance in the representation of a communicative exchange between the times as fantastical in many of Peter Ackroyd's novels, in which counterfactuals are employed to promote the conservative vision of a 'cultural catholicism', or, in the case of Salman Rushdie, who confronts historical and imaginary temporal experience in order to introduce alternative versions of history into his story-telling (30-31).

The effect of this shift, according to Fernand Braudel, was "to dissect history into various planes, or, to put it another way, to divide historical time into geographical time, social time, individual time" (*The Mediterranean and the Mediterranean World in the Age of Philipp II* 21). In the late twentieth century the biological sciences have similarly linked the long duration of evolutionary time to individual lifetime with the effect that notions such as "evolutionary plasticity" have boosted individual expectations of longevity and have extended or even displaced the human life-span.[4] In a recent essay Fredric Jameson has therefore employed the image of "an immense elevator that moves up and down in time" for the historical novel, arguing that "historicity today [...] demands a temporal span far exceeding the biological limits of the individual human organism" ('The Historical Novel Today, Or, Is It Still Possible?' 301).

As described by Gérard Genette, the intricate temporal relationships in literary narrative can be placed against these different concepts of time in history and science.[5] These relationships also have repercussions for the question of representing the historical, which twentieth-century historical theory acknowledges as "the gap between history as past reality and history as present representation" (Kunow, 'Simulacrum as Sub-Text' 24). As far as the contemporary is concerned, the relationship between time and the 'real' constitutes a similar double bind, since "the paradox of the now has *always* been a problem of representation, for to present it is necessarily to *re*-present it, thus introducing a crucial delay, a splitting of temporality":

> The instant of the 'now' always eludes the grasp, can never be self-identical: it is either no longer or not yet present. This effect can be marked as a loss, as the impossibility of seizing the present time. It can be transposed to the definition of an era, one given epochal coherence by rendering 'lost' temporality in spatial forms as displays of nostalgia or pastiche. Or else the difference at the heart of the 'now' can be seen as a *constitutive* and *productive* heterogeneity, a circulation of multiple times within the single instant.
> (Luckhurst and Marks, 'Hurry up Please It's Time' 3; emphasis in text)

Writing against what they perceive as the "panic narratives" that beset cultural theory at the end of the twentieth century in what amounts to an apocalyptic dismissal of history and time, Luckhurst and Marks reconceptualize the contemporary in its multiple relationships to time (4). In the relationship between literature and different notions of time, the doubling of perspectives in the representation of history in relation to narrative, then, as both historiography and story-telling, is at issue.

---

4   On the notion of evolutionary plasticity, see Gems, 'Eine Revolution des Alterns' 31. See also Stephen Katz, who has argued that in the late twentieth century the periods of childhood, middle age and old age have collapsed into a "simulated life-span" which stretches middle age into an almost timeless longevity ('Imagining the Life-Span. From Premodern Miracles to Postmodern Fantasties' 70).

5   In his foundational text of narrative theory, *Narrative Discourse* (1972), Genette distinguishes three major subcategories of narrative temporality: first, the concept of 'order', signifying departures from chronology; second, 'duration' as the variable speed or the "effects of rhythm" in narrative texts (88); and third, 'frequency', which concerns the relations of iteration and condensation between story and discourse (113).

From Moments of Childhood to Evolutionary Time in Ian McEwan's Writings

The question of whether the contemporary world can be rendered in fiction at all is a recurring concern for Ian McEwan. In a recent article he discusses how, when his faith in fiction falters he tends to prefer the knowledge represented by modern science:

> Bring me the cosmologists on the creation of time, the annalists of the Holocaust, the philosopher who has married into neuroscience, the mathematician who can describe the beauty of numbers to the numbskull, the scholar of empires' rise and fall, the adepts of the English civil war.
>
> (McEwan, 'Faith' n. p.)

The return to faith comes when a random sentence reveals to him "fiction's generous knack of annotating the microscopic lattice-work of consciousness, the small print of subjectivity" ('Faith' n. p.). In what McEwan describes metaphorically as his periods of suspended 'belief', he rates the knowledge associated with modern science higher than his own principal form of artistic expression. The language McEwan uses for representing his returning 'faith', moreover, relegates fiction to a mere illustration of scientific knowledge.

During the last decade Ian McEwan has responded in articles and interviews directly to a number of contemporary issues, assessing, for instance, the terrorist attacks of 9/11 as "a failure of the imagination, of the moral imagination" (Whitney, 'Faith and Doubt at Ground Zero' n. p.). Moreover, McEwan has linked his approach to the literary imagination explicitly to his interest in science, combining "the curiosity of science and the morality of the imagination with the possibilities of literature, and with the novel in particular" (Salisbury, 'Narration and Neurology' 884). As his essay 'Literature, Science, and Human Nature' (2001) indicates, his interest in Darwinian evolutionary psychology has repercussions also on his views on time, the contemporary, and history. Before turning to this essay, however, I will investigate McEwan's approach to time in some of his earlier novels.

McEwan's work is frequently divided into the earlier dark short stories and novels that focused primarily on the mental landscape of adolescents and earned him the tag 'Ian Macabre', and the more affirmative and optimistic recent work. His relationship to time becomes manifest, first of all, in the question of his artistic development. Contrasting Ian McEwan's novel *The Child in Time* (1987) with his earlier work, Malcom Bradbury sees this novel as a turning point for being "a work where previously private and psychic concerns become directly public and political ones" (*The Modern British Novel* 430). Cautioning that "[t]he simple narrative of linear development will not do", Dominic Head highlights the constant effect of McEwan's fiction to produce a sense of unease in the reader (*McEwan* 7). Furthermore, while the scope of narrative voices has certainly broadened throughout McEwan's writing career, it is significant that he continues to return to the "unique rhetorical standpoint" he associates with adolescence, which has provided him with "a point of view which is somehow dislocated, removed" (Ricks, 'Adolescence and After' 20).[6] This can be seen, for instance, in the extended view *Atonement* presents of the thirteen-year-old Briony's misguided perceptions. The idea of a fundamental change or transformation between the earlier and later texts, then, can be reformulated as a shift within his continuous interests. Not unrelated to McEwan's fascination with the early stages of life, this shift has been described as a relocation from psychoanalysis to evolution as the 'guiding science':

> McEwan's presiding interest has always been psychology, and, like many scientists of his generation, he has shifted his intellectual allegiances. At first, he studied perversity; now he studies normality. His first god was Freud. Now it is Darwin.
>
> (Zalewski, 'The Background Hum' n. p.)

McEwan's approach to the novel has also been distinguished from what was conceived in the late 1980s as a postmodern aesthetics of self-reflexive hybridity (Head, *McEwan* 15). Instead, his interest in the historical has more firmly been related to a realist aesthetics that links the historical to the contemporary. When he explores, for instance, the trajectory of post-war Europe in *The Innocent*, set in the mid-Fifties in Berlin, he responds also to the changing climate at the end of the 1980s and, most particularly, to the fall of the Berlin Wall.[7] Nevertheless, *The Innocent* is also grounded in the earlier fiction's psychoanalytic interest in the macabre and in the perspective of the early adult's 'innocence'. The protagonist Leonard Marnham is initiated into the secret workings of intelligence services and, at the same time, into the intricacies of a first love relationship. After his sexual initiation he considers that "the line that divided innocence from knowledge was vague, and rapturously so" (60), while his slightly older lover, the German woman Maria, continues to think of him as an innocent even after he has frightened her by acting out his domination fantasies. Innocence is swept away

---

[6]   In this early interview, first published in 1979, McEwan further explains his view of adolescents as "an extraordinary, special case of people; they're close to childhood, and yet they are constantly baffled and irritated by the initiations into what's on the other side - the shadow line, as it were" (Ricks, 'Adolescence and After' 20).

[7]   The different reference frame from that of the postmodern or metahistorical, in which McEwan's earlier work is being read in the early twenty-first century, is further illustrated by the publication of a German translation of *The Innocent* as part of a series of historical thrillers by the weekly journal *Die Zeit*. The focus in the short commentary attached to the novel by a *Zeit* journalist is on the historical evidence for the tunnel built by British and American intelligence agencies and on the historical figures mentioned in the novel, while there is a conspicuous absence of aesthetic considerations. The conception of the series is described thus on the cover of the book: "Besondere Ereignisse aus der Geschichte haben von jeher Anlass zu aufregenden Erzählungen gegeben. Die *Zeit*-Edition „Historische Kriminalromane" versammelt zwölf der spannendsten Kriminalromane aus den unterschied-lichsten Epochen, vom alten Rom über das Mittelalter bis zum Kalten Krieg. *Zeit*-Autoren erläutern in einem exklusiven Anhang die gesellschaftlichen und politischen Hintergründe der jeweiligen Epoche und zeigen, wo die Wahrheit im Roman endet und die Fiktion beginnt." While this conception illustrates the return to a neat distinction between fiction and fact that seems to promise a kind of realism untouched by either modernism or postmodernism, it elevates McEwan's novel to a place among the twelve most thrilling historical crime novels.

effectively when Leonard and Maria kill Otto, Maria's violently intrusive ex-husband, in an act of self-defense, but decide afterwards to dismember and dispose of the corpse in order not to be charged with manslaughter. The prolonged scene of the dismemberment constitutes a nauseating narrative pause, which is framed by the depiction of the young couple's engagement party. It is narrated through the perspective of Leonard's consciousness in an exchange of backward and forward loops, while he cruises the city with the two suitcases containing the dismembered corpse in an impossible attempt at gaining a reassuring pattern of behaviour in movement: "He needed a sequence, a story. He needed order. One thing after another. He boarded the bus and found a seat" (157).

The effect of a nightmarish timelessness produced by this narrative sequence as well as the use of a stream-of-consciousness technique links McEwan's writing to a modernist aesthetics. This is also invoked in the quotation from Kafka's unfinished short story "Der Bau" ("The Burrow", first published posthumously in 1931), in which a mole-like being burrows through an elaborate system of tunnels it has built over the course of its life. The reference transfers a sense of futility to the historical tunnel depicted in the novel.

If *The Innocent* places the surreal representation of guilty acts against the realism of its historical setting, *The Child in Time* is McEwan's most explicit engagement with the meanings of time and his most extended treatment of childhood. The novel centers on protagonist Stephen Lewis's loss of his three-year-old daughter Kate during a visit to the local supermarket. It is set in a dystopian near future which clearly resembles the Thatcherite epoch in which the book was written. On his way into the countryside, where his wife Julie lives as a recluse, Stephen experiences a disturbing scene which he cannot explain: He sees his parents as a young couple in a pub he passes. In contrast to the event of Kate's disappearance, which is narrated in the retrospection of Stephen's continuous brooding return to the catastrophic loss of his child after two years have elapsed, the scene of apparent time travel is dramatized in the narrative present. The vision of his mother in a time prior to his own existence transforms the adult Stephen himself into a 'child in time'. The shock of the experience propels him back emotionally into his own childhood and causes a complete temporal dislocation: "he had nowhere to go, no moment that could embody him, he was not expected, no destination or time could be named" (66).

Generically, *The Child in Time* is a science-fiction novel whose only slight temporal difference opens up representative freedoms while the narrative remains firmly grounded within a realist concern with the contemporary - a strategy similar to that employed in *The Innocent* as far as the historical is concerned. In terms of narrative time, the novel draws on many of the categories distinguished by Genette, thus producing the effect of a complex interweaving of flashbacks and anticipation, reiterated moments and descriptive scenes that evoke a sense of different duration within the story. Furthermore, in ascribing a variety of meanings to childhood on different levels of the plot the novel provides an extended commentary on time.

On one of these levels Stephen's time warp can be read as a momentary regression into childhood that is followed by an equally temporary moment of sexual fulfillment, which Stephen experiences as a provisional redemption of the meaning of time. The time warp experience is reiterated in the novel several times, underlining different stages in the protagonist's development from his initial, static immersion into his grief to a progressively more active return to his own life in time. The first of these returns is in a conversation with Thelma, an academic physicist and the wife of his friend Charles Darke. When Stephen tells Thelma about his strange experience, she embarks on a tutorial on time by pointing to the experiential evidence for the relativity of time before drifting off into a (non-narrated) excursion into her more specific theories, on which Stephen cannot follow her. As Thelma eventually concedes: "I can't help you with your hallucination, Stephen. Physics certainly can't" (136). Nevertheless, the conversation between the two does have the effect to psychologize Stephen's experience, which they "agreed to call [...] hallucination" (139).

Stephen also tells his parents about his unusual experience, disguising it as a remote childhood memory. While his father denies any memory of the scene, his mother remembers and locates it in a time before Stephen's birth. In a second conversation, alone with his mother, she responds to the topic by incorporating her version of the scene into an account of her own life story:

> I can see it now as clearly as I can see you. There was a face at the window, the face of a child, sort of floating there. It was staring into the pub. It had a kind of pleading look, and it was so white, white as an aspirin. It was looking right at me. Thinking about it over the years, I realize it was probably the landlord's boy, or some kid off one of the local farms. But as far as I was concerned then, I was convinced, I just knew that I was looking at my own child. If you like, I was looking at you.
>
> (McEwan, *The Child In Time* 207)

In contrast to Stephen, his mother gives meaning to her apparently magic experience by transforming it into a crucial moment of self-assertion: "So this was her responsibility and this was her time. This was the moment for her to be decisive" (208). In the last chapter of the novel, which has the quality of a fairytale, Stephen is finally able to do the same with his 'hallucination', understanding it as a reaffirmation of "meaningful time" (251). In its closure with a scene in which Julie gives birth to their second child, *The Child in Time* sentimentally places continuation, repetition, the cyclical time of pregnancy, the second birth as "a secular nativity play" (Spice, 'Thatchershaft' n. p.), against the darker vision of its dystopian setting. In thus depicting Stephen as the passive *Bildungroman* protagonist who is shocked out of his frozen state of grief by an experience that leads to his temporary regression into childhood and his eventual return to an adult life in time with the help of female mentors, temporal displacement is redirected into meaningful time in a narrative of private fulfilment.

However, Stephen's successful readjustment to adult life is contrasted with the figure of his friend Charles Darke, whose permanent regression into childhood leads to madness and, ultimately, suicide, thus illustrating the impossibility of reconciling the private and public realms. The topic of childhood is also used to sketch the imagined society's conservative politics: As a writer of children's books, Stephen has been asked to become a member of a government committee on child-care, described as a central political concern. This plotline is given prominence by the novel's chapters being headed by excerpts from an imaginary governmental child-care handbook that indicates a very restrictive view on childhood. The commission's work is ultimately revealed as futile when it becomes known that the handbook had been written years in advance of the committee's work by Charles Darke, then a junior minister, at the prime minister's request. Stephen's consequent disillusionment with his public work matches his private developmental plot, in which "the committee meetings had ceased to represent a refuge of organized time in a chaos of wasted days" (183).

Charles Darke, by contrast, regresses from a successful public figure - he publishes Stephen's first book, then changes to a promising career in politics - into the ridiculous image of a forty-nine-year-old school-boy. When Stephen encounters his former friend for the first time after he has retreated from public life to the country in order to act out his mad return to childhood, his "old-fashioned appearance" reminds him of photo-graphs of World War II evacuees (123). After Charles's suicide, Thelma provides a psychological explanation for his obsession, interpreting another photograph, in which Charles "looks like a scaled-down version of his father - the same suit and tie, the same self-important posture and grown-up expression. So perhaps he was denied a childhood" (240).

The image of the middle-aged Charles in short trousers imitating a ten-year-old school-boy represents a time confusion, which the novel pathologizes in the psychoanalytic terms of regression and denial. This jumbling of temporal categories associates Charles also with the well-known trope of the 'old child' in the Victorian novel. Paul Dombey in Dickens's *Dombey and Son*, equally described as "old-fashioned", enacts a pose of premature old age when he is depicted as the mirror image of his father: "They were the strangest pair at such a time that ever firelight shone upon. Mr. Dombey so erect and solemn, gazing at the blaze; his little image, with an old, old face, peering into the red perspective with the fixed and rapt attention of a sage" (98). Paul Dombey is compared to an uncanny fairy-tale being, while his inability to grow up is resolved in the narrative by his death in childhood. In *The Child in Time*, Charles Darke's suicide is explained with his inability to come to terms with the contradictions of adulthood, and, ultimately, as his "running out of time" (239).

The novel represents childhood as a temporal marker of development, to which further distinctions are added: those between the normal and the pathological, the private and the public, between loss and fulfillment. Childhood becomes a frame of reference in this novel for the multitude of meanings attached to time, bringing together also the different temporal dimensions of the *Bildungsroman* and the Science Fiction genre. *The Child in Time* has also been read as a novel of ideas centrally concerned with "the languages of science and literature", and, more particularly "the temporal discourse of the new physics" (Marcus, 'Ian McEwan's Modernist Time' 87, 86). As we have seen, however, Thelma introduces theories of time deriving from physics into the con-versation about Stephen's hallucination, only to dismiss them in their inability to explain it.

If this early novel, then, can be read as celebrating the complexities and chaos, the harmonies and nightmares of life in time, its playfulness concerning the real disappears from the more recent work. In *Saturday* (2005), the middle-aged neurosurgeon Henry Perowne, who is the novel's central consciousness, reflects on "the so-called magical realists" his daughter has asked him to read. Rejecting the introduction of fantastic ele-ments into fictional writing as the mere childishness of its authors, Perowne recollects the protagonist of McEwan's earlier novel: "One visionary saw through a pub window his parents as they had been some weeks after his conception, discussing the possibility of aborting him" (67). In spite of the familiar narratological distinction between protagonist and author, implied or real, it is surprising how much the fictional neurologist Perowne's position resembles that of its fiction-writing author. When McEwan describes his faltering faith in fiction, his more permanent dismissal of experimental fiction is followed immediately by "the virgin birth of magical realism" he describes himself as having always been "low church on" ('Faith' n. p.). It is only a scepticism about "realism herself" that really worries the novelist.

In 'Literature, Science, and Human Nature', McEwan affirms his belief that Charles Darwin is one of the greatest scientists ever, emphasizing that Darwin's work is as approachable as that of a novelist. He regards Darwin's idea of a "universal human nature" as being supported by "the exercise of imagination and ingenuity as expressed in literature", defining literature as "encoding both our cultural and genetic inheritance" (11). McEwan's position in the classic two-cultures debate between art and science, initially formulated in C. P. Snow's 1961 lecture, is associated with what the publisher John Brockman called "The Third Culture", borrowing Snow's term to aggressively promote a new public culture that is represented by "the 'modern synthesis' of evolutionary biology, that is to say biochemical genetics and Darwinian natural selection" (Amigoni, "'The Luxury of Storytelling'" 156). Among the "Third Culture" thinkers promoted by Brockman as the new public intellectuals are the evolutionary biologist Richard Dawkins and the cognitive psychologist Steven Pinker.[8] In his association with these thinkers and by publishing his essay in the collection *The Literary Animal* (2005), McEwan further demonstrates his allegiance with a version of evolutionary literary criticism that opposes itself to any kind of post-structuralist cultural and literary theory, finding instead in biology "the determining causes of culture" (Salisbury, 'Narration and Neurology' 895). In this context, language as well as literature are being thought of "as a genetic inheritance marked by evolutionary adaptations", which represents "a return to the real, [...] although in a determinedly non-Lacanian sense" (893).

In his essay McEwan considers some of the claims made for a change in 'human nature' throughout history, citing with disapproval Virginia Woolf's ironic announcement that human character changed "[o]n or about December 1910" ('Literature, Science, and Human Nature' 12). Other examples given are T. S. Eliot's theory of the 'dissociation of sensibility' that traces change to the metaphysical poets of the seventeenth century, and Philippe Ariès's claim, in his social history of childhood, that human emotions shifted during the eighteenth century (13). Seeing the motivation behind these different historical claims in their desire for "locating the roots of our

---

8   In 2006, McEwan contributed a talk to an event at the London School of Economics, which was organized to celebrate thirty years since the publication of Dawkins' book *The Selfish Gene*. In 2008, an exchange between McEwan and Steven Pinker was recorded concerning "what is actually happening when people engage in conversation" (McEwan/Pinker, 'Shadow Lines' 180). In an interview McEwan rejects "the indulgent pessimism of the liberal arts culture. That's why I've come to value the company of scientists. [...] Science is organized curiosity, which is fundamentally an optimistic state [...]" (Cook, Groes, and Sage, 'Journeys without Maps' 151). For a detailed review of McEwan's immersion into the "Third Culture" debate see also Amigoni ("'The Luxury of Storytelling'" 155-159).

modernity" (13), McEwan dismisses them as the "secular equivalent of a creation myth", adding that "[l]iterary writers seem to prefer an explosive, decisive moment, the miracle of a birth, to a dull continuum of infinitesimal change" (14).

The "principle of radical periodization on which the very concept of modernity rests", that is at issue here, has been questioned from within literary history as a binary thinking that constructs an earlier period such as the Middle Ages as the "temporal other" against which the 'modern' then defines itself (Johnston, *Performing the Middle Ages* 2). McEwan, however, aims at a more radical substitution, when he chooses the long duration of evolutionary time over the more rapid pace of human history. Affirming the extended biological perspective on history, he ends his essay on a note of futurist enthusiasm for the biological sciences. While literature "has always, knowingly and helplessly, given voice to" the universalism McEwan regards as "our common nature", the biological sciences are "now entering another exhilarating phase" in which they "are set to explore [this universalism] further" (19).

History, Science and Authoritative Narration in *On Chesil Beach*

If McEwan's position in the "Third Culture" debate links him to a way of thinking about science, culture and literature that is curiously unhistorical in its almost missionary rejection of 'social constructivism'[9], I will read these alliances against his novel *On Chesil Beach*, focusing on the implication the evolutionary perspective has for the construction of time and history in this narrative. Among the examples McEwan cites as claims made for a fundamental change in human character, he includes also the decade of the Sixties, in which "similar apocalyptic generational claims" to those in Virginia Woolf's announcement were made:

> Human nature changed forever, it was claimed at the time, in a field near Woodstock in 1967, or in the same year with the release of *Sgt. Pepper*, or the year before on a certain undistinguished street in San Francisco. The Age of Aquarius had dawned, and things would never be the same again.
>
> (McEwan, *On Chesil Beach* 12)

In order to avoid the apocalyptic tone characterizing such hyperbolic announcements of historical change, McEwan positions his novel at the beginning of the decade, at a moment in time that precedes the significant social changes associated with it. As he explains in a promotional video for the novel, the beach is a guiding metaphor for the imminent changes: "So it is as if they stand on a kind of shore, a beach, a beach-head of change" (*Out of the Book*).

On Chesil Beach takes place on a late evening in mid-July in the early Sixties, the wedding night of Florence Ponting and Edward Mayhew. Their sexual inexperience and mutual misunderstanding leads to their separation immediately afterwards. The short

---

[9] See Amigoni, "'The Luxury of Storytelling'" 157: "'Third Culture' intellectuals and evolutionary literary critics see their mission as rescuing literary studies from 'social constructivism' and restoring the field to the standards of truth and clarity expected by a new, scientifically driven public culture."

novel, like many of McEwan's texts, focuses on a singular event to examine it in all its consequences. The central scenes between the two protagonists on this special night are interspersed with a number of flashbacks that investigate their separate childhoods and their briefly shared love story, ending with an extended flashforward. Some of the reviewers have raised the question of narrative voice. Colm Tóibín, for instance, draws attention to a "quasi-Victorian passage" he regards as a characteristic of the "middle style" McEwan employs in the novel to balance "distance and irony, without creating too much of either" ('Dissecting the Body' n. p.). This is the passage he quotes: "It is shaming sometimes, how the body will not, or cannot, lie about emotions. Who, for decorum's sake, has ever slowed his heart, or muted a blush?" (86).

This remark, in the voice of the narrator, is introduced in the third part, which returns to the scene of the wedding night, focusing on Florence's consciousness. It is situated in the immediate context of Florence experiencing a first moment of physical sensation, which is set against her fear of being abnormally uninterested in sex, and is, thus, invested with considerable significance. The phrasing seems anachronistic, with the references to "decorum" and the "blush" recalling the eighteenth-century discourse on sentiment, in which bodily expressions were regarded as more reliable than words. The idea of emotions as involuntary, automatic responses of the body, also refers back to Darwin's theory of the universality of emotional expression. It is Darwin's book on *The Expression of the Emotions in Man and Animals* that is McEwan's main inspiration for promoting the idea of a universal human nature. While McEwan concedes that emotions are partly culture- and time-specific, he regards the insight into their universality as something that has to be rediscovered in the twenty-first century: "Still, behind the notion of a commonly held stock of emotion lies that of a universal human nature. And until fairly recently, and for a good part of the twentieth century, this has been a reviled notion." ('Literature, Science, and Human Nature' 10). Furthermore, the anachronistic phrasing of the comment is placed against the more clinical language which follows it, in which the narrator gives a detailed diagnosis of Florence's experience of "the beginnings of desire, precise and alien" (87).

As this brief analysis indicates, the narrator in *On Chesil Beach* shifts between anachronistic reference and scientific tone, while guiding the reader through the frequent transitions from Florence's to Edward's mental processes. In its concern with early adulthood, depicting Florence's and Edward's meeting when both of them consider themselves as living in a state of suspended time, "waiting fretfully for [their] life to begin" (52), the novel picks up McEwan's continuous interest in liminal stages, in the beginnings of lives and, in this case, of a decade. The complex treatment of time also links the novel with his earlier texts. Narrative time is slowed down in the scenes of the wedding night to achieve an effect almost of 'real time'; acceleration and deceleration are balanced throughout the narrative to provide the background histories for understanding its protagonists, while the flashforward at the end of the novel constitutes a disturbance of time in its excursion into the lost possibilities of 'what-might-have been'. However, it is the narrator, I argue, that is this novel's most distinctive feature. This narrative voice with its alternating perspectives on the two protagonists also determines the novel's approach to time and history.

Some of the narrator's complexities are already indicated by the novel's two opening sentences: "They were young, educated, and both virgins on this, their wedding night, and lived in a time when a conversation about sexual difficulties was plainly impossible. But it is never easy." (3) As Jonathan Lethem points out in his review of the novel, the second sentence brings up the question of "[w]ho speaks, and from what historical vantage?" He further argues that the afterthought presented by the narrator entrenches the events depicted in the novel "in the oceanic retrospect of a ruminative mind, even as they claim to universalize the lovers' predicament, to forgive them their place in the history of sexual discomfort" ('Edward's End' n. p.). The attributes Lethem uses for this narrator indicate the spectrum of characteristics we encounter in the novel's narrative voice: the "ruminative mind" suggests not merely the superior knowledge of an omniscient narrator but also the more specific thought processes this narrator engages in. These encompass the diagnostic precision used in the passage analyzed above, with which the narrator dissects not only the two protagonists' physical reactions but also their interiority. The "oceanic retrospect" brings together another two characteristics of the narrator: his knowledge is based on the historical distance which distinguishes him from his protagonists; and his omniscience is "oceanic", exceeding even the encyclopedic knowledge of many late-Victorian narrators in its formidable extension into the sea and, thus, into natural history.

In an affirmation of his narrative authority, McEwan has rejected the first-person narrative of some of his early work in favour of a third-person voice: "Although the narrator of *On Chesil Beach* is not a character you could describe, or has any past or future, it is a presence which assumes the aesthetic task of describing the inside of two people's minds. Then the reader can make a judgement" (Cook, Groes, and Sage, 'Journeys without Maps' 154).[10] McEwan suggests here that the narrator is an objective presence with a definable aesthetic task, on whom the reader can rely for his or her own judgement. By contrast, the versatile manipulations of the novel's personalized narrator undermine this notion of objectivity. Neither the film camera nor psychoanalysis serve as models for this narration of consciousness, as they do in the unobtrusive mediation of the modernist novel. Instead, the narrative voice in *On Chesil Beach* is a strongly felt presence, an assertive mediator who looks from a number of different angles at his narrative objects.

Taking an inventory of these different perspectives, I wish to distinguish between the historical and the aged narrator, the scientific narrator, the ventriloquist and the translator. The historical perspective is evoked when the narrator indicates the difference of the historical setting. This includes comments on the "history of the English cuisine" for which the early Sixties are "not a good moment" (4). The protagonists' dutiful consuming their less than inviting meal sparks off an excursion into cultural history: "It was precisely because they were adults that they did not do childish things like walk away from a meal that others had taken pains to prepare. It was dinner time, after all. And being childlike was not yet honourable, or in fashion" (18). Other examples include the fascination with measuring intelligence during the Sixties, and the decade's relative inexperience in the language of self-analysis and

---

[10] The quoted passage from the interview begins with this assertive statement: "I want narrative authority. I want Saul Bellow, I want John Updike, I want Chekhov, I want Nabokov and Jane Austen. I want the authorial presence taking full responsibility for everything." (154)

psychotherapy (16; 21). It is in the novel's first part that the narrator chronicles historical difference most frequently while construing the specificity of its historical setting.

The 'aged narrator' refers to a specific form of historical perspective in those instances when the narrator's superior knowledge is an aspect of the narrator's being staged as having advanced beyond the age of the protagonists. These interventions are related to the narrator's comments on transitional points in Edward's adolescence. The narrative of Edward's childhood culminates in a conversation with his father, who tells him, at the age of fourteen, that his mother was "brain-damaged" since her skull was fractured by the heavy metal door of a train (69). This accident occurred when Edward was five, and a fantasy of normality was being upheld during his childhood. His father's revelation is depicted as "a turning point in Edward's life" (71), who begins to experience himself as different from his family and, particularly, his mother. The narrator diagnoses this change, historically, in his reference to the recently invented term 'teenager', drawing at the same time on a difference in lifetime and giving the impression of an older narrator who looks back at someone else's youth: "The term 'teenager' had not long been invented, and it never occurred to him that the separateness he felt, which was both painful and delicious, could be shared by anyone else" (74). Another example also refers to an instance of Edward's emerging self-knowledge, in which he discards an earlier self-image under the influence of a more intellectual male friend. The narrator's comment again focuses on the experiential dimension of historical difference: "He was making one of the advances typical of early adulthood: the discovery that there were new values by which he preferred to be judged" (95).

With the attribute 'scientific' I refer to the diagnostic, almost clinical language the narrator employs to set out the 'core problem', the misunderstandings between the two lovers, in order to dissect their behaviour or emotions. An example for this mode is the depiction of Florence's first physical sensation of pleasure in almost clinical detail. In another instance the focus is on Edward's rising anger in reaction to Florence's escape to the beach. Before switching to Edward's mental processes, the narrator describes how he conjures positive memories of Florence in an unsuccessful attempt to fend off his destructive emotion (132-33). These memories, which take up most of the novel's fourth part, are set against the minute analysis of Edward's fight against "the pull of contrary emotions". Examples of a scientific perspective also include summaries of Edward's and Florence's problem, which the narrator gives at various stages of their story:

> One of their favourite topics was their childhoods, not so much the pleasures as the fog of comical misconceptions from which they had emerged [...]. From these new heights they could see clearly, but they could not describe to each other certain contradictory feelings [...].
>
> (McEwan, *On Chesil Beach* 6)

> And what stood in their way? Their personalities and pasts, their ignorance and fear, timidity, squeamishness, lack of entitlement or experience or easy manners, then the tail end of a religious prohibition, their Englishness and class, and history itself. Nothing much at all.
>
> (McEwan, *On Chesil Beach* 96)

If the novel's opening lines can also be read as the rudimentary outline of its contents in the form of an experimental setting, the two passages above show how this experiment evolves. The first quotation further defines the starting point from which the narrative proceeds: the two lovers have left their childhood behind and have gained an amount of self-knowledge while they are only partially aware of "certain contradictory feelings" which will become part of the problem. The second passage gives an ironic review of all the aspects that stand in their way, summarizing the specific historical detail the narrative has uncovered so far. McEwan's interest in contemporary science informs the direction taken by the novel's 'scientific' mode. The major science is biology, which has invaded "the territory of novelists" since both share their interest in explorations of consciousness and the emotions: "Emotions like anger, shame and even revenge are studied in beautifully constructed experiments" (Cook, Groes, and Sage, 'Journeys without Maps' 148). The narrator's scientific mode in *On Chesil Beach*, then, can be read as a novelist's 'beautifully constructed' experiment.

The narrator as 'ventriloquist' appears in the numerous passages in which a transition is made between the narrator's external perspective and the two protagonists' thought processes. The two dominant modes of narration are also reflected in the different language used for the characters' consciousness. Edward, who has obtained a degree in history, is more frequently described in the historical mode, whereas Florence, the musician, is given a more abstract intellectual voice that is associated with the scientific mode. In the role of 'translator' the narrator depicts the thoughts and feelings of the characters which they are unable to express themselves due to a lack of knowledge - sexual knowledge, self-knowledge and knowledge of their partner. These translations appear to be motivated by a desire to make the reader understand the characters' predicament, but they can also have a patronizing and condescending effect.

The versatility of the narrative voice in *On Chesil Beach*, then, can be seen as a return to the omniscience of the Victorian narrator that is informed by the universalism and materialism of evolutionary biology at the beginning of the twenty-first century. Bringing together scientific and historical modes, the narrator also provides a perspective on time that incorporates the short history of the human lifespan within the long duration of evolutionary time. This is illustrated by the novel's ending which updates Edward's life story to the present in fast motion. In a parody of the Victorian novel's panoramic overview of its characters' life after the plot has ended, the narrator accelerates time to summarize Edward's life, placing the catastrophic wedding night into a historical perspective. In contrast to the temporal shifts between slow, scenic narration and the accelerated background histories which ask for the reader's understanding of the two protagonists, the fast-forward motion across Edward's life has a judgmental effect. Along with a brief chronicle of the important events in his life, Edward's different assessments of Florence and their separation are given as he ages. His memory of her becomes an invitation to think about the different possibilities for his life, until he comes to understand, in *his* sixties, that her "self-effacing proposal" - she asks him to have sex with other people, proposing a kind of open marriage - was "quite irrelevant. All she had needed was the certainty of his love, and his reassurance that there was no hurry when a lifetime lay ahead of them" (165-66). The accelerated review of a life in time, together with the conjectures on 'what-might-have-been', produces the effect of futility, of a life that has been wasted. The authority of the narrator is taken a step further in the novel's last paragraph in which omniscience is supplemented by judgement:

> This is how the entire course of a life can be changed - by doing nothing. On Chesil Beach he could have called out to Florence, he could have gone after her. He did not know, or would not have cared to know, that as she ran away from him, certain in her distress that she was about to lose him, she had never loved him more, or more hopelessly, and that the sound of his voice would have been a deliverance, and she would have turned back. Instead, he stood in cold and righteous silence in the summer's dusk, watching her hurry along the shore, the sound of her difficult progress lost to the breaking of small waves, until she was a blurred, receding point against the immense straight road of shingle gleaming in the pallid light.
>
> (McEwan, *On Chesil Beach* 166)

The drama of this last scene lies in the narrator's placing the conjecture of a different, happier outcome of the two lives dissected at the moment of a tragic failure of sexual and emotional communication against the long duration of geological formations. By reducing Florence to "a blurred receding point against the immense straight road of a shingle gleaming in the pallid light", the endless extension of the beach and the sea heightens the sense of futility that the acceleration of human time has already evoked. In a novel that accumulates images of continuity to evoke its particular historical setting of peaceful stability against a background of imminent change, the flash-forward at the end as well as the closing focus on the long duration of evolutionary time are precisely calculated to dislodge any historical certainties.

Resisting the Sense of an Ending: Julian Barnes's Terminal Moments

It is in Ian McEwan's focus on liminal moments, on the beginnings of life in time, as I have argued, that the trajectory of his engagement with the historical and the contemporary is expressed. In his later work, an assertion of narrative authority is linked to a fascination with evolutionary biology and its extended temporal perspective, a perspective that disrupts historical time. By comparison, Julian Barnes approaches life in time from the opposite end, combining an interest in endings - the end of life, old age - with a resistance to narrative closure. Barnes acknowledges his continuous fascination with death and his fear of it, which he allows to be obsessive only in the context of contemporary culture's denial of death: "[...] I realize it's an obsession compared to how other people don't think about the matter. It's something that I was aware of from the age of thirteen or fourteen, I suppose, and it's with me every day" (Guignery and Roberts, 'Julian Barnes: The Final Interview' 161).

In his recent writings Barnes's concern with the end of life, with death, grief and loss, has become especially prominent.[11] He has approached these themes from different angles and in different genres. In the introduction to his translation of the nineteenth-century French novelist Alphonse Daudet's illness narrative, *In the Land of Pain*,

---

11   On this, see also my essay "'At times it feels as if life is the greatest loser': Old Age, Death and Grief in Julian Barnes's Later Works.".

Barnes notes that in spite of Daudet's insight "that pain [...] drives out language", the memoir shows him "writing close to his death" while avoiding any "illusions about immortality" (v; xiv). Barnes's short story collection *The Lemon Table* (2004) engages with old age in a comic as well as serious style that represents its absurdities and shortcomings, resisting the sentimental idea of an accumulation of wisdom towards the end of life. Dark comedy also characterizes Barnes's non-fictional reflection on his own fear of death, *Nothing to Be Frightened Of* (2008). Like most of Barnes's writing, this text defies generic categories and has been described as "a maverick form of family memoir" that is "so bursting with voices that it seems almost to be a novel" (Lively, 'Before Darkness Falls' n. p.). In his search for an antidote to his fear of death, Barnes again addresses the question of artistic immortality. He calls this idea into doubt, however, by juxtaposing it with the long duration of geological conceptions of time that ultimately defeat the time scope relevant to a writer's afterlife (76). Like McEwan, Barnes draws on the contemporary narrative of genetic determinism, but places it, ironically, against a stubborn sense of himself as an individual and a writer. With reference to Richard Dawkins he formulates the paradox "that individualism - the triumph of free-thinking artists and scientists - has led us to a state of self-awareness in which we can now view ourselves as units of genetic obedience" (93-94). Whether one regards the evolutionary perspective on life - summarized by Barnes as "the blind and fortuitous process which has blindly and fortuitously produced us" - as depressing or elevating, Barnes suggests that "death has an obstinate way of denying us the solutions we imagine for ourselves" (94).

A concern with such terminal moments, however, is already evident in Barnes's early work. *Staring at the Sun* (1986) connects the fascination with flight and the fear of it with a similarly ambiguous approach to death. It opens on a scene in 1941, in which the British Sergeant-Pilot Tommy Prosser sees the sun "as it rose from the waves for the second time that morning" (2). This "ordinary miracle" of the twice-risen sun is related later on to Prosser's death in the skies, when he fulfills his dream of climbing towards the unreachable sun. This initial image links the narrative to the Icarus myth, while the title also refers to the folk belief that staring at either the sun or death is fatal. Apart from this metaphorical link between death and flying, both of which are depicted as defying "rational understandings of human limit" (Tate, "'An Ordinary Piece of Magic'" 54), like McEwan's *The Child in Time*, the novel provides an unusual perspective on narrative time. Its three parts follow the life of Jean Serjeant from her childhood in the 1920s to her very old age in 2021, thus shifting the plot from a historical perspective on the Second World War to the science-fiction setting of the early twenty-first century. Jean Serjeant's progress into a centenarian takes place in an almost carefree manner, indicating her atheist's unconcern with old age meaning approaching closer to death. While she is more interested in the question of how "you tell a good life from a bad life, a wasted life" (139), it is her middle-aged son Gregory who is obsessed with the question of "a good death" (134). The novel's final section, set in the year 2021, shows Gregory in exchange with the publicly funded computer program TAT ("The Absolute Truth") trying unsuccessfully to elicit answers concerning his enquiries after God, death and the afterlife (146). While this section anticipates some of the comic queries of *Nothing to Be Frightened Of*, the novel ends with a characteristically ambiguous return to its beginning, employing the metaphor of staring at the sun to put even the finality of death into perspective. In the final scene, Jean and her son Gregory board a plane on the eve of her centenary to stare at the sun in the manner taught to her by "Sun-Up Prosser" - by putting "your fingers in front of your face" (194). Bringing together the novel's initial scene of Prosser's "ordinary miracle" of the twice-risen sun with his suicidal fascination with staring at it, Jean's "smile towards this post-mortal phosphorescence" links her view of sunset to a more peaceful version of death (195).

If we compare these texts to Julian Barnes's postmodern historiographic metafiction of the 1980s, it becomes clear that, in spite of their suggestion that the past is ultimately inaccessible, they focus also on the individual's life in time. *Flaubert's Parrot* celebrates the writer Flaubert as a personality and "not just a shadowy figure from whom notable texts have emanated" (Head, "Barnes" 15), whereas *A History of the World in 10 1/2 Chapters* breaks down the different durations of evolutionary, mythical and historical time into specific stories of catastrophes narrated from both human and animal perspectives.

The emphasis on the experiential dimension of historical time becomes most obvious in Barnes's more 'serious' historical novel *Arthur & George* (2005). It tells the story of George Edalji, a solicitor of mixed Parsee and Scottish parentage, who was sentenced to seven years' hard labour for allegedly mutilating cattle. Arthur Conan Doyle became interested in his case and began his own investigations, which eventually led to Edalji's being granted a partial pardon. The self-reflexive foregrounding of subjectivity in the first-person narrative of the earlier historiographic metafiction is replaced here by a third-person narration that shifts between the consciousness of its two historical protagonists, alternating their first names as chapter headings. If, in this novel, Barnes "offers something new, an ingenious combination of realism and postmodern historiography" (Berberich, "'All Letters Quoted Are Authentic'" 122), the narrative voice's authoritative stance is counteracted by its double perspective.

The "Beginnings" of the novel's first part introduce Arthur's vision, linking a child's perspective to the historical self-consciousness of memory: "A child wants to see. It always begins like this, and it began like this then. A child wanted to see. [...] What he saw there became his first memory" (3). It is the first encounter with death, with his grandmother's corpse, that initiates the child Arthur into life in time, into an awareness of history and change. The emphasis on perception, on seeing for oneself, is extended also to the final part of the novel, "Endings", which closes on George's view, as one of the mourners at Conan Doyle's funeral, through his binoculars: "What does he see? What did he see? What will he see?" (357) In this historical novel, then, Barnes links the experience of death to the emergence of historical consciousness, while highlighting also, in the questioning stance of its ending, the subjectivity of the experiential dimension. Providing the historical evidence as well as two subjective perspectives on it, Barnes asks the readers of his novel "to critically assess all narrative and take nothing for granted" (Berberich, "'All Letters Quoted Are Authentic'" 128).

If the more realistic historical novel *Arthur & George* is framed, as I have suggested, by the experience of death, thus linking historical consciousness to the experience of life in time, *The Sense of an Ending* can be read as a different exploration of finality. Although, like McEwan, Julian Barnes is aware of the disruptive consequences of the evolutionary perspective on time, his position seems to be closer to the interplay of determinism and freedom that Frank Kermode has described as the coordinates for human endeavours to produce meaning in his study of 1967, with which Barnes's novel shares its title.[12] This interplay of opposites Barnes sees as central also to the production of meaning in fictional storytelling: "Fiction is made by a process which combines total freedom and utter control, which balances precise observation with the free play of the imagination, which uses lies to tell the truth and truth to tell lies" (*Nothing* 240). *The Sense of an Ending* presents the life review of the unreliable narrator Tony Webster as a retrospective narrative which focuses on moments of misunderstanding, betrayal and selfishness that shape the (re)assessment of an individual life. The novel is also a fictional exploration of the final attempt to find meaning in a life story that is about to end - a constellation which Barnes regards as highly suspicious because of the pressures of meaning-making that finality induces. Barnes rejects the idea that the structure of human life is inherently developmental, and that the progression towards its end entails a progress in the sense of growth, maturity or wisdom. As he has pointed out in *Nothing to Be Frightened Of*, adulthood does not feel like an achievement:

> Rather, it felt like a conspiracy: I'll pretend that you're grown up if you pretend that I am. Then, as acknowledged (or at least unrumbled) adults, we head towards some fuller, maturer condition, when the narrative has justified itself and we are expected to proclaim, or shyly admit, 'Ripeness is all!' But how often does the fruit metaphor hold? We are as likely to end up a sour windfall or dried and wizened by the sun, as we are to swell pridefully to ripeness.
>
> (Barnes, *Nothing To Be Frightened Of* 190)

Barnes's rejection of the fruit metaphor entails a rejection of finitude as meaningful that is in keeping with the formal denial of closure in many of his novels. In *The Sense of an Ending* this takes the form of a narrator's failed attempts to make sense of his own life. Tony Webster is in his late sixties when an unexpected legacy triggers his attempts to revisit some of the central moments in his life, which concern a friend's suicide.

In his emphatic affirmation of the third-person voice's narrative authority, McEwan has also rejected first-person narrative as an invitation to write "badly because this is how a character speaks" (Cook, Groes, and Sage, 'Journeys without Maps' 154). By contrast, Barnes's sophisticated use of an unreliable first-person voice represents Tony Webster's belated coming-of-age as a failure of self-understanding, which is not, however, a failure of narrative authority. The topic of memory and its unreliability as well as the meaning of time are recurrent concerns of its first-person narrator. The novel begins and ends with an enumeration of the same events or moments remembered: at the beginning in the form of a list, at the end narrated as an accumulation of thoughts. The circular structure of the text enacts and counteracts the attempts and failure of its narrator to come to terms with his life in time. The novel is divided into two parts, in the first of which Tony Webster describes a number of incidents during his schooldays and adolescence. While it is clear that the sequence of scenes are the memories of a much older man, they are presented as momentary reminiscences which provide only

[12]   See Kermode, *The Sense of an Ending* 20: "[W]e concern ourselves with the conflict between the deterministic pattern any plot suggests, and the freedom of persons within that plot to choose and do alter the structure, the relations of beginning, middle, and end."

occasional glimpses of a later interpretation the reader reconstructs along with but also in opposition to Tony's narration. In spite of markers of different temporal layers, Tony's narrative hardly gives the impression of a difference in self-knowledge between his younger and his older self.

The narrative of events during Tony's youth ends with the news of the suicide of his admired friend Adrian Finn. As the impact of this event retreats "into time and history", Tony brings us up-to-date with his life in retirement (54). This takes the form of an accelerated life review at the end of the novels' first part reminiscent of the fast-motion update of Edward's life at the end of *On Chesil Beach*. Where McEwan's narrator draws on acceleration, the omniscient overview as well as narratorial judgement, a simi-lar effect of futility is achieved by the contrast between two different durations in Tony's life review. While the scenic description of the events in his youth gives the impression of their happening outside the temporal frame, the brief summary of the 'rest' of Tony's life reinforces the sense of its emptiness. As Michael Wood points out:

> In what looks like a bit of narrative perversity or a joke on the idea of the novel, he moves his story from the time he left university [...] to the time he retired, including jobs, marriage, divorce, a grown-up daughter, in five shortish paragraphs, ending with the remark: 'And that's a life, isn't it?' The answer is yes, but only if you're trying very hard not to have one.
>
> (Wood, 'Stupidly English' n.p.)

Tony's curious lack of perspective and understanding of his own life, the sense that he has missed out on the middle of his life-story, is underlined at the beginning of the novel's second part when he proposes the backward and forward movement in time as a means for promoting such an understanding: "What you fail to do is look ahead, and then imagine yourself looking back from that future point. Learning the new emotions that time brings" (59). This confusion of narrative time with lifetime is confirmed by Tony's preference for "official history that's happened in my own lifetime" because he feels "safer with the history that's been more or less agreed upon" (59-60). Moving backward and forward in narrative time is what the reader has to do in order to recon-struct the patterns and links Barnes provides in *The Sense of an Ending*. As regards temporal movement, in its first part the novel links youth, in a chronology of scenes in slow motion, to accelerated old age, while the second part chronicles Tony's attempt to reverse time, as Barnes employs the narrative patterns of romance, Gothic mystery, and detection to pinpoint his narrator's failures to understand his own life in time.

Unlike *On Chesil Beach*, the novel is only loosely situated in the Sixties of Tony's youth, who, nevertheless, depicts himself as a kind of historical chronicler, who "survived to tell the tale" (56). This self-image is contradicted by the revelations of the novel's second part which make Tony appear as a clueless historian and unperceptive witness. Furthermore, he represents himself as a 'survivor' into old age, a self-image that he contrasts with the early death of his friend Adrian. By idealizing Adrian's brief life as an extraordinary one whose clarity he envies, Tony cruelly sentimentalises the catastrophe of his friend's suicide. This is underlined by his use of the aeroplane crash as a metaphor for clarity in life: "If nothing goes wrong, the tape erases itself. So if you crash, it's obvious why you did; if you don't, then the log of your journey is much less clear" (105). The catastrophic crash of suicide appears, in this metaphor, to be preferable to the ambiguities of later life. Thus Tony's misunderstanding of life in time is illustrated, while his failure to experience loss is depicted as a symptom of this misunderstanding. Treasuring youth, he mistakes its self-confident beginnings for significance while rejecting the uncertainties of life in the middle, or the inevitable effects and losses of the ageing process:

> When you are in your twenties, even if you're confused and uncertain about your aims and purposes, you have a strong sense of what life itself is, and of what you in life are, and might become. Later ... later there is more uncertainty, more overlapping, more backtracking, more false memories.
>
> (Barnes, *The Sense of An Ending* 104-105)

While the impact of the catastrophic event of Adrian's early death is preeminent in Tony's recollections, a sense of an ending also attaches to Tony's description of his first sexual relationship. Focusing on the end of this relationship, Tony's avoidance of deep feelings in his dealings with others is highlighted when Veronica, in the scene of the actual break-up, exclaims in exasperation: "You're meant to say what you *think*, what you *feel*, for Christ's sake, what you *mean*" (38; emphasis in text).

Surprising for a novel that is primarily concerned with the ordinary failures of its average protagonist, *The Sense of an Ending* includes instances of the Gothic. One of these induces a sense of foreboding into Tony's narrative of the events in his youth. This sense of foreboding is inserted into the description of the end of his relationship with Veronica and provides a different perspective on catastrophe. Tony recalls how he witnessed the Severn Bore at Minsterworth with some of his friends, a shock wave seen on the tidal reaches of the river Severn, which empties into the Bristol Channel. He describes the natural spectacle as having an unsettling effect on him that is more unnerving than 'real' catastrophe because it appears to be both 'unnatural' and 'untimely':

> It was more unsettling because it looked and felt quietly wrong, as if some small lever of the universe had been pressed, and here, just for these minutes, nature was reversed, and time with it. And to see this phenomenon after dark made it the more mysterious, the more other-worldly.
>
> (Barnes, *The Sense Of An Ending* 36)

This token of the "otherworldly" with its Gothic intrusion into Tony's ordinary, 'peaceable' life reads retrospectively like a materialization of his bad conscience. It can also be read as a foreboding of the "quietly wrong" things to come, which lead to Adrian's suicide. And it can be linked to Tony's vengeful letter to Adrian and Veronica after he has learned that they have become a couple - a letter which is associated with the everyday Gothic when it 'returns' as evidence in the novel's second part and gives ample "proof, corroboration" of his hurt pride and adolescent revenge (39). Its language is intentionally hurtful and expectably ugly. Tony acknowledges this and is shocked by the confrontation with this instance of his earlier self into a rare moment of introspection:

> [I]t wasn't shame I now felt, or guilt, but something rarer in my life and stronger than both: remorse. A feeling which is more complicated, curdled, and primeval. Whose chief characteristic is that nothing can be done about it: too much time has passed, too much damage has been done, for amends to be made.
>
> (Barnes, *The Sense Of An Ending* 99)

In spite of this insight into the quality of remorse Tony begins to pursue another possibility, guided by his wish to retrace his steps: "What if by some means remorse can be made to flow backwards, can be transmuted into simple guilt, then apologised for, and then forgiven?" (107). This attempt to reverse his life-story, to travel backwards in time, is another indication of Tony's misunderstanding of historical processes, of his mistaking narrative time for life in time.

In what follows, Tony begins to reenact his earlier relationship with Veronica, sentimentally refashioning his memories so that they fit this new romance plot. By inserting Veronica, his uncanny memory of witnessing the Severn Bore, for instance, is transformed into a romantic courtship scene. His attempts at placing "personal time [...] in reverse", however, are defeated by Veronica's refusal to comply (122). Instead, a Gothic mystery plot takes over to frustrate Tony's expectations of romance. The strategy of cumulative revelations, which leads Tony from one (failed) reconstruction of the evidence to the next, recalls the narrative pattern of the detective plot, characterising Tony as a dogged but uninspired Watson. The inconclusiveness of the ending, however, rejects even this pattern for meaning-making. When Tony begins to understand that Adrian's 'legacy' is a disabled son he conceived with Veronica's mother rather than the diary fragment he has misread as "Adrian's rational arguing towards his own suicide" (87), he also rereads his own letter to Adrian. Recalling that he had wished upon him revenge in the form of a damaged child, Tony's remorse returns, this time with the force of the Gothic:

> Remorse, etymologically, is the action of biting again. Imagine the strength of the bite when I reread my words. They seemed like some ancient curse I had forgotten even uttering. Of course I don't – didn't - believe in curses. That's to say, in words producing events. But the very action of naming something that subsequently happens - of wishing specific evil, and that evil coming to pass - this still has a shiver of the otherworldly about it.
>
> (Barnes, *The Sense Of An Ending* 138)

But even this second evocation of the supernatural, in a novel that depicts a "pale English world where the Gothic is literally unthinkable" (Wood, 'Stupidly English' n. p.), is not the last reassessment in Tony's narrative. *The Sense of an Ending* is a novel which shifts and reassembles its narrative elements. In its inconclusiveness, it denies its protagonist the reassurance of a sense of an ending.

Ian McEwan and Julian Barnes address life in time from the different directions of its beginning and endings. In their focus on the catastrophes and failures of ordinary lives their timescapes move along the temporal dimensions of evolutionary and geological, historical and individual time to envision specific versions of the contemporary. Whereas their early work has figured prominently in the postmodern metafictional approach to history and time, their more recent work is invested with a strong narrative authority. Nevertheless, the third-person voice of *On Chesil Beach* and the unreliable narration of *The Sense of an Ending* both produce the effect of a displacement of history - in the extended reflection on a spoiled beginning and in the inconclusiveness of the retrospective search for meaning. While their attitudes to contemporary science's materialist approach to consciousness in time differ, both writers are centrally concerned with a reassessment of contemporary life in time.

Works Cited

Alden, Natasha. 'Words of War, War of Words: *Atonement* and the Question of Plagiarism.' *Ian McEwan. Contemporary Critical Perspectives.* Ed. Sebastian Groes. London: Continuum, 2013². 57-69.

Amigoni, David. "'The Luxury of Storytelling': Science, Literature and Cultural Contest in Ian McEwan's Narrative Practice." *Literature and Science.* Ed. Sharon Ruston. Woodbridge: Brewer, 2008. 151-167.

Anderson, Perry. 'From Progress to Catastrophe.' *London Review of Books* 33-15 (2011): 24-28. Web. 3 January 2014. <http://www.lrb.co.uk/v33/n15/perry-anderson/from-progress-to-catastrophe.html>.

Barnes, Julian. *Nothing to Be Frightened Of.* London: Vintage, 2009.

Barnes, Julian. *Staring at the Sun.* London: Picador, 1987.

Barnes, Julian. *The Sense of an Ending.* London: Cape, 2011.

Barthes, Roland. 'The Discourse of History.' Trans. Stephen Bann. *Comparative Criticism* 3 (1981): 7-20.

Berberich, Christine. "'All Letters Quoted Are Authentic': The Past After Postmodern Fabulation in Julian Barnes's *Arthur & George*." *Julian Barnes. Contemporary Critical Perspectives.* Eds. Sebastian Groes and Peter Childs. London: Continuum, 2011. 117-129.

Bradbury, Malcom. *The Modern British Novel.* London: Penguin, 1994.

Braudel, Fernand. *The Mediterranean and the Mediterranean World in the Age of Philipp II.* Vol. 1. London: Fontana Press, 1972.

Childs, Peter. *Julian Barnes.* Manchester: Manchester University Press, 2011.

Cook, Jon, Sebastian Groes, and Victor Sage. 'Journeys without Maps: An Interview with Ian McEwan.' *Ian McEwan. Contemporary Critical Perspectives.* Ed. Sebastian Groes. London: Continuum, 2013². 144-155.

Daudet, Alphones. *In the Land of Pain.* Ed. and transl. Julian Barnes. London: Cape, 2002.

Dickens, Charles. *Dombey and Son.* Ed. Alan Horsman. Oxford: Oxford University Press, 2001.

Gems, David. 'Eine Revolution des Alterns. Die neue Biogerontologie und ihre Implikationen.' *Länger Leben? Philosophische und biowissenschaftliche Perspektiven.* Eds. Sebastian Knell and Marcel Weber. Frankfurt a. M.: Suhrkamp, 2009. 25-45.

Genette, Gérard. *Narrative Discourse. An Essay in Method.* Ithaca: Cornell University Press, 1983.

Groes, Sebastian, and Peter Childs, eds. *Julian Barnes. Contemporary Critical Perspectives.* London: Continuum, 2011.

Groes, Sebastian. 'Introduction: A Cartography of the Contemporary: Mapping Newness in the Work of Ian McEwan.' *Ian McEwan. Contemporary Critical Perspectives.* Ed. Sebastian Groes. London: Continuum, 2013². 1-12.

Groes, Sebastian, ed. *Ian McEwan. Contemporary Critical Perspectives.* London: Continuum, 2013².

Guignery, Vanessa, and Ryan Roberts. 'Julian Barnes: The Final Interview.' *Conversations with Julian Barnes.* Eds. Vanessa Guignery and Ryan Roberts. Jackson: University Press of Mississippi, 2009. 161-188.

Guignery, Vanessa, and Ryan Roberts, eds. *Conversations with Julian Barnes.* Jackson: University Press of Mississippi, 2009.

Hartung, Heike. "'At times it feels as if life is the greatest loser': Old Age, Death and Grief in Julian Barnes's Later Works." *Narrating Loss. Representations of Mourning, Nostalgia and Melancholia in Contemporary Anglophone Fictions.* Eds. Brigitte Glaser and Barbara Puschmann-Nalenz. Trier: Wissenschaftlicher Verlag Trier, 2014. 141-160.

Hartung, Heike. *Die dezentrale Geschichte. Historisches Erzählen und literarische Geschichte(n) bei Peter Ackroyd, Graham Swift und Salman Rushdie.* Trier: Wissenschaftlicher Verlag Trier, 2002.

Head, Dominic. 'Julian Barnes's *Flaubert's Parrot*.' *British Fiction Today*. Eds. Rod Mengham and Philip Tew. London: Continuum, 2006. 15-27.

Head, Dominic. *Ian McEwan.* Manchester: Manchester University Press, 2007.

Hutcheon, Linda. *A Poetics of Postmodernism. History, Theory, Fiction.* London: Routledge, 1988.

Jameson, Fredric. 'The Historical Novel Today, Or, Is It Still Possible?' *The Antinomies of Realism*. London: Verso, 2013. 259-314.

Johnston, Andrew James. *Performing the Middle Ages from Beowulf to Othello.* Turnhout: Brepols, 2008.

Katz, Stephen. 'Imagining the Life-Span. From Premodern Miracles to Postmodern Fantasies.' *Images of Aging. Cultural Representations of Later Life.* Eds. Mike Featherstone and Andrew Wernick. London: Routledge, 1995. 59-76.

Kermode, Frank. *The Sense of an Ending. Studies in the Theory of Fiction.* Oxford: Oxford University Press, 1968.

Kunow, Rüdiger. 'Simulacrum as Sub-Text: Fiction Writing in the Face of Media Representations of American History.' *Simulacrum America. The USA and the Popular Media.* Eds. Elisabeth Kraus and Carolin Auer. Rochester, NY: Camden House, 2000. 23-36.

Lethem, Jonathan. 'Edward's End.' Rev. of *On Chesil Beach* by Ian McEwan. *New York Times Sunday Book Review*, 3 June 2007. Web. 3 January 2014. <http://nytimes.com/2007/06/03/books/review/Lethem-t.html>.

Lively, Penelope. 'Before Darkness Falls.' Rev. of *Nothing to Be Frightened Of*, by Julian Barnes. *Financial Times*, 1 March 2008. Web. 13 January 2014. <http://www.ft.com>.

Luckhurst, Roger, and Peter Marks. 'Hurry up Please It's Time: Introducing the Contemporary.' *Literature and the Contemporary. Fictions and Theories of the Present*. Eds. Roger Luckhurst and Peter Marks. Edinburgh: Longman, 1999. 1-12.

Marcus, Laura. 'Ian McEwan's Modernist Time: Atonement and Saturday.' *Ian McEwan. Contemporary Critical Perspectives*. Ed. Sebastian Groes. London: Continuum, 2013². 83-98.

McEwan, Ian, and Steven Pinker. 'Shadow Lines.' *Conversations with Ian McEwan*. Ed. Ryan Roberts. Jackson: University Press of Mississippi, 2010. 180-7.

McEwan, Ian. 'Literature, Science, and Human Nature.' *The Literary Animal: Evolution and the Nature of Narrative*. Eds. Jonathan Gottschall and David Sloan Wilson. Evaston, Ill.: Northwestern University Press, 2005. 5-19.

McEwan, Ian. 'When Faith in Fiction Falters - and How It is Restored.' *The Guardian*, 16 February 2013. Web. 3 January 2014. <http://theguardian.com/books/2013/feb/16/ian-mcewan-faith-fiction-falters>.

McEwan, Ian. *On Chesil Beach*. London: Cape, 2007.

McEwan, Ian. *Saturday*. London: Vintage, 2006.

McEwan, Ian. *The Child in Time*. New York: Anchor Books, 1999.

McEwan, Ian. *The Innocent*. London: Picador, 1990.

McEwan, Ian. *Unschuldige*. Transl. Hans-Christian Oeser. Hamburg: Zeitverlag, 2010.

McHale, Brian. *Postmodernist Fiction*. London: Methuen, 1987.

Nicklas, Pascal, ed. *Ian McEwan: Art and Politics*. Heidelberg: Winter, 2009.

Nietzsche, Friedrich. 'Vom Nutzen und Nachteil der Historie für das Leben.' *Nietzsches Werke. Kritische Studienausgabe*. Eds. Giorgio Colli and Mazzino Montinari. Berlin: de Gruyter, 1972. Vol. 3.1. 241-332.

Nünning, Ansgar. 'Crossing Borders and Blurring Genres: Towards a Typology and Poetics of Postmodernist Historical Fiction in England since the 1960s.' *European Journal of English Studies* 1-2 (1996): 217-238.

Nünning, Ansgar. *Von historischer Fiktion zu historiographischer Metafiktion. Band 1: Theorie, Typologie und Poetik des historischen Romans*. Trier: Wissenschaftlicher Verlag Trier, 1995.

Out of the Book: On Chesil Beach. Dir. Doug Biro. Hudson River Films, 2007. Web. 5 January 2014. <http://www.ianmcewan.com/bib/books/chesil.html>.

Puschmann-Nalenz, Barbara. 'Ethics in Ian McEwan's Twenty-First Century Novels. Individual and Society and the Problem of Free Will.' *Ian McEwan: Art and Politics*. Ed. Pascal Nicklas. Heidelberg: Winter, 2009. 187-212.

Ricks, Christopher. 'Adolescence and After.' *Conversations with Ian McEwan*. Ed. Ryan Roberts. Jackson: University Press of Mississippi, 2010. 19-25.

Roberts, Ryan, ed. *Conversations with Ian McEwan*. Jackson: University Press of Mississippi, 2010.

Salisbury, Laura. 'Narration and Neurology: Ian McEwan's Mother Tongue.' *Textual Practice* 24-5 (2010): 883-912.

Spice, Nicholas. 'Thatchershaft.' Rev. of *The Child in Time* by Ian McEwan and *The Book and the Brotherhood* by Iris Murdoch. *London Review of Books* 9-17, 1 October 1987. Web. 4 January 2014. <http://www.lrb.co.uk/v09/n17/nicholas spice/thatchershaft>.

Tate, Andrew. "'An Ordinary Piece of Magic': Religion in the Work of Julian Barnes." *Julian Barnes. Contemporary Critical Perspectives*. Eds. Sebastian Groes and Peter Childs. London: Continuum, 2011. 51-68.

Tóibín, Colm. 'Dissecting the Body.' Rev. of *On Chesil Beach* by Ian McEwan. *London Review of Books* 29-8, 26 April 2007. Web. 5 January 2014. <http://www.lrb.co.uk/v29/n08/colm-toibin/dissecting-the-body>.

Wesseling, Elisabeth. *Writing History as a Prophet*. Amsterdam: Benjamins, 1991.

White, Hayden. *Metahistory. The Historical Imagination in Nineteenth-Century Europe*. Baltimore: The Johns Hopkins University Press, 1975.

Whitney, Helen. 'Faith and Doubt at Ground Zero. Interview Ian McEwan.' *Frontline*, April 2002. Web. 4 January 2014. <http://www.pbs.org/wgbh/pages/frontline/shows/faith/interviews/mcewan.html>.

Wood, Michael. 'Stupidly English.' Rev. of *The Sense of an Ending* by Julian Barnes. *London Review of Books*, 22 Sept 2011. Web. 4 January 2014. <http://www.lrb.co.uk/v33/n18/michael-wood/stupidly-english>.

Zalewski, Daniel. 'The Background Hum: Ian McEwan's Art of Unease.' *The New Yorker*, 23 February 2009. Web. 5 January 2014. <http://www.newyorker.com/reporting/2009/02/23/090223fa_fact_zalewski>.

ANDREW JAMES JOHNSTON

Atonement – Ian McEwan's *Canterbury Tale?*

Ian McEwan's novel *Atonement* can well be considered its author's greatest success. Published in 2001 to a chorus of approval, the novel was nominated for the Booker Prize and later turned into a film starring Keira Knightley and James McAvoy.[1]

Indeed, the book has all the makings of a bestseller. Circling around love and treason, the plot displays all the ingredients of high drama; English upper middle-class life of the 1930s comes in for an opulent, yet consistently morbid and critical portrayal, only to give way to an all the more horrific tableau of World War II: first, the British Expeditionary Force's chaotic retreat to Dunkirk in May 1940, then life on the home front in a London ravaged by war – in a military hospital which turns into a medical variety of hell as droves of maimed and wounded soldiers come flooding back to England in the aftermath of Operation Dynamo. In short, *Atonement* unites most of the traditional elements that have made the historical novel so successful. The book links the individual fates of fictional – yet nonetheless typical – characters to a larger, in this case almost mythical, national destiny. After all, what more mythical event in twentieth-century British history than the evacuation of a total of 338,226 soldiers (including 110,000 French) from the docks and beaches of Dunkirk that took place between 27 May and 4 June of 1940? Its emotional and atmospheric appeal notwithstanding, the novel is also a narrative and intertextual masterpiece of the first order, indeed too much so for some critics. *Atonement* is a work of art that poses questions of fiction and historiography in a confusing, almost enigmatic fashion, thereby raising the issues of both the ethical value and the ethical potential of fiction, and ultimately of narrative itself.

This essay, too, addresses *Atonement's* negotiations of the tensions between ethics and narrative, but it does so through the prism of a particular set of intertextual relations, i.e. Geoffrey Chaucer's *Canterbury Tales*, the relevance of which, to my knowledge, has largely been ignored. As I hope to show, it is through a number of poignant allusions to the medieval English poet's most canonical work that *Atonement* probes deeply into the problem of confession as a means both to discuss the relations between ethics and narrative and to comment on the history of English literature.

The first part of the novel is set in the Tallis family's splendid country house on a scorchingly hot summer day in 1935. It is mainly concerned with the budding romance between young Cecilia Tallis and Robbie Turner, a relationship that inauspiciously

---

[1] *Atonement.* Dir. Joe Wright. Universal Pictures, 2007.

transgresses class boundaries.[2] On the very night the two protagonists discover and declare their mutual love, Lola, Cecilia's pubescent cousin who is currently staying in the house, is raped on the premises. Briony, Cecilia's thirteen-year old sister who is herself on the threshold between childhood and adolescence, mistakenly accuses Robbie Turner of the crime. A precocious and yet oddly naive girl with literary aspirations who provides much of the focalization in the novel's first part, Briony feels that her artistic ambitions have been exposed to ridicule previously in the day. More importantly, she has also witnessed the two dramatic scenes in which Cecilia and Robbie discover their love and reveal it to each other. In both cases, however, Briony arrives at a misinterpretation of her observations, identifying Robbie as a dangerous sexual menace to her sister. While the police conduct their investigation, Briony comes to believe more and more that she actually did see Robbie moving away from the prostrate Lola in the darkness of the nightly park. Based on Briony's testimony, Robbie is sentenced to a long term in prison.

The second part of the novel takes us to northern France in 1940 where, from Robbie Turner's perspective, we witness the chaotic retreat to Dunkirk. Together with two other soldiers, Robbie slowly makes his way to the legendary stretch of coast, experiencing one terrible event after the other. As the story moves on, it becomes more and more obvious that Robbie is concealing a serious wound from his companions. Having eventually reached Dunkirk, the three of them wait for a transport and Robbie progressively slips into a feverish delirium – yet the reader is given to understand that help is on the way. What exactly is going to happen remains open at this point.

The third part of the book takes us to St Thomas' Hospital in London, where an adult Briony is undergoing training as a nurse, just like her older sister before her. We are told of her first and only partially successful literary endeavours: one of them a modernist short story entitled "Two Figures at a Fountain", a narrative revisiting the scene in the hot summer of 1935 when Briony was watching Robbie and Cecilia at the fountain in the park. We experience the hardships of Briony's training, followed by scenes of horror as the wounded suddenly begin to fill the hospital. One afternoon, Briony sets out to attend her cousin Lola's wedding to Paul Marshall, a millionaire and wartime profiteer, and later to call on her sister Cecilia. As is to be expected, after five years without any contact, the encounter with her sister proves painful for all involved, especially after it becomes clear that Cecilia is sharing her dingy room in a working-class house with Robbie, home on leave after apparently surviving Dunkirk. Briony now promises to retract her erroneous testimony in order to rehabilitate Robbie. She has finally come to realize what she now calls "her crime" and is ready to make amends for it. As it turns out, however, there will be legal complications: Briony is now aware that the true perpetrator is none other than the very Paul Marshall her cousin has just married. As Cecilia and Robbie walk away in one direction and Briony in the other, the issue of eventual rehabilitation thus remains unresolved.

The fourth and shortest part of the novel is set in 1999. This part is narrated from a first-person perspective by the celebrated novelist Briony Tallis on the occasion of her

---

2   For a recent reading that insists on the novel's attentiveness to class issues see Karley K. Adney, "These Ghosts Will Be Lovers: The 'Cultural Haunting' of Class Consciousness in Ian McEwan's *Atonement*".

77th birthday. Here, the reader is acquainted with at least three highly disturbing facts: first, that the writer is suffering from dementia, an illness that will soon obliterate her memory; second, that all we have read so far – the novel's three parts outlined earlier – was written by Briony Tallis herself. We have, as it were, been reading a novel within a novel without being aware of it; third, we learn that the semi-conciliatory ending of Part III, giving us Cecilia and Robbie standing next to each other in a London street as Briony heads back to the hospital, is a mere invention of the writer Briony Tallis. Fate, as Briony now tells us, did not grant the characters a shared future in real life: Robbie Turner died of his wounds on the beach at Dunkirk, Cecilia was killed by a direct hit from a German bomb in a Tube tunnel used as an air-raid shelter – and Briony herself would never have dared to face her sister again. As Briony informs us, she only made up the two protagonists' survival as a kind of atonement in order to give their love a future in the realm of fiction, if nowhere else. Thus, the author's atonement for her infantile crime must also remain confined to the fictional sphere.

This final plot twist has considerably exercised the minds of critics and readers alike and is of crucial importance for this essay, too. It is worthwhile dwelling for a moment on these last two pages where the author Briony Tallis – or to be more exact, the fictional author within the text, the character of the novel called Briony Tallis who acts as a first-person narrator – lays her cards on the table:

> It is only in this last version that my lovers end well, standing side by side on a South London pavement as I walk away. All the preceding drafts were pitiless. But now I no longer think what purpose would be served if, say, I tried to persuade my reader, by direct or indirect means, that Robbie Turner died of septicaemia at Bray Dunes on 1 June 1940, or that Cecilia was killed in September that same year by the bomb that destroyed Balham Underground station. That I never saw them in that year. That my walk across London ended in the church on Clapham Common. And that a cowardly Briony limped back to the hospital, unable to confront her recently bereaved sister.
>
> (McEwan, *Atonement* 370-1)[3]

At this juncture, the reader is retrospectively made aware that this development has indirectly been prepared for at several points throughout the novel. When Briony goes to see her sister after the wedding, the narrative voice permits itself some remarks on the relationship of fact and fiction in literature, remarks that linger in the attentive reader's mind, but reveal their meaning only retrospectively. We, the readers, too, have an inkling that even as a young author Briony was occupied mainly with reprocessing the events of the summer of 1935. While working at the hospital in Part III, Briony receives a letter from a famous literary critic of the 20s and 30s, Cyril Connolly, editor of the literary magazine *Horizon*, who offers critical remarks on a short story she had submitted for publication. Again in retrospect, a number of details in this letter reveal that the novel's first part is indeed a revised and expanded version of this short story from 1940.

---

[3]   All quotations from the novel are taken from the following edition: McEwan, Ian. *Atonement*. London: Vintage, 2002.

The first-person narrator Briony is not content with revealing her secret – she also supplies readers with a theoretical interpretation steeped in her own idiosyncratic version of narrative theory. She outlines her particular ethical/narrative predicament in fairly specific terms:

> The problem these fifty-nine years has been this: how can a novelist achieve atonement when, with her absolute power of deciding outcomes, she is also God? There is no one, no entity or higher form that she can appeal to, or be reconciled with, or that can forgive her. There is nothing outside her. In her imagination she has set the limits and the terms. No atonement for God, or novelists, even if they are atheists. It was always an impossible task, and that was precisely the point. The attempt was all.
>
> (McEwan, *Atonement* 371)

As the story is the product exclusively of the author who is the sole creator of its events and characters, there is no higher authority that could absolve her from her sins. She herself must remain the final arbiter.

Readers have come up with widely differing interpretations of this deceptively logical coda and its implications for the novel. There is the large group of critics who read this ending as a brilliant, metafictional and above all things postmodern affirmation of fiction.[4] Critics with a particular interest in the novel's specifically postmodern aspects see themselves vindicated by the plentiful intertextual references in the novel, by its constant allusions to the great novelists of English modernism and their precursors, ranging from Shakespeare, Richardson, Fielding and Jane Austen via Henry James to L.P. Hartley, D.H. Lawrence, E. M. Forster and especially to Elizabeth Bowen and Virginia Woolf.[5] No less postmodern is the way in which the novel skilfully integrates historical sources. Ironically, the issue of source material – repeatedly addressed in the novel via comments by McEwan's fictional author Briony Tallis – became the subject of controversy when the descendants of an author whose memoirs had furnished McEwan with a wealth of detail accused him of plagiarism. A whole number of illustrious co-novelists came to his aid, defending the right of postmodern writers freely to avail themselves of any and all texts that strike their fancy, adapting and transforming them as best may fit their purpose.[6] As a matter of fact, even from a traditional point of view, it is hardly possible to construe a true case of plagiarism since, after all, McEwan does reference his sources. Yet there have also been dissenting voices who see McEwan

---

[4]   Some critics even see the novel's aesthetics and ethics as specifically modernist, as does Maria Maragonis when she declares that the "beautiful, crystalline, perfectly constructed novel deliberately betrays its readers to make the modernist point that all fiction – indeed, all writing – is a kind of betrayal" (Maragonis, 'The Anxiety of Authenticity: Writing Historical Fiction at the End of the Twentieth Century' 148).

[5]   The list of allusions seems to be virtually endless. The Italianate fountain, for instance, where Robbie and Cecilia have their first important encounter is often seen as a reference to Evelyn Waugh's *Brideshead Revisited* (Hidalgo, 'Memory and Storytelling in Ian McEwan's *Atonement*' 84).

[6]   For an insightful analysis of the plagiarism debate concerning *Atonement* in the context of McEwan's anti-postmodernist stance see Alastair Cormack, 'Postmodernism and the Ethics of Fiction in *Atonement*'.

as an aesthetic conservative for whom *Atonement* marks a programmatic farewell to both modernism and postmodernism in literature. For all his gestures towards intertextuality and historical metafiction, they argue, McEwan is actually turning toward a traditional style of narration which he perceives as ethically superior when compared to modernism and postmodernism.[7] In so doing, he relies on what amounts to an almost reactionary image of national identity in literary and cultural terms. To put it differently: based on an emphatic concept of literary Englishness, McEwan turns his back on what he seems to conceive of as the morally irresponsible stylistic, narrative and intertextual frivolities supposedly marking both modernism and postmodernism. And if one considers his subsequent novels, such as *Saturday* and *On Chesil Beach*, this hypothesis only gains in plausibility. Ironically, in *Atonement* it is none other than the *arbiter elegantiarum* of modernist literature, Cyril Connolly himself, who gets to explain to Briony that her modernist short story about a child observing two adults next to a fountain is not merely boring, but fails to convince. Dealing merely with momentary sensory perceptions and emotional states, it lacks action, and thus ultimately what could best be termed a certain moral seriousness. Here, modernist narration is understood as a deficiency in ethical commitment.[8] All things considered, the fictionalized critic seems to suggest, a truly ethical stance must derive from action, not from a mere state of mind. Later on in the novel, Briony the author will agree emphatically. Against this backdrop, the septuagenarian Briony's statements regarding the relationship between fiction and real-life history, between narration and morality can be read as a rejection of an apparently amoral aesthetics, a rejection of postmodernism. Yet a different perspective would argue that, as long as a reader is guided by a sound moral compass, there is no danger of his or her being led astray by a postmodern phantasmagoria created by the literary text's dissolution of the boundaries between history and fiction. However impossible true atonement may be in the realm of fiction – in reality it is quite possible, indeed.

Another issue that proves to be of considerable importance is McEwan's concept of Englishness. I hope to show below that McEwan's investigations into the question of Englishness, too, appear in a more ambivalent light when discussed within the context of his Chaucerian allusions. As a closer look reveals, the novel's representation of Englishness is by no means as celebratory as some professional readers would have us believe. There is, for instance, the national myth of Dunkirk as depicted in Part II: rather than being presented to us as a democratic version of the heroic epic, it appears as a surreal scene of horror. In painting this picture, the aesthetically sophisticated narrative deploys a complex plethora of literary techniques, devices ranging from the strictly documentary to the modernist – devices, that is, that echo a characteristic feature of Part I of the novel, the part which supposedly derives from Briony's modernist short story.

---

[7] For a careful weighing of the postmodern and the traditional elements in the novel and an interesting attempt to establish a synthesis between those two tendencies in *Atonement*, see Stefanie Albers and Torsten Caeners, 'The Poetics and Aesthetics of Ian McEwan's *Atonement*'.

[8] As Brian Finney points out, McEwan himself has, with reference to *Atonement*, commented on "how for him the ideology of modernism (especially its prioritization of stylistic innovation) has hidden moral consequences" (Finney, *English Fiction since 1984: Narrating a Nation* 95).

On top of all this, as Helga Schwalm has demonstrated, Part II contains even more disconcerting elements: time and again we witness reflections on the problem of individual responsibility in the face of historical catastrophe that are conspicuously articulated from Robbie Turner's perspective. In this sense, the myth of Dunkirk seems to serve an exculpatory function as far as Briony is concerned. Against the backdrop of an all-encompassing terror generated at the level of global history, terror of a magnitude far beyond a mere individual's control, her crime appears considerably less heinous (Schwalm, 'Figures of Authorship, Empathy, & The Ethics of Narrative (Mis) Recognition in Ian McEwan's Later Fiction' 179). The problem of individual guilt is shown in all its relativity – for all truly terrible events in history, it could be argued, there is never one single, clearly identifiable guilty party, but rather an intricate network of involved participants and entangled responsibilities. And this, too, is already made clear as early as the end of Part I, and is restated throughout the novel. Briony's crime was possible only because she was, all things considered, still a child unable to cope with the world of adults and their sexuality; because the uncommon heat of the day did away with inhibitions, sharpening emotional sensitivities and hampering rational behaviour; because Cousin Lola, the victim of the rape who should have known better, endorsed Briony's testimony and turned it into the basis for her own love, life and happiness by later marrying her rapist; because Briony's mother could not bear to be confronted with Cecilia's sexuality and love life any more than with the fact that the object of her eldest daughter's affection was, of all things, her cleaning lady's son; because Briony's father was in London, frolicking with his mistress and neglecting the responsibilities of the *pater familias*; because police and courts in class-conscious England were only too eager to focus their suspicion on the cleaning lady's offspring, failing to look for alternative suspects and the evidence they might have left behind; and most of all because Briony was simply mistaken, the victim of an unfortunate delusion. If, from Robbie's perspective on the plains of northern France, the party responsible for the terrors of global history can no longer be determined, the same holds true for Briony's crime. Her guilt is ultimately interwoven with a multifactorial structure of mutually reinforcing influences and conditions which all contribute to mitigating her culpability. And as Robbie's viewpoint has been invented and created by Briony Tallis, the author, in the first place, this amounts to her own indirect exoneration of herself.

The problems of ethics and narrative, of literary tradition and Englishness just sketched gain in even greater complexity if scrutinized through the prism of intertextuality that constitutes one of the book's most potent literary devices. This is all the more important since I am convinced that a decisive, perhaps even *the* decisive, intertextual reference has largely been overlooked by critics.[9] This important set of

---

[9]   A number of diverse medieval and even Chaucerian allusions have been spotted by Mary Behrman but her interest is primarily in Arthurian references (*Chrétien de Troyes*, *Sir Gawain and the Green Knight*) and in allusions to great medieval lovers (e.g. Tristan and Iseult, Troilus and Criseyde). Chaucer's work is, therefore, mentioned primarily as far as *Troilus and Criseyde* is concerned and the *Canterbury Tales* are touched only very briefly and exclusively with respect to Griselda. Behrman's principal aim is to spot motifs of waiting (Behrman, 'The Waiting Game: Medieval Allusions and the Lethal Nature of Passivity in Ian McEwan's *Atonement*' 453-70). Maria Vaccarella draws attention to Briony's self-characterization as a

intertextual allusions first becomes manifest in the description of Briony's world in St Thomas' Hospital at the beginning of Part III:

> The unease was not confined to the hospital. It seemed to rise with the turbulent brown river swollen by the April rains, and in the evenings lay across the blacked-out city like a mental dusk which the whole country could sense, a quiet and malign thickening, inseparable from the cool late spring, well concealed within its spreading beneficence.
>
> (McEwan, *Atonement* 269)

It appears as though the text here were echoing the beginning of the Prologue to Geoffrey Chaucer's *Canterbury Tales*:

> Whan that Aprill with his shoures soote
> The droghte of March hath perced to the roote,
>
> (*The Canterbury Tales*, Fragment I, ll. 1-2)[10]

As we can see, Chaucer's overt message is elegantly inverted. As the German offensive casts its dark shadow ahead, the erotic optimism inherent in the medieval poet's *reverdie*, the literary topos of blossoming springtime, is replaced by a sense of foreboding. Moreover, quite apart from alluding to the *Canterbury Tales*, every reference to April in English literature after 1922 must also inevitably resonate with the opening lines of T.S. Eliot's 'The Waste Land':

> April is the cruellest month, breeding
> Lilacs out of the dead land, mixing
> Memory and desire, stirring
> Dull roots with spring rain.
>
> (Eliot, 'The Waste Land' ll. 1-4)

As McEwan's text makes abundantly clear, however, in *Atonement* this allusion is primarily a reference to Chaucer: this is not about April in general, but about the "April rains", the "cool late spring" and the "spreading beneficence" that Chaucer so impressively brings to the mind's eye in his famous Prologue. Besides, there is another interesting parallel between Chaucer's opening to the Prologue and McEwan's novel as a whole. The novel is as suffused with a specifically national-historical aspect as is the inception of Chaucer's poem. Beginning with an initial vernal eroticism, the introductory lines to the Prologue of the *Canterbury Tales* famously change their trajectory to a different context altogether, namely that of a pilgrimage to the shrine of England's national saint Thomas Becket, the Archbishop of Canterbury martyred on 29 December 1170. But the idea of nationhood is woven even more deeply into the fabric

---

'medical Chaucer' but sees this merely as evidence of "her disproportionate self-confidence" (Vaccarella, "'A Kind of Medical Chaucer': Testimony, Storytelling and Caregiving in Ian McEwan's *Atonement*" 143).

[10] All quotations from Chaucer's *Canterbury Tales* are taken from the following edition: Benson, Larry D., ed. *The Riverside Chaucer*. 3rd ed. with a new foreword by Christopher Cannon. Oxford: Oxford University Press, 2008.

of the pilgrimage, since the very concept of pilgrimage is embedded in the nation's political and administrative topography. The pilgrims converge on Canterbury "fram every shires ende of Engelond", i.e. not only from the farthest reaches of the kingdom, but from the farthest reaches of that kingdom as conceived of in terms of a totality of territorial administrative units. Power, place and penance thus enter into an unholy alliance signalling the degree to which the ethical and the religious is always already enveloped by the political and the national and how this impinges on the poetic. Given McEwan's deep intertextual fascination with Chaucer it is no surprise then that the Middle English "fram every shires ende of Engelond" finds something close to an echo in McEwan's "which the whole country could sense".

Nor do McEwan's allusions to Chaucer end here; on the contrary, the novel's references to Chaucer continue to appear as the text progresses. As soon as one starts looking, quotes from Chaucer and allusions to his work, as well as to medieval English culture in general, fairly pour from the text – evidence that McEwan takes his Chaucer very seriously.

Just how important Chaucer is to McEwan is evinced, for instance, in the following passage that describes how, during her back-breaking training as a nurse, Briony still manages to dedicate half an hour every evening to her writing:

> She was under no obligation to the truth, she had promised no one a chronicle. This was the only place she could be free. She built little stories – not very convincing, somewhat overwritten – around the people on the ward. For a while she thought of herself as a kind of medical Chaucer, whose wards thronged with colourful types, coves, topers, old hats, nice dears with a sinister secret to tell.
>
> (McEwan, *Atonement* 280)

In this passage, the *Canterbury Tales* are explicitly invoked as Briony's literary model, both in regard to her work as an author and to her self-image as a writer. The trappings of a nurse in training conceal "an important writer in disguise" (McEwan, *Atonement* 280), much as the exterior of a late medieval customs official and civil servant disguised Chaucer's social identity as a poet and was deployed to fashion his literary self. And most importantly, neither Chaucer nor his twentieth-century acolyte have any "obligation to the truth".

Even in terms of its topography does Briony's narrative echo Chaucer's account of the Canterbury pilgrimage. Briony's training takes place in one of the oldest hospitals in England, St Thomas', named after Thomas Becket as early as the 13th century – the very saint that Chaucer's pilgrims set out to worship. The text also insists on emphasizing the hospital's specific geographical location. Looking north from its windows, one can make out the Houses of Parliament on the opposite bank of the river Thames. A basic knowledge of London topography assumed, it thus becomes clear that the hospital is to be found in Southwark, the same borough outside medieval London where Chaucer's group of pilgrims assemble for their journey to Canterbury. And when Briony and a fellow-nurse leave the building through the rear entrance, they find themselves in Lambeth Palace Road. Lambeth Palace is, of course, the London resi-dence of the Archbishop of Canterbury, the residence of St Thomas Becket's modern successor in office. It is, as it were, a small piece of Canterbury right outside the gates of the medieval city – and seen from today's perspective, a small piece of Canterbury in the very heart of London. Geographically speaking, the text thus performs the miracle of bilocation. Briony finds herself in the exact place where the pilgrimage to Canterbury begins and, in a sense, also where it should have ended, i.e. in the quarter of London that can be seen as a politico-ecclesiastical extension of Canterbury.[11] It comes as no surprise then that, at the beginning of the novel's epilogue, when Briony is on her way to the Imperial War Museum, the taxi once more takes Briony "towards Lambeth" where she catches "a glimpse of St. Thomas's Hospital" (McEwan, *Atonement* 356). As the narrative prepares for its final surprise, it cannot help but compulsively revisit its Chaucerian topography.

Apart from these strikingly direct references, there is an abundance of less obvious allusions to Chaucer's work and times. I shall mention only some of the most visible: one of Briony's fellow-nurses is called Langland – an allusion to Chaucer's contemporary, the poet William Langland, author of the powerfully penitential religious allegory *Piers Plowman*. On the occasion of their last meeting, her 80-year-old cousin Lola wears a broad-brimmed red hat similar to the one the Wife of Bath famously wears; and the head nurse, Sister Drummond, bears more than a passing – and not entirely suitable – resemblance to Chaucer's Prioress. Nor does McEwan refrain from pointing out the manifold similarities between medieval nuns and the nurses serving in a 20th-century hospital. And even the name of Briony's sister Cecilia may well have been borrowed from *The Second Nun's Tale*, one of the saints' legends in the Canterbury Tales. Moreover, concerns central to the *Canterbury Tales* are invoked in other parts of the novel, too. Thus, Tim Noble has pointed out how Robbie's journey through Northern France resembles a pilgrimage, but one that ends in the grimly apocalyptic scenery of the beaches of Dunkirk (Noble, 'Making Things Up: Narratives of Atonement' 77).

And finally, even in structural terms is there an uncanny resemblance between *Atonement* and the *Canterbury Tales*. Briony's final confession serves as a frame for the narrative of *Atonement* in a fashion not dissimilar from the way the *Canterbury Tales* are framed by the pilgrimage setting. Moreover, just as the *Canterbury Tales* present themselves as something close to a compendium or an encyclopaedia of English narrative genres and styles, so does *Atonement* with its modernist tale within the tale and with its flood of intertextual references that claim the status of an encyclopaedic evocation of English literature. In this context, especially, one might simply argue that Chaucer is deployed once more to invoke a historical ideal of literary Englishness – the ideal of the Great Tradition as founded by the English literary scholar F. R. Leavis between the wars, an ideal on which the classical canon of English literature is founded. After all, it is customary for the Great Tradition to begin with Chaucer (Eagleton, *Literary Theory: An Introduction* 32). But given the insistent presence in the novel of themes such as pilgrimage, confession and penance, themes closely associated with the *Canterbury Tales*, it would seem to be superficial to explain the text's Chaucerian

[11] Ironically, the hospital itself performed a similar miracle since, originally based in Southwark, it was moved to adjoining Lambeth in 1871. But since Lambeth claims only a small stretch of the river bank and Southwark's neighbouring portion of the river bank is even shorter, the move hardly matters in terms of the actual distance traversed.

references purely in terms of an extended intertextual parlour game, or at best an evocation of tradition merely for tradition's sake.

But what exactly is the role that Chaucer is made to perform in this context? What do the allusions to Chaucer accomplish that those to Shakespeare, Austen, James, Woolf and all the rest of the impressive panoply of English literary history do not? And how does Chaucer add to our understanding of the ethical concerns of the narrative conundrum the reader is confronted with at the end?

It appears to me that the references to Chaucer emphasize a much wider range of issues than an exclusive focus on literary modernism and postmodernism would be capable of encompassing. There is the problem of literary atonement, as is prominently displayed in the novel's title itself, and the way that Chaucer time and again negotiates the relation between ethics and narration. When we consider Chaucer's attitude towards the ethics of narrative and of fiction, it is important to keep in mind that he wrote at a time when fiction was not necessarily taken for granted and had to be justified, lest it be condemned as a mere lie and patent untruth. For Chaucer, having "no obligation to the truth" did still matter in ways far more fundamental than it does for (post)modern authors, for whom the liberating potential of fiction has become entirely normal and self-evident. Moreover, truth is a matter of fundamental importance for confessional discourse and, if we are to believe Michel Foucault, confessional discourse itself has been crucial in shaping Western notions of truth and practices of truth-telling as well as Western concepts of subjectivity (Foucault, *The History of Sexuality: An Introduction* 61-2).

At the same time, confessional discourse of all types played a central role in the formation of English literature in the late fourteenth and early fifteenth centuries. Chaucer's contemporary and prime literary interlocutor, John Gower, named his Middle English frame tale narrative the *Confessio Amantis* and Chaucer's most immediate successor, Thomas Hoccleve, introduces a whole variety of confessional settings into his works, e.g. the Prologue to his *Regiment of Princes*, or the authorial voices in a number of other poems such as his *Series*. Middle English authors of Chaucer's time frequently framed literary discourse with confessional discourse in one way or an other, with a fictionalized version of the author playing a pivotal penitential role. These fictionalized versions of the authors tend to be so intriguing because, paradoxically, the more they stress their links to the extra-literary reality of their existence, the more fictional do they actually become. So, it is just before personally encountering the flamboyantly allegorical God of Love in a dream vision, that Chaucer's fictional *alter ego* complains most bitterly and seemingly realistically of his extra-literary toils as a civil servant.

The curious link between confessional discourse and deliberately fictionalized versions of the empirical author is perhaps best encapsulated in the narrative *coup de grâce* that appears to bring Chaucer's curiously unfinished *Canterbury Tales* to an almost violent religious close. At the end of the *Tales*, the poet briefly addresses his audience directly:

> Now preye I to hem alle that herkne this litel tretys or rede, that if there be any thyng in it that liketh hem, that therof they thanken our Lord Jhesu Christ, of whom procedeth al wit and al goodnesse./ And if there be any thyng that displese hem, I preye hem also that they

arrette it to the defaute of myn unkonnynge and nat to my wyl, that wolde ful fayn have
sayd bettre if I hadde had konnynge. / For oure book seith, "Al that is writen is writen for
oure doctrine," and that is myn entente./ Wherfore I biseke yow mekely, for the mercy of
God, that ye preye for me that Crist have mercy on me and foryeve me my giltes;/ and
namely of translacions and enditynges of worldly vanitees, the whiche I revoke in my re-
tracciouns:/ as is the book of Troilus; the book also of Fame; the book of the XXV. La-
dies; the book of the Duchesse; the book of Seint Valentynes day of the Parlement of
Briddes; the tales of Caunterbury, thilke that sownen into synne;/ the book of the Leoun;
and many another book, if they were in my remembrance, and many a song and many a
leccherous lay, that Crist for his grete mercy foryeve me the synne./ But of the translacion
of Boece de Consolacione, and othere bookes of legendes of seintes, and omelies, and
moralitee, and devocioun,/ that thanke I oure Lord Jhesu Crist and his blisful Moder, and
alle the seintes of hevene,/ bisekynge hem that they from hennes forth unto my lyves ende
sende me grace to biwayle my giltes and to studie to the salvacioun of my soule, and
graunte me grace of verray penitence, confessioun and satisfaccioun to doon in this
present lyf,/ thurgh the benigne grace of hym that is kyng of kynges and preest over alle
preestes, that boghte us with the precious blood of his herte,/ so that I may be oon of hem
at the day of doom that shulle be saved./ *Qui cum Patre et Spiritu Sancto vivit et regnat
Deus per omnia secula. Amen.*

                    (*The Canterbury Tales*, Fragment X, ll. 1081-92)

In this passage, several things relevant for readings of *Atonement* all happen
simultaneously. First and foremost, like Briony Tallis in Part IV of the novel, Chaucer
the fictionalized author here speaks to his readers with an immediacy that no longer
permits his audience to see the narrator merely as one of the pilgrims. Instead, what we
now hear is a different voice, one claiming a much closer relationship to the empirical
author Chaucer.

Second, at the very least, there is a structural resemblance between what Chaucer is
doing here and Briony Tallis's statement at the end of her novel. Chaucer performs a
retraccioun, a morally and religiously motivated revocation of his non-religious works –
including the majority of the *Canterbury Tales*, of which this *retraccioun* paradoxically
is itself a part. Chaucer's retraction in the style of a confession claims to be calling most
of his life's work as a poet into question, just as Briony Tallis' confession to the reader
casts doubt on the ethical relevance of her novel. Yet Chaucer's retraction is far more
ambiguous than it appears at first glance. Scholars do not tire of pointing out that this
retraccioun has a paradoxical effect. While the poet busily enumerates and, with very
few exceptions, apparently rejects his works, he simultaneously provides his audience
with an impressively comprehensive catalogue of his oeuvre. The *retraccioun* thus
constitutes a final bid for literary fame. The fact that we do not even know all of the
works mentioned in this list testifies to its very exhaustiveness: it is futile to look for the
"Book of the Lion" in an edition of Chaucer, since this work is lost.

Chaucer's text thus openly indulges in a performative self-contradiction, with the
exact listing of the poet's achievements subverting the tone – and the seriousness? – of
his prayer-like confession. What is supposed to appear as a Christian penitent's
communication with his maker and, simultaneously, a plea for the readers' prayers,
thereby assumes the nature of a self-conscious piece of poetic self-promotion. Even as
the literary voice invites the audience to support the author in his quest for salvation, the

text itself does the exact opposite of what this voice purports to be engaged in. The text establishes a self-confident sense of a literary oeuvre, while the authorial voice calls into question the ethical and spiritual relevance of the major part of that same oeuvre. To a certain degree then, the intentions uttered by the authorial voice must, therefore, be feigned. To put it differently, the seemingly authentic voice focusing exclusively on the ethical and religious value of literature is unmasked as a textual ploy.

In a way, Chaucer's literary penance resembles the medieval genre of the confessio ficti, the confession of a hypocrite, a genre the poet deals with in the character of his Pardoner (Patterson, *Chaucer and the Subject of History* 400). Like the Wife of Bath, with whom he is often compared, the Pardoner delivers a narrative of self-justification in his Prologue. Though in the Pardoner's case, there is precious little to justify – and, indeed, he does not even seem to try. Instead, his confession reads more like an extended boast of his own wickedness, a wickedness all the more damning since he is in the business of selling pardons and indulgences. In other words, the Pardoner earns his livelihood through criminally exploiting the ordinary Christian's desire for salvation. Precisely because the Pardoner is a cog in the later Middle Ages' well-oiled machinery of penance, his own confession largely is about how he is capable of making others confess, though he does so for utterly ulterior motives. And these motives continue to disgust some readers even today. But disgusting though he might appear, the Pardoner proves to be fully aware of the spiritual paradox of his own existence. At one point he explicitly states that, for all the greed and hypocrisy which guide his activities, his brilliant performances as a preacher do, in fact, awaken true contrition in the congregations he addresses and thereby contribute to their salvation. Ironically, his listeners' souls are saved regardless of the fact that his moral persuasiveness is founded on his own greed. It is the emotional effect on the audience, not the preacher's motives that count. The Pardoner's sermons help his audience enter into that state of emotional purity, into the state of contrition, i.e. the unadulterated sorrow for one's own sins, that has, since the Fourth Lateran Council of 1215, been the prerequisite condition for a valid act of penance.[12] As the Pardoner points out in the same breath in which he openly admits both to his greed and his hypocrisy:

> Thus kan I preche agayn that same vice
> Which that I use, and that is avarice.
> But though myself be gilty in that synne,
> Yet kan I maken oother folk to twynne
> From avarice and soore to repente.
> But that is nat my principal entente;
> I preche nothyng but for coveitise.
> Of this mateere it oghte ynogh suffise.

> *(The Canterbury Tales*, Fragment VI, ll. 427-33)

---

[12] For the complex history of medieval confession and especially for the role of the Fourth Lateran Council of 1215 in the shaping of the sacrament of penance see Thomas N. Tentler, *Sin and Confession on the Eve of the Reformation*.

As he says himself, despite his own sinfulness the Pardoner is capable of "maken oother folk to twynne/From avarice and soore to repente." In as much as he provides the necessary state of mind for the successful enactment of the sacrament of penance, the Pardoner is a most effective purveyor of salvation, even though he must assume himself to be ineluctably damned. He reinforces this paradox by concluding that this effect is not, however, his "principal entente". And yet he cannot but be aware of the paradox and make it explicit, as though he might still be entertaining a final hope – a hope against hope, as it were – that his contributions to his fellow-sinners' salvation might in fact open up a loophole to heaven for him. While the fictional Chaucer's own *retraccioun* does not take things remotely as far as does the Pardoner, it clearly exploits a similar sense of performative paradox as it negotiates the tensions between literary and spiritual merit.[13]

How then does the structural resemblance between the ending of the *Canterbury Tales* and that of *Atonement* affect our understanding of the latter?

Let us recall once more what Briony Tallis, the fictional author, has to say about her moral and narrative dilemma:

> There is nothing outside her. In her imagination she has set the limits and the terms. No atonement for God, or novelists, even if they are atheists. It was always an impossible task, and that was precisely the point. The attempt was all.
>
> (McEwan, *Atonement*, 371)

According to Briony, the failure of her literary atonement is due to the basic structural conditions of fictionality. Since the characters she has created are of necessity the products of her own imagination, they must ultimately remain devoid of an autonomous existence and hence incapable of forgiving her. As an almighty creator, Briony claims godlike status – and must, therefore, suffer the consequences. Her suffering does not, however, seem to go beyond a certain point. After all, the 77-year-old writer we encounter at the birthday party that forms the background for her revealing the truth about Cecilia and Robbie is portrayed as a successful celebrity looking back on her life with a high degree of professional and emotional satisfaction. Despite having been diagnosed with dementia, she thoroughly enjoys the hustle and bustle around her, while, for all its tone of regret, her revelation is delivered with the occasional whiff of smugness. After all, this is quite a bombshell to drop on the reader within the final pages of the novel.

Especially against the backdrop of *Atonement*'s many and manifold Chaucerian resonances, the question is thus whether Briony's own analysis of her predicament

---

[13] The allusions to the *Canterbury Tales* and to a specifically medieval topography of London as embodied in Lambeth and St Thomas' hospital does not necessarily mean that McEwan considers himself as a religious writer in the traditional sense. In a number of statements McEwan has explained quite clearly that his preferences lie with what has been called the 'New Atheism'. In McEwan's particular version of this stance the "novel form" is celebrated as a "form of secular religion" that "offers a this-worldly experience of grandeur, consolation, and even redemption" (Bradley, 'The New Atheist Novel: Literature, Religion, and Terror in Amis and McEwan' 22).

really encapsulates all there is to it, or whether it contains, as does Chaucer's retraction, an element of the tongue-in-cheek, whether there are additional paradoxical effects that force us to re-think our response.

Chaucer's own performative paradox in the retraction, we must not forget, can become truly manifest only in the eyes of the very entity he addresses along with God: the reader, the reader whom he speaks to directly: "to hem alle that herkne this litel tretys or rede". This must be a reader fully capable of detecting the discrepancy between the poet's self-conscious evocation of confessional discourse, on the one hand, and his equally self-conscious cataloguing of his *opera omnia*, on the other. In her musings, Briony, the author-narrator of the epilogue seems, however, to be taking very little account of the readers. For her, it is only the relationship between the characters and their creator that appears to be significant, i.e. the God-like power that an author possesses with respect to his literary creation. This might perhaps have been acceptable had *Atonement* been a straightforward, conventional and one-dimensional narrative with a simple plot structure. Yet the ultimate success of Briony's multifaceted intertextual game – or is it McEwan's? – depends on a critical entity capable of registering the full effect of the inextricable contradictions and paradoxical juxtapositions in the novel's maze of focalizers, narrative levels and intertextual references. And that entity must obviously be the reader, factored into this literary equation from the very outset. It is, after all, the reader whom Briony finally entrusts with her confession. And this, I would argue, is the scenario in which some form of atonement can, at the end of the day, be successful. To be sure, atonement is not to be found in a mere plot-twist reuniting the two lovers in fiction while they supposedly perished in real (fictional) life. Instead, atonement, i.e. a sense of redemption, derives from the fact that Briony has fully exposed herself as author-character, and hence her readers, to the horror of the non-atonable. She has done so paradoxically by performatively dedicating a complete novel to the utter and abysmal impossibility of fictional atonement. In purely structural terms, this makes visible the vast extent of her unquenchable thirst for forgiveness, while cancelling out the smugness that seems to accompany her final confession. As we witness a purely fictional eighteen-year-old Briony mustering the courage to face the bitterness and contempt of her victims in the kitchen of a working-class flat, we as readers experience the cathartic effect of this encounter, an encounter that could have served as the perfect climax of the story, were it not for the novel's actual ending. At the end, however, Briony's catharsis appears not merely to be withheld but veritably to be snatched from the reader. What the readers took for straightforward fiction, has now been demoted to the status of a lie within the fiction through "the almost sadistic ingenuity of the novel's final, beautifully delayed revelation" (Bradley, 'The New Atheist Novel' 27). Yet even as readers realize the extent of their loss, they become just as aware of how much they would actually have wanted Briony to be granted this catharsis.[14] As James Phelan has put it, though within the context of a rather different reading:

---

[14]   As Kathleen D'Angelo puts it pithily: "why do we as readers find this version of Robbie and Cecilia's ending particularly satisfying?" (D'Angelo, "'To Make a Novel': The Construction of a Critical Readership in Ian McEwan's *Atonement*" 100).

our emotional trajectory through the problem of the crime and its atonement, however intense and difficult, has been too easy: in retrospect we must admit that we were too ready to believe that Robbie survived the retreat, that Briony's meeting with Robbie and Cecilia would lead to some atonement.

(Phelan, 'Narrative Judgments' 335)

Retroactively, readers are brutally confronted with their own emotional commitment not merely to a happy union of the lovers, but possibly even more so to Briony's redemption. After having retroactively been deprived of Briony's – and our own – catharsis, and the redemption it seemed to promise, we as readers appear to be left with no choice but to accept the second, the Shakespearean part of Briony's self-judgement: "It was always an impossible task, and that was precisely the point. The attempt was all."[15]

But is this really true? After all, the readers' experience is not the same as the fictional author's. Even though Briony, the author-character of the epilogue, may, in purely structural terms, be incapable of truly experiencing the cathartic effect she claims to be craving, we as readers do experience something akin to a catharsis – and we experience it twice! First, when we are offered a scene of redemption within the kitchen-sink-drama setting of Briony's 1940 encounter with Cecilia and Robbie. Second, when we must face our readerly disappointment at realizing that the catharsis we were so ready to embrace is a mere fiction, possibly even a lie, wrapped in a fiction. The very pain of emotional deprivation ushers in an even more radical confrontation with what one might call the ethical desire for closure. Whereas, for the epilogue's Briony, redemption must, indeed, remain unattainable, we as readers actually get a double dose if not of redemption itself, then of the redemptive desire that is its prerequisite. It is our disappointment that paradoxically highlights – and heightens – our wishing for Briony's redemption. As Chaucer's Pardoner has taught us, it is not, first and foremost, the narrator's or the fictional author-character's "principal entente" that matters; rather it is the effect of the Pardoner's sermons – filled to the brim, as they are, with exempla, i.e. fictional accounts of sinners and their fates – that matters. It is the sermons' emotional and spiritual effect on the congregation that pave the road to salvation, not the author's intentions, and certainly not the question of whether the author himself will, in fact, be granted salvation. While neither the Pardoner nor Briony can be granted redemption within the fictional frameworks we encounter them in, the reader will feel something very similar to redemption through the paradoxical emotional reinforcement of a desire first seemingly satisfied and then retroactively destroyed. Despite not working for the fictional Briony herself, *Atonement* is nevertheless capable

---

[15] Elke D'Hoker seems to be following a similar critical trajectory when she argues that it is not absolution that lies at the heart of the literary confession but what "matters is the attempt, the performative process of confessing, which generates and reveals a true story" (D'Hoker, 'Confession and Atonement in Contemporary Fiction: J. M. Coetzee, John Banville, and Ian McEwan' 41). But since D'Hoker focuses on confession as a secular rather than a religious concern, the measure of truth she applies, citing comments Ian McEwan made in an interview, is the "sense of 'reconciliation with self,' 'being at one with oneself'" (ibid. 41-2). Ultimately, D'Hoker's view reduces the novel's message to the psychological satisfaction obviously enjoyed by Briony, the elderly author-character in Part IV of the novel whereas the reader's dissatisfaction at having been duped is not taken into account.

of providing a cognitive equivalent to the emotional and ethical cleansing the reader craves. And as the text's performative paradoxes unfold their meaning in the reader's mind, the reader finds herself/himself extending that sense of desire for redemption toward Briony. This may not quite be the prayer that Chaucer is asking for in his *retraccioun*, but it may still constitute an appropriate response to the performative equivalent of such a request as voiced by someone hoping beyond hope – an emotional response most audiences seem not to have been willing to grant the Pardoner, but one they do seem prepared to grant Briony.

In *Atonement* the history of English Literature is spelt with a huge capital H. From Chaucer's *Canterbury Tales* through the works of Shakespeare and Jane Austen, and so many other representatives of the Great Tradition, English Literature is imagined as engaging with history through the issue of redemption. Literary fiction is shown to have close links to confessional discourse and this close relationship is claimed especially for *English* fiction. Just as the fourteenth-century poet Chaucer embeds his fiction of literary penance within the framing device of a pilgrimage to St Thomas Becket's shrine in Canterbury Cathedral, so does Ian McEwan send his pilgrim to St Thomas' Hospital. But whereas, if only in purely topographical terms, Chaucer's pilgrims never reach the shrine they set out for and Chaucer's Pardoner is given no reason for hope, Briony seems to have succeeded in generating at least some degree of hope through readerly sympathy, as readers feel and sympathetically re-enact within their own souls, with an immediacy they might not otherwise have been capable of experiencing, the sense of disappointment generated through Briony's predicament. Readers may not actually pray for Briony, but they do envelop her with their penitential desire. In as much as Ian McEwan thus appears to be finishing Chaucer's unfinished business, he inserts himself at the very end of English literary history, nay, elevates *Atonement* to the status of its very culmination. Thus, this novel constitutes a historical novel not only in the sense of dealing with historical matter but also in the way it stages itself not merely as a part of the tradition of English literary history, but as something that approaches its redemptive fulfillment. Where Chaucer merely provided a catalogue of his own works, McEwan's all-encompassing intertextual bravura gestures toward an imagined totality of English fiction. But read through the prism of Chaucer's paradoxically tongue-in-cheek retraction, McEwan's bid for literary fame does not look quite as immodest as this conclusion seems to suggest. After all, in a manner that resembles the way in which Chaucer's *Retraction* forcibly reminds us that his literary pilgrims will never actually reach their goal, will never arrive at Canterbury, readers of *Atonement* find themselves experiencing penitential desire most effectively through a paradoxical form of closure ultimately withheld. Here, too, the business can be finished only by remaining unfinished. Like Chaucer's *Canterbury Tales*, *Atonement* thus imagines English literature as a never-ending pilgrimage of penitential desire, a form of desire most acutely felt through an awareness that it can never truly be fulfilled in literature.

Works Cited

Adney, Karley K. 'These Ghosts Will Be Lovers: The "Cultural Haunting" of Class Consciousness in Ian McEwan's Atonement.' *The Ghostly and the Ghosted in Literature and Film*. Eds. Lisa Kröger and Melanie R. Anderson. Newark, DE: University of Delaware Press, 2013. 47-58.

Albers, Stefanie, and Torsten Caeners. 'The Poetics and Aesthetics of Ian McEwan's Atonement.' *English Studies* 90 (2009): 707-20.

Atonement. Dir. Joe Wright. Universal Pictures, 2007.

Behrman, Mary. 'The Waiting Game: Medieval Allusions and the Lethal Nature of Passivity in Ian McEwan's Atonement.' *Studies in the Novel* 42 (2010): 453-70.

Benson, Larry D., ed. *The Riverside Chaucer*. 3rd ed. with a new foreword by Christopher Cannon. Oxford: Oxford University Press, 2008.

Bradley, Arthur. 'The New Atheist Novel: Literature, Religion, and Terror in Amis and McEwan.' *Yearbook of English Studies* 39 (2009): 20-38.

Cormack, Alastair. 'Postmodernism and the Ethics of Fiction in Atonement.' *Ian McEwan: Contemporary Critical Perspectives*. Ed. Sebastian Groes. London: Continuum, 2009. 70-82.

D'Angelo, Kathleen. '"To Make a Novel': The Construction of a Critical Readership in Ian McEwan's Atonement." *Studies in the Novel* 41 (2009): 88-105.

D'Hoker, Elke. 'Confession and Atonement in Contemporary Fiction: J. M. Coetzee, John Banville, and Ian McEwan.' *Critique* 48-1 (2006): 31-43.

Eagleton, Terry. *Literary Theory: An Introduction*. Oxford: Blackwell, 1983.

Eliot, T. S. 'The Waste Land, 1922.' *The Complete Poems and Plays*. London: Faber and Faber, 1969. 59-75.

Finney, Brian. *English Fiction since 1984: Narrating a Nation*. Houndmills: Palgrave Macmillan, 2006.

Foucault, Michel. *The History of Sexuality: An Introduction*. Trans. Robert Hurley. Vol. I. New York: Vintage, 1990.

Hidalgo, Pilar. 'Memory and Storytelling in Ian McEwan's Atonement.' *Critique* 46 (2005): 82-91.

Maragonis, Maria. 'The Anxiety of Authenticity: Writing Historical Fiction at the End of the Twentieth Century.' *History Workshop* 65 (2008): 138-60.

McEwan, Ian. *Atonement*. London: Vintage, 2002.

Noble, Tim. 'Making Things Up: Narratives of Atonement.' *Communio Viatorum* 52-1 (2010): 68-82.

Patterson, Lee. *Chaucer and the Subject of History*. Madison: The University of Wisconsin Press, 1991.

Phelan, James. 'Narrative Judgments and the Rhetorical Theory of Narrative: Ian McEwan's Atonement.' *A Companion to Narrative Theory*. Eds. James Phelan and Peter J. Rabinowitz. Oxford: Blackwell, 2005. 322-36.

Schwalm, Helga. 'Figures of Authorship, Empathy, & The Ethics of Narrative (Mis) Recognition in Ian McEwan's Later Fiction.' *Anglistik und Englischunterricht* 73 (2009): 174-85.

Tentler, Thomas N. *Sin and Confession on the Eve of the Reformation*. Princeton: Princeton University Press, 1977.

Vaccarella, Maria. "'A Kind of Medical Chaucer': Testimony, Storytelling and Caregiving in Ian McEwan's Atonement." *Challenges for the 21st Century: Dilemmas, Ambiguities, Directions*. Eds. Rosy Colombo, Lilla Maria Crisafulli and Franca Ruggieri. Papers from the 24th AIA Conference, Vol. I: Literary Studies. Rome: Edizioni Q, 2011.

RENATE BROSCH

Thomas Cromwell, Our Contemporary: The Poetics of Subjective Experience as Intersubjective Ethics in *Wolf Hall*

From its beginning historical fiction stood in complementary opposition to historiography while literary criticism struggled to distinguish between them. As Ann Rigney points out,

> what defines the historical novel as a genre is precisely the interplay between invented story elements and historical ones. As novels, they are written under the aegis of the fictionality convention whereby the individual writer enjoys the freedom to invent […] a world 'uncommitted to reality'. As historical novels, however, they also link up with the ongoing collective attempts to represent the past and invite comparison with what is already known about the historical world from other sources. […] They are not 'free-standing fictions' […], they also call upon prior historical knowledge, echoing and/or disputing other discourses about the past.
>
> (Rigney, *Imperfect Histories* 19)

Authors have been unusually self-conscious about the genre, supplying paratexts, such as the pseudo-veracity of the 'Author's Note' (Walter Scott) to elucidate the way their fiction intersects with history. Until the present day, authors continue to include commentary, references and disavowals, negotiating the relationship. These inclusions demonstrate an awareness of the strangeness of writing historical fiction. The double nature of the genre as a faithful representation and an imaginative extension gratifies two opposing desires in readers: to actively contribute their share of framing historical knowledge, on the one hand, but also to be hoodwinked into an alternative universe on the other.

Every encounter with history's complexity in narrative pivots on a polarity between the strange and the familiar, between feelings of distance and proximity to historical figures; emphasizing one of these poles too strongly leads to pitfalls of different kinds. A too familiar past construed of cliché and stereotype makes history a usable resource, something that seems to be available without intermediary and translation – a commodity for instant consumption. Looking at the strangeness of history has a different effect: it offers surprise and amazement; such a view of the past detached from present concerns is prone to esoteric exoticism or worse Orientalist notions of superiority (Wineburg, *Historical Thinking and Other Unnatural Acts* 5).

These contrasting options have resulted in an extraordinary spectrum of realizations in historical fictions, including not just 'highbrow' and 'lowbrow' but also quite frequently novels that occupy a middle ground between popular and highbrow fictions.

According to Perry Anderson, it is the particular variability of the genre that sets the historical novel apart from other narrative forms (Anderson, 'From Progress to Catastrophe'). While most literary genres have generated a variety of registers and derive vitality from interactions between high and low, elite and popular forms, the peculiarity of the historical novel seems to be to elude any stable stratification of high and low. The reason lies not just in the development of the genre but also in an oscillating continuum of registers within individual works. As Wineburg points out, the tension is necessary because both aspects of history – the familiar and the strange – are indispensable. We need to feel kinship with the people of the past and we need to realize that their circumstances were different (Wineburg, *Historical Thinking and Other Unnatural Acts* 5-6). Like detective fiction, the historical novel faces the problem of making the familiar entertaining, to create suspense where the outcome is clear. Strategies of popular fiction may help to solve this problem.

Since the 1970s we have been invited to value scholarship that questions the dichotomies on which we rely to organize our knowledge and understanding. It has become a scholarly convention that rigid binary oppositions must be broken down and third spaces between them valorized. With respect to the topic at hand, we have become accustomed to regard as particularly advanced and innovative studies that interrogate the distinction between fiction and history (A. Nünning, 'Verbal Fictions?' 354). It was especially Hayden White's *Metahistory* (1973) and his *Tropics of Discourse* (1978) which inaugurated this radical deconstruction of boundaries in the field. White claimed that "viewed [...] as verbal artefacts histories and novels are indistinguishable from one another", in other words fictions and histories are subject to the same narrative use of language and narrative is never neutral (White, *Tropics of Discourse* 121-22). His view of historiography as emplotted in narrative and shaped by conceptual metaphors opened up an incisive new perspective for historians and proved productive for scrutinizing implicit ideologies in history writing. In literary criticism, this theoretical position lent itself particularly well to an analysis of those narratives which accompanied or even prompted the theory, since postmodern instances of the historical novel themselves made disciplinary, generic and aesthetic boundaries between factual and fictive histories permeable.

In what is often assessed as a 'resurgence of the historical novel as a "serious" genre' after the Second World War (Boccardi, *The Contemporary British Historical Novel* 26), virtually every rule of the classical canon, as laid down by Georg Lukács, was flouted or reversed. Authors no longer aspired to the total representation of a trans-formation of human lives reshaped by social forces.[1] Among other traits, the postmodern historical novel freely mixed times, combining or interweaving past and

---

[1] Georg Lukács describes the historical novel as a simultaneous presentation of historical necessity and of the human experience of social forces. Its extensive, epic representation shows how human beings and their society develop as part of a process which includes and envelops the present. This model of the genre, based on a concept of history as dialectical progress, was built around the formative work of Walter Scott. Lukács's genre theory is part of his larger claims in preference of realist narratives that enable the reader to 'reexperience the social and human motives which led men to think, feel and act just as they did in historical reality' (Lukács, *Historical Novel* 42, see also Jameson, *Marxism and Form* 196-198).

present, paraded the author within the narrative, took leading historical figures as central rather than marginal characters, strewed anachronisms, mixed genres and voices, multiplied alternative endings, and played with counterfactuals. These artistic expressions of postmodernity, famously termed 'historiographic metafiction' by Linda Hutcheon, playfully interrogate and subvert conventional views of the past (Hutcheon, 'Historiographic Metafiction' 5).[2]

Within the paradigms of deconstructivism and New Historicism, any attempt to distinguish fiction from historical narrative is doomed to failure. Dorrit Cohn's claim that the latter are subject to "judgements of truth and falsity" (Cohn, *The Distinction of Fiction* 15) seems entirely discredited in view of the present acknowledgement of the ubiquity of narrative and the notion that "[t]here is no textual property, syntactic, or semantic, that will identify a text as a work of fiction" (Searle, 'The Logical Status of Fictional Discourse' 325). That the past is not a finite accessible entity frozen in history but something that is constantly reshaped and resurrected in narratives as part of a dialogic process between authors, readers and their narratives has become received academic opinion. But the fortunate overlap between literature and theory during the last decades of the twentieth century has ended, and to reiterate Hutcheon's and White's well-known insights does not seem as innovative as it did in the 1980s.

The negotiation of past and present must remain a defining characteristic of the historical novel. This negotiation is not just a matter of content; it is realized in the discourse, perspective structure and diegesis, to name only those elements of the narration which I will comment on in the following. If we look not at the sources or themes of this literature but at its forms and its effects, a more nuanced picture emerges. In Rigney's definition quoted above there is a circumspect reference to the fictionality of historical fictions. Maybe the component that imagination and composition add to the narrative is not as self-explanatory as it appears. After all, the historical novel is bound to history and historiography in terms of content only. Its fictionality comes to the fore in the formal structure of the representation. The license of fictionality is realized in the poetics of the historical novel, i.e. in its formal features, style, discourse, deixis and perspective. Every fictional history is predicated on an idea of its culture; thus it contains a reflection of cultural identity politics. But because historical novels must confront the conventions of fiction as well, their politics are realized partly through their poetics.[3] Reinhart Koselleck therefore demands that an interpretation of a historical novel must give priority to the formal composition and the poetics of representation (Koselleck, *Vergangene Zukunft* 131; qtd. in Geppert, *Der Historische Roman* 153).

In the following case study I try to acknowledge this priority. My example is Hilary Mantel's *Wolf Hall* (2009), an extraordinary novel in which postmodern scepticism

---

[2] Fredric Jameson, by contrast, does not share Hutcheon's optimistic view of the interventionist effects of postmodern writing (Hutcheon, 'Historiographic Metafiction' 5). For Jameson, the historical novel has "fallen into disrepute and infrequency" because capitalist media society has deadened a sense of history. In postmodernism historical fiction resurrects history only in a ludic or 'pastiche' manner (Jameson, *Postmodernism* 284).

[3] „Die Poetik des historischen Romans interpretiert ihre historische Seite nahezu ausschließlich als stoffliche Gebundenheit, während die jeweils ausgeführte Form der Darstellung das fiktionale Element enthält" (Schabacher, *Topik der Referenz* 94).

towards historical truth manifests itself in a muted manner: obvious counterfactuality or metafictionality is avoided, but the narrative technique is innovative nevertheless. I want to account as precisely as possible for the extraordinary success of this novel in creating suspense although all its major events and characters are well-known. I am convinced that this success results from a peculiar mixture of styles and registers: *Wolf Hall* combines the narrative techniques of high modernism with those of contemporary popular fictions, it presents a hero-story in a complicated narrative perspective, with the result that its peculiar mixture of fanciful and plausible accounts of the past are legitimized by their subjectivity. By examining the way tense, deixis, characterization and description work, I aim to grasp the peculiar contemporaneity of the hero figure.

A cautionary note seems necessary at this point: I do not advocate a formalist analysis as an end in itself, I hope that my response-oriented interpretation can map how form translates into function, or, in other words, how the poetics of representation informs its politics. The idea that 'the content of a work of art stands judged by its form' is part of the dialectical materialist methods of Fredric Jameson and the Marxist critics he discusses approvingly in *Marxism and Form* (55). I believe that textual analysis can demonstrate the effect of a novel's narrative technique not only in individual terms but in terms of its contribution to cultural discourse as well. In my understanding, fictional narrative also monitors intersubjectivity by addressing the reader, instructing her to react to it in a preferred way. My reading is thus based on the assumption that the formal and stylistic aspects of a novel which determine the experience of the reader influence its social and ethical function as well. This is not a new position, it is an argument that goes right back to Lukács himself but is being further developed at present by critics such as Martha Nussbaum and Timothy O'Leary. I would, however, offer the suggestion that the historical novel is perhaps the genre best suited to produce the kind of reading experience that occasions what O'Leary terms 'ethical transformation' (O' Leary, *Foucault and the Art of Ethics* 15; see also Jameson, *Marxism* 173).

It is the privilege of the historical novel to revise traditional historiography, to question conventional assumptions governing a dominant view of the past, and to shift centre stage things and people hitherto neglected. At the same time, writing historical novels can be understood as what Jan Assmann calls a commemorative practice ('kulturelle Mnemotechnik') which invokes a counter-present ('kontrapräsentisch'), so that its projections of historical values and ideas are placed against contemporary ones (Assmann, *Das kulturelle Gedächtnis* 227). *Wolf Hall's* revision of history as well as its engagement with present-day values hinges on its protagonist. The novel's choice of main protagonist has baffled critics: He is Thomas Cromwell, the political councilor of Henry VIII. Cromwell was widely hated in his lifetime and he makes a surprising fictional hero today. His main activities in law, financial and bureaucratic administration are not obvious material for fiction. Indeed, "the pop-Foucauldian worldview of much historical fiction since the 1980s would see his bureaucratic innovations as inherently sinister" (Tayler, 'Henry's Fighting Dog').

Some periods have fired the imagination of later generations in such a way that they have become favourites of historical writing; one of these is certainly the time of Henry VIII. For historians, the central issue here is the 'Tudor Revolution', as the historian Geoffrey Elton calls it, by which the British state supposedly won independence from foreign and ecclesiastic rule. For historical fictions, Henry's divorces and wives have proved fertile ground for generations of British readers, movie goers and TV viewers. As a special chapter in Jerome de Groot's recent study of the historical novel proves, the story of Anne Boleyn has been a favourite which is returned to constantly, in partic- ular in historical romances aimed at a female market (de Groot, *The Historical Novel* 69-78). Anne Boleyn shares with Thomas Cromwell an adequate amount of gaps in biographical information that has allowed novelists great latitude in exploring sensation, intrigue and passion, representing either woman's martyrdom or her ambition and cruelty.

In these fictions Cromwell has typically featured as Machiavellian arch villain who manipulates and tortures when engineering the break with Rome to pursue his own power. According to de Groot "this important figure has been reduced in popular cul- ture to a plotting bureaucrat spy-master" (de Groot, *The Historical Novel* 74). But even in the scholarly *Oxford Dictionary of National Biography* he is 'tyrannical' and 'unprincipled' in his policy, and displays a combination of 'cruelty' and 'abject submissiveness' in his behavior at court (*DNB*, 'Cromwell, Thomas' 200). One recent biographer, Robert Hutchinson, portrayed Cromwell as a corrupt proto-Stalinist and in Robert Bolt's *A Man for All Seasons* he sadistically hounds a saintly Thomas More to his death of martyrdom. More and Cromwell were enemies, and cultural memory has taken More's side.

Mantel's novel reinterprets both historical figures: her Cromwell seeks reconcilia- tion between religious extremists, whereas her More seeks absolute conformity. Mantel's Cromwell is not vengeful: when he interviews More in the Tower, he wants to give him an opportunity to save his life, as we find out from his inner deliberations which Mantel invented contrary to historical evidence (*Wolf Hall* 591-92; *DNB*, 'Cromwell, Thomas' 199). Mantel's More is vain, arrogant and unrelenting. In attempting to extinguish both Tyndale and his influence, he holds torturing heretics or tricking them into a confession to be a 'blessed' act. "It is a shocking revision of this reader's pieties, brilliantly done", admits Claudia FitzHerbert (FitzHerbert, review of *Wolf Hall*).

The comment points to one of the main functions of the genre, its intervention with tradition. However, in the reading of this long novel, it becomes increasingly clear that not history is the important thing but memory, "the construction and interpretation of the past from the point of view of the present" (V. Nünning, 'The Invention of Cultural Traditions' 73). *Wolf Hall* seems to engage less with historiography than with other historical fictions. Its target is not serious history writing but the bulk of popular histori- cal fictions which have compressed the Reformation controversies into an opposition between Cromwell and More. Yet it references no identifiable fiction in particular but the way cultural memory as a collective resource preserves the past. In contrast to historiography, cultural memory is conceived as "a virtual space which is organized by rituals, semiotic objects and systems and processes of oral, written and visual communication" (Gymnich, Nünning, and Sommer, 'Gauging the Relation between Literature and Memory' 3). By fictionalizing history, historical novels can affect cultural memory, that elusive storehouse of images which shapes the shifting ground of a culture's identity. Cultural memory centres around significant events and larger-than- life figures. As John Fowles points out, "What Robin Hood was, or who he was, in the dim underwoods of history, is unimportant. It is what folk history has made him that matters" (Fowles, 'On Being English but Not British' 158). By constructing and deconstructing these icons, historical novels participate in the constant rewriting of memory. *Wolf Hall* rehabilitates Cromwell against traditional icons like More.

For this revisionist approach to cultural memory the novel needed to make Cromwell a hero. It does this with great aplomb: Cromwell's mind is the filter for everything that happens and Cromwell's mind is in many ways a modern mind, a mind of today. The novel's narrative perspective maintains a strict intra- and homodiegetic focalization, so that everything is seen through Cromwell's eyes.[4] It is Cromwell's perception that guarantees textual coherence and defines the vision of the world represented since it sets the limits of what is possible within this world. The narrative technique of *Wolf Hall* thus stands in direct opposition to traditional conceptions of the genre.

In her defense of the fundamental distinction between history and fiction, Dorrit Cohn insists that the difference lies in the area of voice, i.e. in perspective and focalization. She claims that authors of 'serious', 'scholarly' history or biography would never quote a character's thoughts other than their own (Cohn, *The Distinction of Fiction* 117). As Philippe Carrard has noted, Cohn overstates her case somewhat; historians do sometimes surmise their characters' thoughts (Carrard, 'The Distinction of Historiography' 128). But the point remains valid that fictions raise greater expectations of intimate, lived experience. Lukács was aware of the problem when he opined that historical narratives will focus on mediocre characters of no great distinction and that famous historical figures will be oblique or marginal (Lukács, *The Historical Novel* 33, 39). Besides a Marxist objection to histories of great men or their ideas, the central position of famous historical individuals undermined, for Lukács, the genre's aim to present social transformation in the light of 'everyday lives' and 'lived experience' (Jameson, *Marxism and Form*. 194). This reticence with regard to 'real' famous people is still noted in a recent description of the practice: 'historical novels often tend to eschew dramatizing the lives of well-known "real" figures' (de Groot, *The Historical Novel* 10).

The intention behind focusing on fictitious rather than historical persons is to offer an individual perspective on well-known events. But by concentrating on fictive characters in period settings and thus introducing character interest into known facts, historical novels encounter further problems: they have to confront the gap between factual history and lived experience. One strategy to skirt the problem of truth and invention is to make the perception of events an explicitly subjective one. This strategy was not recommended in traditional studies of the historical novel. According to Peter Demetz, for instance, there are good reasons for having a distanced narrator to survey, order, and reflect the events. In making a character's experience central to the narrative, authors would sacrifice a panoramic overview and with it analysis and assessment. Moreover, Demetz claims that the articulation of emotional preverbal experience in well-shaped verbal composition would appear absurd (Demetz, *Formen des Realismus* 25).

---

[4]   In a single brief moment of inconsistency, *Wolf Hall* describes Cromwell from an external perspective at the beginning (Mantel, *Woolf Hall* 31). I am not sure how to explain this short departure, especially as Mantel recently criticized young British novelists for their "inability to keep the viewpoint steady" (McIntyre, *Point of View in Plays* 1).

Significantly, the historical novel did not favour modernism's representation of interior consciousness. According to Fredric Jameson, modernism's subjective form of narration with each consciousness a 'closed world' is a regrettable 'monadic relativism'. Hence a reason for the genre's distance to modernist forms might be that a primacy of immediate subjective perception makes the representation of 'social totality' impossible (Jameson, *Postmodernism* 412).

What Demetz and Jameson perceive as an oddity *Wolf Hall* embraces with a vengeance: it emplots history as a history of the mind, choosing to offer its readers not only a 'real' historical person as central hero figure but to concentrate exclusively on an imaginative rendering of his individual perception, thus creating an engulfing illusion of proximity to the focalizer. This enables the novel to fuse two traditions – the popular and the serious. As mentioned above, it is constitutive of the historical novel that the values, norms and beliefs of the fictional world and those of the reader do not match. Many conventional historical novels aim to minimize the mismatch. *Wolf Hall* tackles the task by taking us directly into the perception of its central character. Yet, its success does not necessarily prove Jameson wrong, because its strict focalization does not replicate modernism's commitment to the primacy of interiority. As I will try to demonstrate, its poetics of subjective experience serves to make the personality of Cromwell mysterious rather than to disclose it.[5]

On the one hand, homodiegetic focalization turns Cromwell into one of the most appealing and enlightened characters of the period. On the other, it is clear from the start that he is as cunning as legend has it and his flashback memories when he is Cardinal Wolsey's backstairs manoeuvrer hint at an unsavoury past. While we are invited to participate in his perception and 'mind style' we are also intrigued by his ambiguous personality (Semino, 'A Cognitive Stylistic Approach to Mind Style in Narrative Fiction' 97). This is a strategy familiar from contemporary crime novels, in which the appeal of the hero rests on his fascinating resemblance to the criminals he is pursuing. This double nature is made manifest in a startling use of ekphrasis: the novel recounts the painting of Hans Holbein's famous portrait of Cromwell now in the Frick collection in New York, which offers the reader a powerful aid to visualization. Since homodiegetic focalization omits the external appearance of the focalizer, a portrait scene can be a reminder of an alternative assessment. According to *Wolf Hall*, the painting shows a shrewd, unfriendly man, holding a folded paper "like an upturned dagger". Characteristically laconic, Cromwell comments, 'I look like a murderer'. And his son answers, 'Didn't you know' (Mantel, *Wolf Hall* 527).

To even the balance, Mantel elaborates the scant historical evidence concerning his early life by imagining a miserable childhood for Cromwell as the son of a violent

---

[5] My concept of focalization in this article is a broad one, including not only visual perception but also incorporating all kinds of mental processes of the character who focalizes as in Manfred Jahn's 'Windows of Focalization'. As Jahn's model indicates, focalization may be predominantly associated with the representation of consciousness, but it does not necessarily have to depict interiority and self-reflexion.

blacksmith in Putney.[6] The novel begins with an empathy-producing episode in which he is almost kicked to death by his raging, alcoholic father. Technically, the primacy of individual perception which Jameson thinks detrimental to historical narratives is rigorously pursued:

> So now get up.
> Felled, dazed, silent, he has fallen; knocked full length on the cobbles of the yard. His head turns sideways; his eyes are turned towards the gate, as if someone might arrive to help him out. One blow, properly placed, could kill him now.
> Blood from the gash on his head – which was his father's first effort – is trickling across his face. Add to this, his left eye is blinded; but if he squints sideways, with his right eye he can see that the stitching of his father's boot is unravelling. The twine has sprung clear of the leather, and a hard knot in it has caught his eyebrow and opened another cut.
> (Mantel, *Wolf Hall* 3)

As this is the novel's first paragraph, we do not even know who 'he' is. The passage makes no allowances for the convention of an accessible beginning; instead, it takes the reader right into Cromwell's experiencing consciousness. Subsequently, we will discover the fractured syntax and present tense of interior monologue, but interior monologue is normally rendered in first person or elided first person. *Wolf Hall* renders an interior monologue voice in third person, thus producing an extended novel-length experiential perspective. The use of 'he' is unusually difficult and confusing in this novel as countless commentators on the internet complain. The deixis of grammatical person is supposed to synchronize a text's references with the articulating or narrating voice; and the third person pronoun, in contrast to the first person pronoun, requires a referential noun in the near vicinity in order to be identifiable.[7] In *Wolf Hall* deixis is obscure because Cromwell's thoughts are given in the third person, and hence 'he' is

---

6   That his father was a blacksmith as well as a shearer of cloth and kept a hostelry and brewing house in Putney is confirmed by the *Oxford Dictionary of National Biography* ('Cromwell, Thomas' 192).

7   Traditional linguistic analysis explains anaphoric use of personal pronouns as 'referring back to' an antecedent mention of a character by name. On this view, the mind would search back through text read earlier like a computer to find out which person 'he' or 'she' refers to by a 'slot-filling' approach. But this is not how we read, as Catherine Emmott has shown (Emmott, 'Consciousness and Context' 86). In contrast to a computer, "we do not just retain in our minds a character's name for assigning future pronoun slots, we […] form a mental representation of the character" (Emmott, 'Consciousness and Context' 87). This requires 'visualization', retaining an image as long as the character remains relevant to the narrative. Mention of a pronoun, immediately brings forward the visualization held backstage of the mind. If a pronoun is indeterminate, we have to quickly try the fit of possible characters and decide for the most plausible. Merely recovering the most proximate mention of a suitably gendered character by name, would in a lot of cases not lead to a satisfying result. Through activating our visualization of characters and our hypotheses for their behaviour which are available in our working memory we can decode efficiently and correctly (Brosch, 'Visualisierungen in der Leseerfahrung' 58). This shows yet again that a categorizing approach which understands deixis as anchoring devices is inadequate. Instead of regarding deixis as a stable factor in narrative, we must consider the dynamics of deictic shift theory.

easily confused with references to other male characters. The confusing use of personal pronouns creates small spaces of dissonance for the reader who is jolted out of an easy immersive reading for illusion.

Since everything is focalized through Cromwell's eyes, the novel lacks postmodern multiple perspectives. Yet it does not recuperate the distanced narration typical of realist historical novels either. Instead of presenting a narrator or character who looks back on the story he tells, explaining and justifying actions and events, Mantel has chosen to make the experiencing Cromwell the focus of the whole unfolding chain of events. Her choice is partly motivated by characterization: Cromwell is genial and urbane, but also reticent and sly; he has a dark and violent past to hide and would never tell his story to anyone. Moreover, he is not given to self-examination and his motivations are never fully analyzed. This is an issue I will return to. More technically, the focalization opens the experiencing eye *in actu* to the reader, his now and here limits the horizon of his perception and restricts his insight into the consequences of his actions. The effect of these defamiliarizations is to place the reader at a remove from well-known Tudor history into a veritable maelstrom of unpredictable events.

Ordinarily, historical novels purport to explain history from a later perspective. The narrative technique of *Wolf Hall* denies us this latter-day advantage while it demands a considerable knowledge of early modern English history. We are caught in the experiencing moments of Cromwell and in his lack of knowledge of the future. Cromwell is ignorant of what is to come and while we are developing an immense liking for him our fears for his future increase. *Wolf Hall* thrusts us into history, not as a linear procession of events, but as an ongoing cognitive process accompanied by reminiscences, hopes and speculations as well as misapprehensions, "we are not looking back at a path through time, but trying to find our way onward, and uncertainty reigns" (Caines, 'Arrange One's Face'). We have to constantly resort to extratextual frameworks of knowledge to supplement the story. The effect is dramatic irony with a vengeance. As educated readers, we know most of Cromwell's future, his fall from fortune and his execution, yet the protagonist-focalizer knows only the past, the present and possibilities. This is narrative strategy in the service of irony, and it reaches its apex at the very end of the novel, when Cromwell is at the height of his power. He has started to fancy Jane Seymour and a brief visit to *Wolf Hall*, the Seymour family seat, sounds promising: "'Five days,' he says. 'Wolf Hall'" (Mantel, *Wolf Hall* 650). That is the last sentence of the book, and portentous with regard to events to come. From the depiction of the Seymour family we know that Wolf Hall is a site of scandal, a place where men prey on women and the old on the young. It is also the place where – according to history – Jane first caught Henry's eye. Thus the portentous name that recalls Hobbes's phrase *homo homini lupus* serves as a reminder of uncomfortable events that fall outside the book's time scheme.[8]

After the beating which opens the novel, Cromwell runs away from home and we meet him next 30 years later. Of the years in between we only learn what Cromwell's recollections reveal, which is not much: some years as a mercenary in France, some

---

[8]   At the time this essay was written the sequel to the novel had not been published. Now that it is, it has become apparent that the author is just as reluctant to let her hero die as I assume readers to be.

more with bankers in Florence, some time as a clothier, some more as a lawyer. As we also follow his winding quest for his own lost history in vivid flashbacks, what surfaces in fragments from the past are often acts better forgotten. In an early episode we see him evading an imagined attack by Wolsey with the swiftness of somebody who is used to assassins lurking in the shadows. In explanation he admits that he has killed a man (Mantel, *Wolf Hall* 71-73). We witness the working of memory not as an interior self-reflexive activity but as a conscious construction: "It is early in their association and his character as invented by the cardinal, is at this stage a work in progress" (Mantel, *Wolf Hall* 73). The novel foregrounds the topic of memory by staging Cromwell's recollections as a significant aspect of his self-fashioning.

On the continent, Cromwell has mastered an Italian technique that allows him to store stunning amounts of information in his memory (Mantel, *Wolf Hall* 79). He knows the entire New Testament by heart. In another ekphrastic scene his skill is linked to classical descriptions of *ars memoria*. He memorizes the seating of guests at a dinner table as in the famous legend of Simonides, signaling to the educated reader the future downfall of aristocratic society. Thus the protagonist performs acts of memory that are at the core of the novel's engagement with the past, reminding readers how dependent we are on iconic items from cultural memory and how refreshing it can be to rearrange these.

Figuring out this Byronic hero of the 21st century is made attractive for the reader through the discrepancy between what we are told and what we know. The discrepancy would be difficult to cope with if our comprehension depended on his focalized narrative alone. But fortunately, as Alan Palmer shows, this is not the case; from constant practice in real life, the reader is able to construct 'continuing consciousness' for a variety of mental realities in different characters simply from descriptions of their behavior and from the content and inflection in their speech.[9] *Wolf Hall* makes this organizational process difficult, but because we are not only adept but particularly clever at reading other minds from external appearances, we enjoy relativizing Cromwell's perception of himself once we have learnt to sort out the text's attributions. In spite of the necessity to prime the reader at the beginning of a narrative, the beginning of the story proper in chapter II already exhibits all the difficulties of *Wolf Hall's* extravagant narrative technique:

> II: Paternity 1527.
> So: Stephen Gardiner. Going out, as he's coming in. It's wet, and for a night in April, unseasonably warm, but Gardiner wears furs, which look like oily and dense black feathers; he stands now, ruffling them, gathering his clothes about his tall straight person

---

[9]   Our ideas of characters' minds are not restricted to those passages where these characters are focalizers or to their episodes of inner speech, otherwise we would – in a novel like *Wolf Hall* – never know what is going on. As readers in general we adjust our 'fictional encyclopaedia' to contain the knowledge of all the characters. Indeed, this is what we derive a lot of our enjoyment in reading from, that we perceive the differences and conflicts between the different characters' views of story worlds and generate hierarchical relations to them. Epistemic imbalance between the characters generates plot and drives the reader's interest. According to Palmer, the readers' representation of an actual story world is most of the time more accurate than any single character's view (Palmer, *Fictional Minds* 197).

like black angel's wings.
'Late,' Master Stephen says unpleasantly.
He is bland. 'Me, or your good self?'
'You.' He waits.
'Drunks on the river. The boatmen say it's the eve of one of their patron saints.'
'Did you offer a prayer to her?'
'I'll pray to anyone, Stephen, till I'm on dry land.'
'I'm surprised you didn't take an oar yourself. You must have done some river work, when you were a boy.'
Stephen sings always on one note. Your reprobate father. Your low birth. Stephen is supposedly some sort of semi-royal by-blow: brought up for payment, discreetly, as their own, by discreet people in a small town. They are wool-trade people, whom Master Stephen resents and wishes to forget; and since he himself knows everybody in the wool trade, he knows too much about his past for Stephen's comfort. The poor orphan boy!
(Mantel, *Wolf Hall* 17)

Suspense, then, is generated in *Wolf Hall* primarily through the mystery of its hero which readers will seek to unravel. Several stylistic features serve to enhance this appeal to a detecting reader: the fragmented syntax of interior monologue stalls the attribution of observations to their proper fictional referents. The problem is later aggravated by the presence of at least as many Thomases in the story as Henry VIII had wives: Wolsey, More, Cranmer, Cromwell, Howard (Third Duke of Norfolk), Wriothesley (First Earl of Southampton). Grammatical modes disguise identities; like low-born Cromwell, readers are outsiders who have to learn to decode the intricacies of court society. When Cromwell asks, "'Me or your good self?'", the text may be said to ironically address the uncertainty about identities which is at the core of its deictic difficulty for the reader.

Besides the third person pronoun, further deictic difficulties slow down the reading process because they demand constant attention to grammatical constructions. For one thing, Cromwell's references to himself ('your reprobate father') are in second person, perhaps mentally quoting Gardiner, and therefore do not grammatically match the experiencing narration. While we are turning back pages to make sure we know who said or did what, we are temporarily removed from the fictional world. Moreover, in the passage above we may note an unfamiliar combination of tense with adverbial deictic markers. The momentariness of narration in the present tense is foregrounded by the use of a sports reporter 'now' as if referring to an actual ongoing event ('he stands now' 17).[10] In order to imagine the situation, we have to step into Cromwell's shoes, as it were, for the moment. *Wolf Hall* does not allow a fictionalizing distance; everything is actual in the mind of Cromwell and the emphasis is squarely on his here and now.

For a historical novel the present tense is still somewhat unusual, but to *Wolf Hall*'s experiential approach it is brilliantly appropriate. It creates a sense of momentariness that seems natural and genuine (*sensu* Fludernik) in the oral concurrent reporting of

---

[10] Linguists speak of a typical 'clash' between the deixis of the verb and adverbial deixis, when the verb is in the past tense and the temporal or spatial adverb signifies the present, as in 'they were now here, in Rome' or 'today was Christmas' (Sitta, *Deixis am Phantasma* 106). But this normal incongruence is familiar to readers (Sitta, *Deixis am Phantasma* 107).

certain forms of journalism ('he is crossing the fifty yard line' or 'sources close to the president report'). In fact, the current frequency of the present tense in other literary narratives is probably due to the influence of the media. Moreover, writers probably assume that the present tense implies immediacy, its very name suggesting a story-time close to the reader's present. The narrative preterite, by contrast, signals that the narrated events are past and its subject absent. As the more traditional mode for fiction, past tense includes all other times and gives the reader the feel of having a vast temporal-spatial panorama at his or her disposal.[11] This used to be an asset for a historical novel, and nineteenth-century authors took full advantage of it. Today, its illusionary quality, resulting from the commodious arrangement the reader's imagination makes within the fictional world, is exactly the reason why many writers shun the past tense, writers who have rejected the idea of *grands récits* and wish to make their readers aware that they are partaking in one version of (fictional) history only. In historical novels the attraction of the present tense doubles because it can undermine the sense of total access to the world of the past recreated in fictional form.

For this purpose the present tense is ideal: it massively disturbs the experience of continuity, making narration disjunct, leading from one moment to the next and excluding global temporal reference. The present tense in narrative is more focused on moments or episodes than the past tense; "it sacrifices the larger time-field to achieve keen, close focus" (Le Guin, *Steering the Craft* 73). Therefore the present tense implies discontinuity; it could be called a narrative tense of less authority.

The cognitive effect of an omniscient authorial narrator is that the represented events appear as the result of a deliberate act of selection and combination which has taken place on a different (higher) diegetic level from that of the fictional story world. The narration in *Wolf Hall*, by contrast, resembles the unordered, associative impressions of lived experience. Whereas authorial narration in the past tense facilitates an effortless organization of the temporal flow and a connection of divers settings and events, stream of consciousness in the present tense seems to be a record of unfiltered perceptions and thoughts. The latter form of writing to the moment resists structural organization.[12] The text's central voice is thus subtly feminized by this apparent lack of authority over the novel's plot on the level of discourse, a move which can be assumed to increase its attractiveness for present-day readers. The reader is already aligned with the focalizing

---

[11] Narratologists have traditionally claimed that it is extremely easy for the reader to navigate the fictional world once set down in the narrative past tense. All the other tenses (past perfect, future perfect and the various moods and forms of the verbs) follow naturally and logically from the initial sentence, enabling easy access to times before and after the narrated moment for the reader (Le Guin, *Steering the Craft* 73). But in recent years the use of the present tense has become much more widespread, so that readers are probably accustomed to it.

[12] I am referring to the level of discourse, not to the story, in which plotting in the form of court intrigues is a forté of Cromwell's. As Alison Case has pointed out, "in conventional novelistic narrative [...] 'plotting', that 'activity of shaping' is performed first and foremost by the narrator [...] In relation to the reader, plotting is an act of authority [...] Since some of the most consistent threads in Western gender ideology concern women's purported inability to take purposive action – to be goal-oriented – and the inappropriateness of their assuming certain kinds of authority over others, it should come as no surprise that women's relationships to narration are often problematical" (Case, *Plotting Women* 12).

Cromwell since both share the task of having to discover coherence in a seemingly contingent world.

In order to make a coherent construction of chronology possible for the reader, *Wolf Hall* provides dates as chapter headings. Like the dynastic charts and character lists, these dates reference an extratextual framework of knowledge. In combination with the difficult deixis, the effect of these paratexts is to undermine the urge to immerse oneself in a historical world. An anti-illusory experience of discontinuity in narrative gives readers time to reflect their immediate emotional responses to characters and events.

In summary the contradictory narrative techniques include: the fragmented syntax of interior monologue, but not its first person mode; the third person and character-specific word choices of free indirect discourse ('erlebte Rede'), but not its past tense; the homodiegetic and intradiegetic focalization of I-narration without I-narration; the narration of consciousness without (or with little) self-reflection. Perhaps it is simplest to say that *Wolf Hall* is a book-length interior monologue in the third person.

Thus Hilary Mantel uses focalization and deixis in *Wolf Hall* for remarkably ambiguous or even contradictory effects: on the one hand, the deixis and defamiliarizing narration undermine the sense of illusion; on the other, focalization immerses us in Cromwell's version of the world. In combination, however, the two effects establish a strong attachment to the protagonist. The deictic indeterminacy demands a slow, attentive and reflective reading, in which the necessary synchronizing of deictic references with the reader's imaginative spatialization and chronology is accomplished. Interior focalization with its disjunct and momentary experientiality in present tense reinforces the strong bond between reader and focalizer.

What is especially remarkable about Cromwell as a focalizer is an effect created by his peculiar visual perception. Quite often his observation is focused on a minute and irrelevant detail; thus in the scene quoted from the novel's very beginning he sees the stitching on his father's boots while being kicked almost to death by him. Particularly in moments of crisis such as this, Cromwell's eye is drawn by an innocent object, thereby offering the reader a starling pictorial counterpart to the strife that is going on. The technique is familiar from movies where huge close-ups also serve to divert the spectator's attention from circumstances as well as to intensify relations to the individual or object zoomed in on. Cromwell's surprising images and metaphors vitalize the narrative by prompting the reader to visualize: and to visualize is to remember (see *Wolf Hall* 464).

Participating in the mental life of a character in this way can lead to identification, a mode of reading often encouraged by popular historical novels but disparaged in literary criticism. However, *Wolf Hall* does not employ all the strategies that encourage identificatory reading. In one particular respect focalization here contradicts expectations trained on modernist novels of consciousness: Cromwell never investigates his own emotions. Although the entirely modern English the characters speak disguises this, *Wolf Hall* is thoroughly grounded in extensive knowledge about the early modern world; and in this world the pursuit of self-knowledge was suspect to say the least. Cromwell's mind style is so thoroughly different from our contemporary individualist thought as to make homodiegetic focalization almost a defamiliarizing device. In the quote from chapter II (1527), for instance, he might have wondered why Stephen Gardiner is always insulting him, he might have admitted to being hurt. None of this is mentioned: his mind is busy imagining the point of view of others, a mental occupation so prominent and central to his character that it prevents him from thinking about himself. In spite of the dominant interior monologue mode, Cromwell's mind is not given to acts of pure self-expression or self-examination, but works primarily in the interest of observation and awareness of others. We never exit his perceptions, but these perceptions are not constrained by a modernist notion of isolated 'subjectivity-first consciousness'. Instead, he is constantly engaged in processes of third person ascriptions in reading and judging other minds. *Wolf Hall* seems determined to demonstrate Alan Palmer's contention that "thought is consummately social: social in its origins, social in its functions, social in its forms, social in its applications. At base thinking is a public activity [...]" (Palmer, *Fictional Minds* 11).

It is one of his likable characteristics for present-day readers that Cromwell intuitively performs this imaginative identification with others; it is a less endearing aspect of his character that he explicitly realizes the manipulative advantage this kind of imagination may bring: "Possibly it's something women do: spend time imagining what it's like to be each other. One can learn from that, he thinks" (Mantel, *Wolf Hall* 44). In many scenes we are allowed to watch him making good use of this knowledge. In the following passage, Cromwell acts like a detective by giving the emperor's ambassador Chapuys a piece of information and then watching coolly while Chapuys makes futile attempts to conceal the anxiety it causes him.

> October: monsieur Chapuys, the Emperor's ambassador, comes to Austin Friars [Cromwell's home] to dine [...] Rising from the table, Chapuys praises the food, the music, the furnishings. One can see his brain turning, hear the little clicks, like the gins of an elaborate lock, as he encodes his opinions for his dispatches to his master, the Emperor.
>
> (Mantel, *Wolf Hall* 322)

The two characters are engaged in competitive intermental thinking, each trying to out-think/out-read the other. Chapuy's mind is transparent to Cromwell; the perspective conveys to the reader the idea that his insight into other characters is more accurate than vice versa. The mental advantage Cromwell has is further compounded through his metaphors for his adversary's mental calculations: 'clicks', 'gins' and 'lock' which suggest a mechanistic act of shutting down something, images of both fatuousness and restrictiveness. And this metaphoric reification provides a memorable image of a conflict situation in which one party is at a decided mental disadvantage. This is what is constantly happening in Wolf Hall. Cromwell is assigned the superiority of a detective: his views of other characters are presented as intellectually superior, emotionally detached, ironically amused as well as rational and intuitive. The others, like Chapuys, are made to seem not only prevaricating and deceitful but also inept in attempting to pull the wool over Cromwell's eyes.

In consequence, this Cromwell remains a disconcerting mystery for the people around him. His own sister cannot add him up; rumours about dangerous activities during his lost years abroad make it easy for courtiers to believe in the earnestness of his threats. The novel stresses his unstable personality not only through the use of the confusing personal pronoun 'he'. In employing many variants of Cromwell's common name it also hints at multiple selves: "Thomas, also Tomos, Tommaso and Thomas Cromwell" (*Wolf Hall* 71). That "[h]alf the world is called Thomas" (*Wolf Hall* 68) presents itself as an opportunity to Cromwell who "withdraws his past selves into his present body" (*Wolf Hall* 71). As Michael Caines notes in a *TLS* review, "[i]t is the compound nature of this formidable figure that intrigues Wolsey and King Henry himself, that scares the noblemen and ultimately renders him a blank to himself as well" (Caines, 'Arrange One's Face'). I am not sure if Caines is right in this respect; the novel does not really allow us to ascertain what Cromwell thinks of himself.

It does, however, show us *how* Cromwell thinks: in poetic and vivid images. He appears to accept 'an occult history of Britain', according to which there was once an island on 'the edge of the known earth' which became known as Albina, bloodied at birth, and how demons and princesses gave rise to a race of giants who "spread over the whole landmass" (Mantel, *Wolf Hall* 65). At the same time, he belongs to the new inquisitive, open-minded and scientifically informed men of his time. Cromwell has gathered most of his knowledge in his travels outside England and shows interest in new ideas, such as those of Copernicus and Machiavelli. With these preoccupations the novel registers the exploding knowledge and increasing sense of uncertainty in the early modern world. It is hardly surprising that the novel frequently refers to the shifting nature of reality, this "quaking world" where "nothing [...] seems steady" and certainties can be changed in an instant (WH 522, 327). The early modern revolution in social and scientific knowledge systems creates a new sense of reality.

> Kratzer [...] draws the sun and the planets moving in their orbits according to the plan he has heard of from Father Copernicus. He shows how the world is turning on its axis, and nobody in the room denies it. Under your feet you can feel the tug and heft of it, the rocks groaning to tear away from their beds, the oceans tilting and slapping at their shores, the giddy lurch of Alpine passes, the forests of Germany ripping at their roots to be free.
> (Mantel, *Wolf Hall* 495)

As Ben de Bruyn notes, the novel does more than *describe* the sense of an ever-widening world: it *evokes* it in numerous panoramic scenes where the entire city or country seems to be crumbling at the edges (91). The images work amazingly well for present readers, resembling computer games graphics or computer generated film scenes. Filmic writing is able to capture the dissolution of old worlds and the emergence of new ones, as reflected in Cromwell's consciousness. But it is not just technical virtuosity that makes the representation work, it is also the cognitive framework readers bring to the text; the sense of upheaval and shifting reality is uncannily familiar from fiction and discourse about the present.

An unstable world requires flexible minds, and "*Wolf Hall* pits the agile mind of Cromwell against unwavering attitudes like More's" (de Bruyn 92, see WH 228). Rather than voice opinions or issue statements when considering the larger context of his times, Cromwell tends to ask questions. He is a foreigner to all the fanaticism and fundamentalism of early modern England; especially tolerant in religious matters. Some critics see him as a covert Protestant who runs uncharacteristic risks to protect the more militant adherents of the movement from the heretic-burning (Smith, 'Henry VIII got the Wives, but Cromwell got the Power'). This reading of Cromwell as a subversive agent for Protestantism misses the novel's innovative take on history. And it misses the message for which the remarkable technical achievement of this novel is so appropriate: Cromwell is not a pious, not even a religious person. His support for reformers comes from his basic tolerance and from the thoroughly secular grounding of his thought. He is disgusted by superstition and superiority alike, condescending neither to poor people, nor to women or children. Male chauvinism is as foreign to his mindset as the outdated feudal arrogance of the privileged. In enduring their jibes at his low birth, Cromwell reflects that,

> The world is not run from where he [Henry Percy, the dull-witted Earl of Northumberland] thinks. Not from his border fortresses, not even from Whitehall. The world is run from Antwerp, from Florence, from places he has never imagined; from Lisbon, from where the ships with sails of silk drift west and are burned up in the sun. Not from castle walls, but from counting houses, not by the call of the bugle but by the click of the abacus, not by the grate and click of the mechanism of the gun but by the scrape of the pen on the page of the promissory note that pays for the gun and the gunsmith and the powder and shot.
>
> (Mantel, *Wolf Hall* 378)

Mantel's Cromwell is a representative of an unstable world where his unprecedented rise from humble origins is possible. He embodies the cultural shift from religious to secular and from class-bound to meritocratic thinking. He seems confident that noble blood and feats of arms will soon count for less than lines of credit and nicely balanced books (Tayler, 'Henry's Fighting Dog'). In such anachronistic reflections Cromwell anticipates the fading of aristocratic power and the dawning of the capitalist system. Mantel is indebted to G.R. Elton in whose histories of the English Reformation Cromwell is the master mind behind Henry's break with Rome. Elton credited Cromwell with a vision of how the separation could consolidate the nation. Mantel's novel follows Elton in this estimation of Cromwell's outstanding achievement, yet it downplays exactly the political and administrative sector in which his most important work was done according to Elton's narrative of Tudor history. There is little if any mention here of the real Cromwell's use of the printing-press in a concerted campaign in print to vindicate his policies, as Caines notes. We do not have to follow parliamentary proceedings or consecutive amendments of bills and applications; instead we can enjoy court intrigues and battles of wit. Instead of collecting tedious arguments for the sovereignty from legal compilations, which the historical Cromwell seems to have done rather well, Mantel's Cromwell interprets Henry's nightmares for him in order to persuade him that he has merely to assert sovereignty. On the whole she avoids the historian's celebratory emphasis on nation-building by emphasizing the originality of Cromwell's viewpoint.

> Wherever one touches him, one finds originality and the unconventional […] he disdained pomp and cultivated a plain accessibility which reflected his genuine interest in other people. An exceptionally lively mind hid behind the formidable façade and expressed itself in vigorous and witty speech, his conversation charmed even his enemies and he had great natural gifts as an orator.
>
> (Elton, *Reform and Reformation* 169-70)

Elton's characterization finds its way into the novel, which refers to his enormous memorizing capacity, demonstrates his wittiness in brilliant repartee and elaborates on Elton's list of accomplishments by making him a thoughtful, considerate family father and friend. In consequence, *Wolf Hall's* Cromwell becomes an omnicompetent figure, "at home in courtroom or waterfront, bishop's palace or inn yard. He can draft a contract, train a falcon, draw a map, stop a street fight, furnish a house and fix a jury" (Mantel, *Wolf Hall* 31). In contrast to his Tudor contemporaries, Mantel credits him with many attributes that we tend to admire today: intercultural competence (he is fluent in many languages), financial and legal genius, psychological insight, physical courage, wit and last but not least a greater interest in others than in himself. The novel rewrites Cromwell's character so that he becomes more our contemporary than More's. On the one hand, he stands for secular scepticism and pragmatic relativism instead of moral principles, for intercultural competence instead of faith in an essential national identity. Unencumbered by strong convictions, he is not impressed by status without intellectual quality. On the other hand, he is an intimidating physical presence with no hesitations about using violence and capable of employing quite sinister methods in eliminating his enemies. He also is a transnational economic genius who seems to endorse proto-capitalist ideas: "Study the market. Increase the spread of benevolence. Bring in better figures next year" (Mantel, *Wolf Hall* 365). Here as elsewhere, his rhetoric belies a ruthlessness that extends well beyond the business sphere.

Interior monologue serves to disguise the historical inaccuracy of Cromwell's modern sympathies. Since the narrative makes significant demands on readers to perform a mind-reading activity similar to Cromwell's own, the process of relativizing his personality is gradual. Naturally, Cromwell's interior focalization records his maneuvers without disapproval. We do, however, become increasingly aware that we are getting only his side of things. In one scene at court, we witness his brutal manhandling of an unwelcome follower, but the narrative glosses over the violence of his action because focalization screens us from an outside evaluation (Mantel, *Wolf Hall* 370). For a large part of our reading experience, then, we happily enjoy something postmodernity has made unfamiliar –a narrative with a hero. Through the emphasis on the present moment Cromwell becomes an object of sympathy, but the careful reading which the narrative technique necessitates gradually dissolves the hero figure into a thoroughly ambiguous personality so that it dawns on us that we may have been misled in trusting his first person ascriptions.[13] Gradually we learn to accept the novel's accumulating hints and clues that the character of Cromwell may not be to his outside world what he appears to be on the inside to himself. The irritation produced by deictic

---

[13] I suppose some critics would call this 'unreliable narration'. I hesitate to employ this convenient term which can cover anything from self-delusion to downright mendacity. In typical novelistic unreliability, like Henry James's *The Ambassadors* – every narratologist's favourite example of internal focalization – we are made aware of the narrator's judgmental superiority to 'poor Strether' from the start. James's novel flatters our intellect and our generosity because we can feel superior to the focalizer and pride ourselves that we like him, nevertheless. In *Wolf Hall* we admire the focalizer inordinately, but have to gradually learn to distrust his judgement. In realizing that our own perceptions were wrong – in spite of the hindsight of historical distance –, we recognize our own delusions and gullibility.

indeterminacy and the resulting incomplete deictic shifts appears to be desired; the narrative is exquisitely designed to produce a hesitant, sceptical reading, unsure of itself and the meanings it is projecting.

Cromwell's complex personality presents a challenge that produces most of the novel's suspense. Yet in the end, the sum of his historical parts does not add up; he appears a complicated compound of likable and legendary characteristics. In offering this compelling indeterminacy at the centre of its construction of character, the novel not only rejects the notion of a psychologically rounded character, but also educates its readers that identity is unstable, a process rather than an entity, and – above all – that it depends on interpersonal construction.[14] We meet a historical figure that is not a definitively characterized identity but a performance that requires our participation in the process of reading. Identity cannot be constituted without an Other who questions its existence. In this case the position of the Other is filled by the reader who completes, empathizes, hypothesizes, casts into doubt and reconceptualizes Cromwell's identity. A commonly assumed roundness and unity of subjectivity is undermined by our own very act of reading. Thus the novel rejects the traditional 'subjectivity first' model of the mind – polemically called "the Robinson Crusoe model of epistemology" (Jones, 'Philosophical and Theoretical Issues in the Study of Deixis' 27) – and educates us to not only perceive but exercise the mind as an instrument of interpersonal awareness and cultural learning "equipped with needs for dialogic, intermental engagement with other minds" (Trevarthen, 'Intersubjectivity' 417).

Because Cromwell does not know the future, the reader is not just in the midst of history but in the midst of a subjective experience of history. The events of the novel force Cromwell not only to imagine a future England, but to correct a fraudulent history of the nation informed by religious prejudice. "Because [England] is in a state of flux, in fact, the nation cannot be definitively mapped" and hence "history, too, cannot be definitively mapped" (de Bruyn 94, see WH 646). *Wolf Hall* evokes the experience of history through participation in the reading process.

It seems to be the hallmark of serious historical novels to direct some message to the present day via its description of the past. The two time-planes of historical fictions – the protagonist's present and the reader's present – are joined in a cause-and-effect relationship. In this sense, *Wolf Hall* tells the success story of capitalism and the transformation of the incipient nation state's financial administration. This affirmative message is undermined only by the psychology of an intersubjective reading of its proto-capitalist hero's character. Realizing that we, as readers, have been complicit in constructing a hero to our liking, we are reminded that our judgements can be misled, and that they may be based on false values. *Wolf Hall* encourages us to examine our values in the construction of identity. By casting us in the role of the Other, the novel produces a dynamic dialectic of the familiar and the strange; it makes us aware of the moral responsibility involved in interpreting other people and the past. Instead of the

---

[14] Current work on the intersection of philosophy with evolutionary neurobiology insists that our ability to understand others and to empathize is what drives human cognition and enabled the emergence of culture (Swirski, 'Me First or We First' 160). Likewise, "[t]he notion of deictic egocentricity" that deictic structures reference everything to an 'ich-Origo' have been abandoned in favour of relational deictic shift theory (Fuchs, *Remarks on Deixis* 42).

limited postmodern project of juggling alternative histories, *Wolf Hall* asks us to transcend what Jameson calls 'monadic relativism' and interrogate the ethics we would value in literary and historical 'heroes' (Jameson, *Postmodernism* 412).

De Groot has suggested that the historical novel represents an alternative strand in the rise of the novel in general, an alternative "concerned with social movement, dissidence, complication and empathy rather than the more individualistic novel form we are familiar with, born of autobiographical, personal, revelatory narratives" (de Groot, *The Historical Novel* 2). Of course, a single case study like this does not warrant a judgement on the validity of this historical hypothesis. It does, however, allow me to conclude that the reading practices which *Wolf Hall* invites have a communal effect of the sort that de Groot describes. I believe that the novel not only deals with intersubjective processes but that its reading promotes intersubjectivity: Readers willing to tackle the dense, complex and sometimes opaque deixis of this novel are rewarded with massive affective involvement. Thus, in spite of its ruthless and opportunist protagonist, the novel not only discusses but actively invites pro-social versions of self-definition through its narrative technique. This encouragement of interpersonal empathy and understanding might be considered a highly desirable effect in a real world where cognitive and emotional involvements beyond individual and national identity boundaries are often found wanting. The outstanding achievement of *Wolf Hall* is to captivate the reader with the popular appeal of its hero, whose mind we can enter only to ultimately reject egocentric subjectivity in favour of an alternative focus on an intersubjective construction of identity.

Works Cited

Anderson, Perry. 'From Progress to Catastrophe: Perry Anderson on the Historical Novel.' *London Review of Books* 33-15 (2011). 6 June 2012. <http://www.lrb.co.uk/v33/n15/perry-anderson/from-progress-to-catastrophe>.

Assmann, Jan. *Das kulturelle Gedächtnis: Schrift, Erinnerung und politische Identität in frühen Hochkulturen.* München: Beck, 1992.

Boccardi, Mariadele. *The Contemporary British Historical Novel: Representation, Nation, Empire.* New York: Palgrave, 2009.

Brosch, Renate. 'Visualisierungen in der Leseerfahrung.' *Visualisierungen: Textualität - Deixis - Lektüre.* Eds. Renate Brosch and Ronja Tripp. Trier: Wissenschaftlicher Verlag Trier, 2007. 47-87.

Bühler, Karl. *Sprachtheorie: Die Darstellungsfunktion der Sprache.* Jena: Fischer, 1934.

Caines, Michael. 'Arrange One's Face.' Rev. of *Wolf Hall*, by Hilary Mantel. *Times Literary Supplement*, 15 May 2009. Web. 6 June 2012.<http://entertainment.times-online.co.uk/tol/arts_and_entertainment/the_tls/article627083.ece.>

Carrard, Philippe. 'The Distinction of Historiography: Dorrit Cohn and Referential Discourse.' *Narrative* 20-1 (2012): 125-31.

Case, Alison. *Plotting Women: Gender and Narration in the Eighteenth and Nineteenth Century Novel.* Charlottesville: University Press of Virginia, 1999.

Cohn, Dorrit. *The Distinction of Fiction*. Baltimore: Johns Hopkins University Press, 1999.

De Bruyn, Ben. *Wolfgang Iser: A Companion*. Berlin: de Gruyter, 2012.

De Groot, Jerome. *The Historical Novel*. The New Critical Idiom. London: Routledge, 2010.

Demetz, Peter. *Formen des Realismus: Theodor Fontane: kritische Untersuchungen*. München: Hanser, 1964.

Dictionary of National Biography. 'Cromwell, Thomas, Earl of Essex (1485?-1540).' Eds. Leslie Stephen and Sidney Lee. 22 vols. Oxford: Oxford Univesity Press, 1968.

Elton, Geoffrey R. *Reform and Reformation: England 1509-1558*. London: Arnold, 1977.

Emmott, Catherine. 'Consciousness and Context.' *New Essay in Deixis: Discourse, Narrative, Literature*. Ed. Keith Green. Amsterdam: Rodopi, 1995. 81-97.

FitzHerbert, Claudia. Rev. of *Wolf Hall*, by Hilary Mantel. *The Telegraph*, 25 April 2009. Web. 26 June 2012. <http://www.telegraph.co.uk/culture/books/bookreviews/5207969/Wolf-Hall-by-Hilary-Mantel-review.html>.

Fludernik, Monika. *Towards a 'Natural' Narratology*. London: Routledge, 1996.

Fowles, John. 'On Being English but Not British.' *Texas Quarterly* 7-3 (1964): 154-62.

Fuchs, Anna. *Remarks on Deixis*. Heidelberg: Groos, 1993.

Geppert, Hans Vilmar. *Der Historische Roman: Geschichte umerzählt – von Walter Scott bis zur Gegenwart*. Tübingen: Francke, 2009.

Gymnich, Marion, Ansgar Nünning, and Roy Sommer. 'Gauging the Relation between Literature and Memory: Theoretical Paradigms – Genres – Functions.' *Literature and Memory: Theoretical Paradigms, Genres, Functions*. Eds. Ansgar Nünning, Marion Gymnich, and Roy Sommer. Tübingen: Francke, 2006. 1-10.

Hutcheon, Linda. 'Historiographic Metafiction: Parody and the Intertextuality of History.' *Intertextuality and Contemporary American Fiction*. Eds. Patrick O'Donnell and Robert Con Davis. Baltimore: John Hopkins University Press, 1989. 3-32.

Jahn, Manfred. 'Windows of Focalization: Deconstructing and Reconstructing a Narratological Concept.' *Style* 30-2 (1996): 241-67.

Jameson, Fredric. *Marxism and Form: Twentieth-Century Dialectical Theories of Literature*. Princeton: Princeton University Press, 1971.

Jameson, Fredric. *Postmodernism, or, the Cultural Logic of Late Capitalism*. London: Verso, 1991.

Jones, Peter. 'Philosophical and Theoretical Issues in the Study of Deixis: A Critique of the Standard Account.' *New Essay in Deixis: Discourse, Narrative, Literature*. Ed. Keith Green. Amsterdam: Rodopi, 1995. 27-48.

Koselleck, Reinhart. *Vergangene Zukunft: Zur Semantik geschichtlicher Zeiten*. Frankfurt a.M.: Suhrkamp, 1989.

Le Guin, Ursula. *Steering the Craft: Exercises and Discussions on Story Writing for the Lone Navigator or the Mutinous Crew*. Portland: The Eighth Mountain Press, 1998.

Lukács, Georg. *The Historical Novel*. Boston: Merlin Press, 1962 [1937].

Mantel, Hilary. W*olf Hall*. London: Fourth Estate, 2010.

McIntyre, Dan. *Point of View in Plays: A Cognitive Stylistic Approach to Viewpoint in Drama and Other Text-Types*. Amsterdam: Benjamins, 2006.

Nünning, Ansgar. '"Verbal Fictions?": Kritische Überlegungen und narratologische Alternativen zu Hayden Whites Einebnung des Gegensatzes zwischen Historiographie und Literatur.' *Literaturwissenschaftliches Jahrbuch. Neue Folge* 40 (1999): 351-80.

Nünning, Vera. 'The Invention of Cultural Traditions: The Construction and Deconstruction of Englishness and Authenticity in Julian Barnes's *England, England.*' *Anglia: Zeitschrift für Englische Philologie* 119-1 (2001): 58-76.

Nussbaum, Martha C. '"Finely Aware and Richly Responsible': Literature and the Moral Imagination." *Love's Knowledge: Essays on Philosophy and Literature*. New York: Oxford University Press, 1990. 148-67.

O'Leary, Timothy. *Foucault and the Art of Ethics*. New York, London: Continuum, 2002.

Palmer, Alan. *Fictional Minds*. Lincoln: University of Nebraska Press, 2004.

Rigney, Ann. *Imperfect Histories: The Elusive Past and the Legacy of Romantic Historicism*. Ithaca: Cornell University Press, 2001.

Schabacher, Gabriele. *Topik der Referenz: Theorie der Autobiographie, die Funktion 'Gattung' und Roland Barthes'* Über mich selbst. Würzburg: Königshausen & Neumann, 2007.

Searle, John. 'The Logical Status of Fictional Discourse.' *New Literary History* 6-2 (1975): 319-32.

Semino, Elena. 'A Cognitive Stylistic Approach to Mind Style in Narrative Fiction.' *Cognitive Stylistics: Language and Cognition in Text Analysis*. Eds. Elena Semino and Jonathan Culpeper. Amsterdam: Benjamins, 2002. 95-122.

Sitta, Georg. *Deixis am Phantasma: Versuch einer Neubestimmung*. Bochum: Brockmeyer, 1991.

Smith, Wendy. 'Henry VIII Got the Wives, but Cromwell Got the Power.' Rev. of *Wolf Hall*, by Hilary Mantel. *Washington Post*, 6 Oct. 2009. Web. 12 July 2012. <http://www.washingtonpost.com/wpdyn/content/article/2009/10/06/AR20091006 2905.html>.

Swirski, Peter. 'Me First or We First: Literature and Paleomorality.' *Philosophy and Literature* 35-1 (2011): 150-67.

Tayler, Christopher. 'Henry's Fighting Dog.' Rev. of *Wolf Hall*, by Hilary Mantel. *The Guardian*, 2 May 2009. Web. 12 July 2012. <http://www.guardian.co.ukbooks/2009 /may/02/wolf-hall-hilary-mantel>.

Trevarthen, Colwyn. 'Intersubjectivity.' *The MIT Encyclopedia of the Cognitive Sciences*. Eds. Robert A. Wilson and Frank C. Keil. Cambridge: MIT Press, 2001. 415-19.

White, Hayden. *Metahistory: The Historical Imagination in Nineteenth-Century Europe*. Baltimore: Johns Hopkins University Press, 1973.

White, Hayden. *Tropics of Discourse: Essays in Cultural Criticism*. Baltimore: Johns Hopkins University Press, 1978.

Wineburg, Sam. *Historical Thinking and Other Unnatural Acts: Charting the Future of Teaching the Past*. Philadelphia: Temple University Press, 2001.

MARGITTA ROUSE

'There'll just be progress of a sort': Elegizing the Historical Novel in Jim Crace's *Harvest*

At a time when the historical novel is as diverse, popular and commercially successful as it has never been before, it seems peculiar, if not paradoxical, that writers might choose to elegize the genre through its very medium. Jim Crace's highly acclaimed novel *Harvest*, first published in 2013, questions our desire to know and explain 'the' past in terms of (technological and economic) progress where events line up as a series of novel achievements. This essay sets out to show that the novel critically comments on the literary tradition it depends upon by presenting an elegiac progress narrative that is as much outside of history as it is within. I wish to argue that ultimately, *Harvest* is a timely elegy not only on the classical form of the historical novel as chiefly associated with Walter Scott, but also on its various postmodern, meta-fictional adaptations that (re)create history by attempting to give voice to the marginalized, the forgotten and the dispossessed.

Depicting the catastrophic destruction of a post-plague/pre-industrial village community at a time when collectively managed crop farming is about to be replaced by sheep farming, Crace's novel is decidedly political. The story is told by the voice of Walter Thirsk, a modest, yet literate, farmer, who describes how his village community is displaced before the sheep have even arrived. Like the narrator, the local landowner and authority to the villagers, Master Kent, is recently widowed, and since his wife left him no children her property passes to her distant cousin, Master Jordan. Initially, it appears that Kent is a man who enjoys country life and would protect the 'old' ways if he could, yet the new heir, townsman Jordan, regards the common as unprofitable, and Kent placidly follows his lead. At the end of harvest time, Jordan arrives, and he and Kent secretly consolidate plans for the property's future. It is not the arrival of Jordan and his men that occupies the foreground of Walter's story however, but that of a family of squatters seeking new livelihoods within the community's bounds, and the presence of a mapmaker in Kent's employ. His charts of the community's land are to form the basis for the coming agricultural reforms. Ominous events surrounding the squatters and the mapmaker culminate in the village's destruction.

What is remarkable about Crace's progress narrative is that it eschews both temporal and spatial specificity, while it revels in historical detail as regards agricultural life much of which is invented nevertheless. As Crace explains, he took liberties with historical details precisely because historiography itself gave him license to do so: "Not all the natural history in the novel is trustworthy; I have invented the names of animals and birds because in Tudor times there wouldn't have been a universal way of describing things" (Crace, *Picador Podcast: Jim Crace*). This is not to say that the novel is reliably set in the Tudor period. Neither realistic nor fantastic, *Harvest* evokes an unstable, unsettled time and place in the double sense: No dates or place names are provided or can reliably be inferred (no famous historical persons appear); only the characters' surnames (Saxton, Kent, Rogers) suggest we are in England, while the wealthier protagonists' attire resembles Tudor fashion. The novel's events generally call to mind the complex and controversial history of land enclosure in England during which common land was seized by the wealthy and tilled land was successively converted to pasture, effectively depopulating vast areas of land and concentrating former peasants in towns and cities. This was a comparatively long process, which began in the fourteenth century as collective forms of ownership gave way to agricultural privatization. The so-called depopulating enclosures took place in lowland England in the fifteenth and sixteenth centuries and were paralleled in the eighteenth-century Scottish Highland Clearances. Land reforms on a grand scale ended in the late-eighteenth and early-nineteenth centuries with the so-called parliamentary enclosures (see Turner, *Enclosures* 193-4). Historians agree that the enclosures irrevocably changed the socio-economic make-up of England's agricultural communities. However, there is considerable debate on whether the land reforms increased agricultural productivity and thus aided England's economic modernization, benefitting society at large, or whether they constituted "a pure enough case of class robbery" (Turner, *Enclosures* 195).

Crace's novel does not so much explore the consequences of depopulation – the narrative breaks off once the village is destroyed – but takes snapshots of Walter's musings as to why the catastrophic events befall his village and what their consequences will be. As he tries to make sense of confusing incidents, we get an insight into the ways in which his community is organized. As the present-tense narrative voice arranges itself as a competition between first person singular and first person plural, we witness Walter struggling to defend the collective idea of the open field system while advancing his own interests.

Evidently concerned with historical and ecological development though it is, the novel gravitates towards the allegorical, even biblical – it is no accident that the rural community, simply named 'The Village' in a stretch of land called 'The Land', is annihilated in precisely seven days. Crace's story thus begs the question as to what it is that ultimately sets the novel's events in motion, and engineers 'progress'. Despite its scriptural subtext, the story is certainly not governed by a teleological thrust, nor does it suggest that 'progress' is inevitable. We will see that all talk of progress in the novel itself serves to draw attention to the politics of what Rita Felski has called 'doing time', the ideological practices of assessing time and history in terms of novelty and advancement and the socio-political consequences of such practices (Felski, *Doing Time: Feminist Theory and Postmodern Culture*).

Harvest's linguistic choices, too, present us with a remarkable mix of the realistic and the fantastic. In presenting his own version of what economic historians have termed 'the tragedy of the commons', Crace's modest narrator uses highly aestheticized, lyrical language, which has not failed to irritate or fascinate a single reviewer. An unusual blend of pastoral and anti-pastoral with dystopian overtones, *Harvest* thus flaunts its literariness by being more akin to a long poem of lament than the historical novel as we assume to know it. I wish to argue that it is precisely through its acute literariness that *Harvest* develops its socio-political, and specifically elegiac, take not only on historical fiction's arguable predilection towards historical realism and its concomitant view of progress but also on the genre's postmodern articulations of what could be regarded as realist desires.

The Trouble with Realism

Even though deconstructionist claims that 'reality' is a socially constructed phenomenon are now widely accepted, the question as to how it 'really' was (or might have been) still haunts critical engagements with historical fiction. What seems central to historical fiction as it is traditionally discussed, is the genre's apparent tendency to confront temporal alterity with a set of familiarizing strategies that will make depictions of the past seem credible to us, or rather: that will make the past accountable to us. To illustrate this claim we need only take a look at a recent introduction to the genre: For Jerome de Groot, historical narratives' 'intergeneric hybridity and flexibility' are such that they may build upon the frameworks of "romance, detective, thriller, counterfactual, horror, literary, gothic, postmodern, epic, fantasy, mystery, western, children's books" (de Groot, *The Historical Novel* 2). If there is a defining trait of historical fiction at all, he argues, it is precisely its generic flexibility and hybridity. Where historical fiction is similar to other forms of novel-writing is that it "shares a concern with realism, development of character, authenticity" (4). Historical fiction fundamentally differs from novels set in the present in that readers are "slightly more self-aware of the artificiality of the writing and the strangeness of engaging with imaginary work which strives to explain something that is other than one's contemporary knowledge and experience: the past" (4).

De Groot does not discuss whether such heightened awareness of the literary made possible through texts 'explaining' the past is created by the novels' 'concern with realism', by their striving to overcome historical difference using 'realistic' means, or by readers' (frustrated or fulfilled) desires for authenticity when reading historical fiction; nor does he explain why literary self-awareness ought to be less pronounced in novels set in our present. It is unlikely in fact that de Groot intends to suggest anything of the kind, not least because his discussion also includes postmodern forms of historical fiction which may freely intermingle past and present, celebrate anachronisms, or provide alternative endings to the same story; and these are aesthetic means which are regarded as typical of any kind of postmodern writing. If the related notions of realism and authenticity here creep into de Groot's argument in a manner both undefined and unquestioned, this is most likely the effect of a critical discourse on the genre which has traditionally been drawn to the views and tastes of its most illustrious theorist, György Lukács, as presented in his seminal *The Historical Novel*. As Perry Anderson puts it: "Any reflection on the strange career of this form has to begin there, however far it may then wander from him" (Anderson, *From Progress to Catastrophe* 28). And for Lukács, the novel rose to superior heights through nineteenth-century realism, a development for which he saw a precedent in Walter Scott's writing.

As is well known, in presenting Walter Scott's *Waverley* as the origin of the historical novel and precursor to nineteenth-century realism, Lukács also established the lens through which historical fiction was to be evaluated: fidelity towards historical 'truth', achieved through a realistic, that is, spatio-temporally concrete, portrayal of a society. Importantly, such a portrayal depended on an analysis of the society's development in time which enabled historical consciousness in the first place. For Lukács, the "artistically faithful image of a concrete historical epoch" was invented by Scott: "What is lacking in the so-called historical novel before Sir Walter Scott is precisely the specifically historical, that is, derivation of the individuality of characters from the historical peculiarity of their age" (Lukács, *The Historical Novel* 19).

While this is not the place to paint an exhaustive overview of Lukács's legacy in critical approaches towards historical fiction, it is important to show that his influence has clouded an understanding of the acute temporality of spatio-temporally evasive worlds or worlds of alternative temporalities, especially in pre-Scottian fiction, and also beyond; in fact it has served to accentuate a binary opposition of the realistic (here as the temporally concrete) versus the fantastic/symbolic (as gravitating towards the temporally elusive). Yet both modes can serve similar, as well as competing, attitudes towards the historical, and they can be combined or played out against one another in order to deconstruct a specifically modern understanding of progress and of what constitutes temporal alterity. As will become apparent, Jim Crace's medievalist analysis of a social crisis in *Harvest*, which operates at a level of spatio-temporal concreteness that could be regarded as realistic and fantastic at the same time, is a case in point. Before I return to *Harvest*, it is pertinent to take a closer look at Lukács's politics of time and the way it has been appropriated in more recent criticism, in order to understand why spaces of alternative temporality are often viewed as ahistorical or atemporal worlds and have thus escaped students of historical fiction more than they deserve.

For Lukács, not even the "great realistic social novel of the eighteenth century", even though it "accomplished a revolutionary breakthrough to reality for world literature", was able to capture temporal change: "The contemporary world is portrayed with unusual plasticity and truth-to-life, but is accepted naïvely as something given: whence and how it has developed have not yet become problems for the writer" (Lukács, *The Historical Novel* 19). He argues that the apparent lack of focus on temporal development in pre-Scottian fiction also affects the portrayal of place; writers such as Swift, Voltaire or Diderot create realistic contemporary worlds "in a 'never and nowhere'", but "they do not see the specific qualities of their own age historically" (20). Seeing the specific qualities of the present time historically, for Lukács, means understanding time in terms of progress, or having "a clear understanding of history as a process, of history as the concrete precondition of the present" (21). He posits that it was the German post-Enlightenment writers such as Goethe or Heine who, in the wake of the European 'mass experience' of the French Revolution, first enabled a specific literary awareness of historical and social changes, even if a discourse on the rise and fall of societies had been in place since antiquity. Answering "the need of men to comprehend their own existence as something historically conditioned" (24), post-revolutionary European writers participated in a mass-project of nation-building: They popularized the idea of mass armies. Their efforts ultimately also facilitated new "judgments on economic conditions and class struggle" (25), and with it new ideologies of what constitutes historical progress. Lukács explains that progress could now be understood (and experienced) in the Hegelian sense as the result of opposing social forces: "history itself is the bearer and realizer of human progress" (27), and revolutions in history are regarded "as an indispensable component of human progress" (29). The Hegelian view of history as a dialectic process constituted the basis for a new Humanism, which could not, however, "transcend the limits of that age – except in fantastical form, as was the case with the great Utopians" (29).

Scott's great accomplishment as seen by Lukács is that his novels use realistic, that is, representational, ways to promote the awareness of historical development in his readers: Scott advanced the understanding of the *necessity* of historical progress by dramatizing the social circumstances of a "'middling' merely correct and never heroic 'hero'" (33). In Scott's novels known historical figures often appear but play only a marginal role; instead, events are played out through undistinguished 'historical-social types' (35), protagonists who represent the clash of opposing 'social trends and historical forces' (33). The mediocre hero is of the utmost importance for representing this contest effectively, since he may come into contact with both warring forces, but need not be drawn passionately to either side. His sympathies might change, 'waver', while, simultaneously, the popular side of historical change can be evoked: "by disclosing the actual conditions of life, the actual growing crisis in people's lives, [Scott] depicts all the problems of popular life which lead up to the historical crisis he has represented" (38). And it is only when the reader has understood the social determinants of the historical condition depicted, that the great historical hero enters the narrative and solves the crisis. By this point Scott has established sympathy in the reader for both sides of the conflict: "the broadly drawn social struggles which precede the appearance of the hero show how at just such a time, just such a hero had to arise in order to solve just such problems" (38). In a nutshell, the great novelty of Scott's writing according to Lukács is that it was capable of infusing the achievements of eighteenth-century realism with a new historical consciousness and its affirmative view of progress.

Lukács claims that the historical novel as inspired by Scott had its great phase before the 1848 revolutions; in the late nineteenth century and beyond, novelists "no longer have any immediate social sense of continuity with the prehistory of their own society" (244), and the genre enters a degenerative phase in which history serves for little more than decorative purposes. He does see a laudable revival of historical fiction in the 1930s, where under the tenet of a new Humanism anti-fascist writers explored the pressures of the present in historical settings; however, it is precisely their tendency to "turn the past into a *parable of the present*" which ultimately works against the paradigm of the classical form which promoted "real historical concreteness" (338).

It follows from Lukács's argument that his partiality towards realism is more an aesthetic preference than a condition for the representation of 'historical truth' (the understanding of progress), since he grants that Utopian writers before Scott were able to overcome the 'limits' of their age in fantastical form. Nevertheless, his insistence on the realistic form as the ideal, if not only, form to represent history *accurately* as a series of necessary and inevitable revolutions has worked to marginalize allegory, symbolism and various forms of fantastic writing in discussions of the form. Not utopian fiction or allegory but the Scottian model as theorized by Lukács serves as the discursive springboard for any engagement with historical fiction, and this is true also for discussions of postmodern historical novels which typically avoid aesthetic choices associated with literary realism.

In asking how we are to interpret the existence of postmodern forms of the historical novel, Perry Anderson cites Fredric Jameson's 'powerful suggestion' that fabulous inventions of the past "rattle at the bars of our extinct sense of history, unsettle the emptiness of our temporal historicity, and try convulsively to reawaken the dormant existential sense of time by way of the strong medicine of lies and impossible fables, the electro-shock of repeated doses of the unreal and the unbelievable" (cited in Anderson, *From Progress to Catastrophe* 26). If 'lies and fables' are needed to uncover a 'dormant' historical consciousness, does this not suggest that realistic means, by contrast, serve historical credibility, the real, and with it an 'awakened' historical consciousness, one that both Jameson and Anderson appear to prefer?

It is important to stress that in discussions of what constitutes historical consciousness Lukács's influence is not simply restricted to the role of realism (and with it the necessity of progress). His idea that Scott invented a form that allowed for a novel sense of temporality through which the past could now be understood as culturally distinct, as 'Other', remained uncontested until very recently. Discussing science fiction, Jameson, for example, still confirms that previous periods and other genres were unable to accomplish such a feat, by taking recourse to Lukács's theoretical approach. Jameson stresses, along with Lukács, that it was the rise of capitalism which demanded "a different experience of temporality from that which was appropriate to a feudal or tribal system, [...] a concrete vision of the past which we may expect to find completed by that far more abstract and empty conception of some future terminus which we sometimes call 'progress'" (Jameson, *Progress Versus Utopia; or, Can We Imagine the Future?* 149). Jameson believes that science fiction, as a genre that emerged when the classical historical novel was declining, responds to the rise of a new historical consciousness as "a form which now registers some nascent sense of the future, and does so in the space on which a sense of the past had once been inscribed" (150). In other words, the new genre inherits the literary space of realism once occupied by the historical novel with a key difference: It imagines possible future worlds instead of recreating past ones.

What is interesting here is that although Jameson agrees with Lukács that the historical novel was a response to a novel experience of temporality that suggested novelists *could* grasp the past in its specific otherness, he is not tempted to draw a similar conclusion for science fiction. He does not suggest that the new genre might give us 'real' or representational images of an actual future; rather he sees its function as "to defamiliarize and restructure our experience of our own present, [...] transforming our own present into the determinate past of something yet to come" (151). And in so doing, he argues, science fiction's specific temporality is akin to that of utopian fiction, or rather, it is science fiction's purpose to articulate a "constitutional inability to imagine Utopia itself" (153). Significantly, he comments here on the very genre that Lukács found could transcend eighteenth-century 'limitations' of expressing historical consciousness and which could – by implication – render a sense of temporality which also grasped the past as a cultural 'Other', albeit in fantastical form. It is striking that even under the auspices of poststructuralist theory it is no contradiction for Jameson that the classical historical novel as a construction of the past, that is, a narrative that cannot *truly* provide access to the past, would still point to a profound experience of the past's alterity, whereas literary constructions of the future or of otherworlds cannot achieve a similarly deep experience of temporal Otherness.

More recently, radical distinctions between fantastic and realistic temporalities have been questioned, especially by studies drawing attention to Lukács's 'gender-blindness' (Wallace, *The Woman's Historical Novel* 11). Diana Wallace observes that women writers were excluded from Lukács's theory, not least because their writing does not suit the model of historical progress as the inevitable result of opposing social forces. She argues that his theory of the historical novel is based on crises traditionally perceived as 'masculine' such as wars, conquests and revolutions, and that it thus privileges what she calls a 'male-defined model' of history (15). Pointing out that women writers' alternative views of history in fact precede and influence Scott, Wallace cites Katie Trumpener's work, which shows that eighteenth- and early nineteenth-century historical novels by writers such as Jane West or Sophia Lee provided a contrastive foil for Scott (15). West's novel *The Loyalists: An Historical Novel*, published two years before Scott's *Waverley*, may not only be the first to feature the term 'historical novel', but also introduces a protagonist called 'Sir William Waverley' whose political sympathies waver between warring camps in the English Civil War (15). The key difference: West's novel offers a critical view of progress, whereas Scott's 'adaptation' chooses an affirmative one (15).

In excluding women's writing from his survey of the historical novel, argues Wallace, Lukács excludes alternative assessments of temporal change. She posits that historical fiction appears in a very different light if it is seen in the context of women's writing. She directs our attention to Umberto Eco's classification of historical fiction as a possible alternative to Lukács's taxonomy, since Eco also includes genres which have traditionally attracted more women writers (genres which Lukács ignores) and which do not depend on a particular notion of progress with its associated 'realistic' temporalities.

In his more inclusive approach Eco distinguishes between three different 'ways of narrating the past': The first is "*romance*, and the examples range from the Breton cycle to Tolkien" (Eco, *The Name of the Rose: Including the Author's Postscript* 533); this category presents "[t]he past as scenery, pretext, fairy-tale construction, to allow the imagination to rove freely" (533). Eco stresses that "a romance does not necessarily have to take place in the past; it must only not take place in the here and now, and the here and now must not be mentioned, not even as allegory. Much science fiction is pure romance. Romance is the story of an *elsewhere*" (533). Thus, Eco's model allows for narrative set-ups in which specific pasts may be narrated as presents or as futures, as long as they are not recognizable as taking place in our immediate present. His second category is what he calls "the swashbuckling novel: [...] This kind of novel chooses a 'real' and recognizable past, and, to make it recognizable, the novelist peoples it with characters already found in the encyclopedia [...], making them perform actions that the encyclopedia does not record [...] but which the encyclopedia does not contradict" (533). The third form is what he calls 'the historical novel'; here, "it is not necessary for characters recognizable in normal encyclopedias to appear [...]. What the characters do serves to make history, what happened, more comprehensible" (534). Eco clarifies that "[e]vents and characters are made up" and that they have a didactic purpose to illuminate the past in ways that history books do not (534).

Wallace's pointer towards Eco is important because his taxonomy draws attention not only to a wider range of historical narratives and their gendered dimension but also to premodern forms of historical fiction. Premodern genres are typically seen as eschewing the realistic, yet they are explicitly included in Eco's model; in a way similar to women's fiction they have been marginalized in discussions of the historical novel. Clearly, Eco's distinction between romance, swashbuckler and historical novel proper does not emphasize the political or ideological dimension of aesthetic choices as much as Lukács's approach does, but it singles out three specific fictional levels of spatio-temporal concreteness as measured against an encyclopaedic attitude towards historical specificity. In so doing, Eco does not so much propose a clear-cut set of categories corresponding to specific assessments of temporal change but rather points towards a continuum of spatio-temporal recognizability within which any attempt to narrate the past is located. As Eco's categories do not depend on an evolutionary and period-biased notion of historical consciousness and/or progress, they allow for a multitude also of decidedly political functions that varying degrees of historical concreteness might have in any given text and period.

It is not coincidental that it was medievalists like Eco who have, in recent years, unmasked the period-bias encroaching on much of literary theory, a bias that also underpins Lukács's thinking. It may suffice to mention only a few examples of medievalist attempts to liberate the Middle Ages from the marginalizing project of teleological periodization: Carolyn Dinshaw, for example, has emphasized the need to recognize not merely the distinct and potentially contradictory histories of individual social groups but also different affective responses to time that coexist with one another. By asking "what it feels like to be a body in time, or in multiple times, or out of time", she has introduced a notion of multi-temporality to literary studies which, firstly, resists the notion that historical time moves as a single, one-directional evolutionary progression, while it secondly acknowledges the complex nature of temporal inflection in premodern literature (Dinshaw, *Temporalities* 109). Another example is Andrew James Johnston's work, which shows that some of the clichéd notions of periodization informing the modern idea of temporal change driven by revolutionary force derive from narrative tropes through which medieval writers already contemplated their own period's temporality (Johnston, *Performing the Middle Ages from* Beowulf *to* Othello 1–22, 312–17).

Jim Crace's *Harvest* presents a fictional world which may seem spatio-temporally evasive at first glance. As Sam Leith argues in a *TLS* review of the novel: "The surfaces of Crace's story are presented as realism; its structure is more like myth" (Crace, *Closed Communities*). This is all as it should be. However, I would like to challenge his conclusion that such a narrative setup ought to be regarded as ahistorical and apolitical. Leith claims that: "Politics and economics don't enter: This is a fall from Eden. The usurping outsiders are cruel baddies; the organic unities of the pre-enclosure commons appear as an unproblematic good. The case for sheep farming is never really made." By contrast, I wish to show that biblical and mythical structures do not oppose a political reading of the novel. At close inspection, *Harvest* presents a multi-temporal response to economic progress recalling premodern and early modern literary traditions and their engagement with historical sensibilities.

Harvest: Deconstructing Biblical Temporalities

In pointing towards Genesis, Leith evidently draws attention to an important subtext of *Harvest*. The novel's spatio-temporal set-up is complex however. *Harvest* blends realistic and fantastic modes of narrating the past with their related temporalities and suffuses them with biblical temporalities that are introduced only to be deconstructed soon after. In so doing, the novel adapts multi-temporal modes of storytelling that can already be found in medieval literature. As Elizabeth Dutton reminds us, medieval mystery plays, for example,

> draw power and meaning from a time frame in which scriptural events, heavy with eschatological significance, are nonetheless translatable into a contemporary setting. The cycles – and near-cycles – share a vital drive to translate scriptural narrative to the time, and also place, of their audience [...]. This anachronism probably possessed subversive potential: contemporary abuses of power are implicitly criticized.
>
> (Dutton, *The Croxton Play of the Sacrament* 61)

Most striking in terms of creating a multi-temporal response to the history of land enclosure is Crace's decision to condense a story of economic progress to a single week and also limit the narrated space to a small rural community, thereby giving an old-testament 'feel' to the progression of events in time which line up as a narrative of inverse creation. Yet the story does not simply recreate a backward-looking, 'mythologizing' Edenic fall; number symbolism and images from the Revelation of John are also present throughout. Significantly, the Revelation is already a temporal adaptation of Genesis in that it uses the pattern of inverse creation to paint a vision of the future. Further, the structural possibilities of inverse creation have been exploited by historical novelists as illustrious as Umberto Eco (in *The Name of the Rose*); the pattern therefore suggests itself as a structural device by which the tradition of historical fiction itself can be highlighted as one of the narrative's concerns.

In *Harvest*, the biblical feel initially works to undercut the immediacy of the present-tense narrative. Precisely seven days are needed to completely ruin the village and drive away all of its 58 inhabitants as well as the few outsiders who come into contact with the cottagers in the course of the story. Throughout the novel there are frequent references to the seven-day progression of events, ensuring that the biblical subtext is not missed by readers. Condensing the plot in this way and having the narrator persistently (re-)count the days has the effect that the narrative seems both temporally specific and timeless.

Importantly, biblical references in the story are plenty but are never used to refer to a teleological model of history, nor are they used to imply deep spirituality on the part of the protagonists. Quite to the contrary, the novel stresses that its villagers are almost without God; as narrator Walter Thirsk lets us know as he recalls the third day of events, the nearest church is a day's ride away; there is a spot of land designated for the building of one, but somehow it never gets built – partly because the community is too poor to raise the necessary funds to pay a priest, but also because the farmers do not feel an urgent spiritual need. In fact, they are quite happy without God's presence:

> No, we dare to think and even say among ourselves, there'd be no barley if we left it to the Lord, not a single blade of it. Well, actually, there'd be no field, except a field of by-blows and weeds; the nettles and tares, the thorns and brambles He preferred when He abandoned Eden. You never find Him planting crops for us. You never find us planting weeds. But we still have to battle with His darnel and His fumiter, we have to suffer from His fleas and gnats and pests. He makes us pay the penalty of Adam.
>
> (Crace, *Harvest* 27)

To some extent, religious discourse in the novel serves a realist agenda – in that it fulfills modern expectations of premodern attitudes towards faith (e.g. premodern images of self depend strongly on Christian parameters), but it never panders to the cliché of excessive premodern spirituality. There is no suggestion anywhere in the story that the destruction of livelihoods should be regarded as the result of disobedience, blasphemy or the villagers' lax attitude towards spiritual matters. Because this is so, scriptural references appear all the more to complicate the ideological undercurrents of Walter's progress narrative.

On a superficial level, the references could be (mis)understood as serving the (equally clichéd) idea of secularization as a marker of modernity. Kathleen Davis has shown that our modern politics of time is questionable in that it depends to a significant degree on a secular/spiritual divide which constructs a sacred-feudal Middle Ages as a pre-political Other to secular-capitalist-democratic modernity (Davis, *Periodization and Sovereignty: How Ideas of Feudalism and Secularization Govern the Politics of Time* 1-22). If the novel followed such temporal politics it would be easy to argue that the cottagers' somewhat 'modern' attitude towards faith signifies the due/inevitable shift from medieval (apolitical) feudalism to early modern (democratic) capitalism. However, *Harvest* forestalls such simple conclusions for at least two reasons: Jordan promises the building of a church in anticipation of future prosperity. The novel may of course tentatively evoke the onset of a 'new' Protestant work ethic in the Weberian sense, an ethic which would measure God's grace in future prosperity, but it is clear to the narrator that this is a wealth (and thus grace) from which the cottagers will not benefit as they are driven from the land. And Walter does not conclude that God has left the farmers *now* that the destruction of their livelihoods is imminent. He suggests that having to work the land is the price for Adam's original sin; he idealizes neither the villagers' future, nor their present or past lives. An Eden *abandoned* by God is their past, present and future; there is also no mention of an Edenic patria that awaits the dead upon resurrection. This lack of a future heaven is clearly evident in that Walter never refers to Christian ideas of the afterlife even though he has recently lost his wife Cecily and mentions her frequently as he chronicles his bereavement, "mourning her in tiny episodes" (Crace, *Harvest* 154). Cecily's loss prefigures the loss of agricultural life as Walter knows it – mourning Cecily, he dwells on his personal past while contemplating the community's demise.

Secondly, socio-economic change as described in *Harvest* entails the loss of quasi-democratic structures, that is, the destruction of the open-field system of communal farming. Progress does not bring with it social/democratic forms of agriculture; rather, the introduction of sheep farming is introduced without consulting those who are affected the most. Local landowner Kent vaguely informs the cottagers without letting them know of reform's radical consequences. Choosing a time of boisterous merrymaking, the harvest festival, Kent holds a speech in which he disguises the village's future as a "dream which makes us rich and leisurely" (31). Avoiding the word 'sheep' his dream paints a world in which "all his 'friends and neighbors' – meaning us – no longer need to labor long and hard throughout the year and with no certainty that what we sow will ever come to grain" (30). Walter, who is the only person to stay sober that night, has no doubt that: "He means to throw a halter around our lives. He means the clearing of our common land" (30). Walter muses that Kent has no other choice since his former property rights have gone to Jordan. Yet as Walter learns later to his disappointment, Kent sides with Jordan. And Jordan maintains that the villagers are to blame and to be punished for having made "the clock stand still". He states: "Their mischief is to shade my path. I'll not pardon them for that" (144).

It is evident here that the novel sheds a light on the ways in which economic change – progress – is justified by blaming the poor for their socio-economic conditions even if these are beyond their control. As will become clearer in the course of my argument, the novel thus depicts the community's destruction not as the result of economic necessity but of various questionable ethical choices disguised as a narrative of modernization. Without idealizing the open-field system these choices are presented as the result of class and gender advantages and associated with the exploitative politics of capitalism.

What is important in this context is that even though Walter Thirsk, a simple farmer, tells *his* version of events, the novel does not suggest that giving voice to the dispossessed goes some way to establishing some form of historical 'truth'. Historiography is cast instead as an opaque and contradictory web of unreliable, (un)ethical narratives which invites political use with questionable outcomes. The powerful do not simply take advantage of the supposedly blameless lower classes – in Crace's novel all protagonists have questionable ethics, including the narrator.

Ethical choices are demanded of all protagonists by three diffuse forces pressing onto the community that are all implicated in its destruction: ominous happenings, the family of squatters, and the presence of mapmaker Earle. All these forces relate to one another in some way, although Walter can never establish in which way precisely. And it is his futile search for a connection that his narrative highlights. During the course of the story it becomes evident that it is certainly not these forces themselves that chiefly work towards the village's rapid undoing. Rather, it is the various conflicting narratives constructed around them which both work towards, and simultaneously veil, the aristocrats' project of engineering change the way it suits them. In this way, narration/storytelling is presented as the domain of political ethics.

The story begins with Walter's description of ominous happenings. Introducing destructive light emerging from darkness in the first sentence, the novel establishes the model of inverse creation spelling apocalyptic doom: "Two twists of smoke at a time of year too warm for cottage fires surprise us at first light, or at least they surprise those of us who've not been up to mischief in the dark" (1). One of the fires destroys the barn belonging to Master Kent; the second fire has been lit by the squatters to signal their arrival. The community abides by a law according to which strangers may claim the right to settle within the community's bounds if they manage to erect a shelter and light a fire undisturbed by anyone. The model of inverse creation demands that the two fires are discovered in the early hours of a 'day of rest' (1) after the harvest has already been brought in; as events progress, the harvest is ruined entirely and by the seventh day the land is left without animals and people. "It's simply quiet and undisturbed, attending to itself, an Eden with no Adam and no Eve" (206). At the end of the story, Walter sets fire to the manor house – he is the last to leave the village, following the squatters at a distance who, having claimed the remains of the already displaced cottagers' possessions and having burnt what they cannot take, are on the move again. How things will develop from here remains uncertain.

Importantly, the two destructive fires at the novel's beginning and further two at the novel's close also connote the concept of witnessing that is central to John's Revelation. The two witnesses of the apocalypse can kill with fire all those who try to harm them; even as they are killed by the beast they regain their lives after three and a half days. As will become apparent, the figure of the witness structures *Harvest*'s engagement with the tradition of historical fiction: Walter is a witness who does not witness reliably. This is made clear at the novel's beginning when Walter claims to know that two local ruffians set fire to the barn but chooses to remain silent, while leaving the reader in doubt as to how dependable his allegations are. The family of newcomers, who consti- tute the second threatening force mentioned above, are 'fugitives from sheep' (110); ironically they are themselves victims of land enclosure and witnesses to its effects. The village, "a kingdom of close relatives where anyone who is not blood is married to someone else who is" (16), treats them harshly as unwelcome intruders. The family is blamed for laying the barn fire even if evidence is thin and there are local suspects, too; the two men are sentenced to a week in the pillory whereas the woman is to lose her long hair. Unintended by the villagers, the elder man dies during this first night in the pillory; nobody prevents his death, although the need to make him more comfortable had been evident at least to Walter who delays his resolve to help the man until it is too late. The family's maltreatment is followed by fear of retribution on the part of the cottagers, and there are yet stranger happenings (Kent's horse Willowjack is brutally slaughtered) – but the exact circumstances of the subsequent events cannot be clarified either. Soon, the woman's attractiveness is used to evoke the spectre of witchcraft, not only to account for inexplicable events, but also to justify the newcomers' treatment, which the villagers themselves feel is unkind and unjust. Narrow-minded lack of compassion – a missing sense of solidarity with one's more unfortunate kinsmen in addition to a gender-bias – is thus presented as facilitating the ethical climate that aids the aristocrats' progress narrative.

Employed by Kent to chart people, animals, fields, hills, rivers, streets, and buildings in order to prepare for the arrival of sheep, mapmaker Philip Earle is the third uncanny presence distressing the villagers, since nobody except Kent understands what his activities signify. Walter sums up the first impression of the man the farmers call 'Mr Quill': "We could not help but stare at him and wonder, without saying so, if those scratchings on his board might scratch us too, in some unwelcome way" (4). It is here, that another important biblical subtext is established in reverse fashion. Earle is something of an artist-cum-scientist: a creator who plays the fiddle skillfully, finds delight in the landscape's beauty, is versed in the use of brushes, quills and paints (hence his nickname), and takes an interest in plants which he collects for his personal 'Natural History' (61). Earle, who is physically handicapped, needs help to make his map, which is why Kent asks Walter, his former man-servant and 'milk cousin' (Walter's mother was Kent's wetnurse), to assist with the mapmaking. Earle teaches Walter to craft the vellum he needs for his task, and he also asks him to 'name' the land and everything that is on it. As a self-declared lover of words, Walter is the ideal person to aid him. Unlike his neighbours, for whom "an iris bulb [is] pig fodder" and "celandines [are] not a thing of beauty but a gargle for an irritated throat" (56), Walter appreciates the beauty not only of words but also of plants and can name each single one. Since Walter feels that some of the names Earle collects are too plain to be written down, he embellishes some and invents others, and Earle is delighted with Walter's wisdom. As Earle begins to teach his craft to Walter, he also rekindles Walter's love of the land which the latter has learnt to fear as unforgiving, inflexible and tormenting. Several passages in the novel synaesthetically present mapmaking, writing, and farming as sister arts, blending a love of colours, shapes, smells, and sounds as Earle and Walter go about their work. Yet as Walter takes pleasure in naming, and Earle in Walter's verbal creations, the two become a team of accomplices in the aristocrats' project of introducing the land reform – a change both understand as a threat to the people. When Walter takes a look at a finished chart for the first time, he secretly concludes: "There is something in these shapes and lines, in these casual, undirected blues and greens, that, for all their liveliness, seems desolate" (102).

Walter's musings over Earle's charts show how much he is in fact aware of the manipulative power of cartography: "Mr. Quill's true account of here and now is not as honest as he hopes. He's colored and he's flattened us. No shadows and no shade. [...] The land is effortless: a lie" (102). Walter points out that the maps also affect the temporalities of his world: "He hasn't captured time: how long a walk might take; how long a piece of work might take; how long the seasons must last" (102). But it is easy for him to appreciate Earle's 'beautiful' paintings "fulsomely for what they are as pretty things, a kind of vision of the world – our little world, in fact – that I have never seen before and which has left me moved and oddly breathless" (102). It seems here that the professions of mapmaker, natural historian (represented by Earle) and storyteller, poet as well as philologist/historian (represented by Walter) are allegorized in a quasi-Platonic sense: lured by their love of word and image, the poet-artists/historians let themselves be used in the service of lies and destruction.

Again, an ethical problem is at the root of Walter's apparently complacent attitude towards imminent 'progress'. As both Kent and Earle confide in Walter, the latter is the only cottager who learns what concrete changes await the community – but he decides to keep this knowledge a secret from his neighbours, hoping to become Earle's assistant in the future. The privileging of personal ambition over the common good is thus offered as a further factor determining the ethical climate for progress-as-destruction as depicted in *Harvest*.

Witnessing and the Politics of Blame

The figure of Philip Earle is important as it symbolically stands in for the role of the arts not only in promoting change (with potentially detrimental consequences) but also in critiquing it. During the harvest festival, Walter had observed: "Mr. Quill the fiddler is shaping us again, making us congruent and geometrical with his melodies as he has done with his charts and ink" (33). Having made all the necessary arrangements for the making of his map, from the crafting of vellum to the mixing of paints, townsman Earle cannot however complete his work. It appears that he had been trying to criticize events, however he is murdered. Creation is portrayed in the novel as being destructive, but it is itself destroyed; Adam is not created and then names what he sees; here, the land is named, then the creator of charts is vilified, disappears from the scene and is found dead.

Mr. Quill's murder happens quietly, unobserved by anyone; the description of events in the foreground is, meanwhile, occupied with the witch hunt against the strange woman and her accomplices who are suspected to have brought about Willowjack's death (i.e. potentially all villagers, even the children, and also Earle). While the narrative merely gestures towards the increasingly violent treatment of the alleged arsonist-horse-killers and anyone who might sympathize with them (eventually all farmers except Walter flee from the village to escape the terror), readers are implicitly invited to speculate who is responsible for Earle's fate. We witness Walter searching the village grounds for the missing surveyor, making one doubtful guess after the other. Many of his guesses involve the mysterious woman since he is certain that she arouses sexual fantasies in all the male protagonists. Yet the three parties, the aristocratic landowners, the cottagers and the squatting woman seem equally suspect, and again, there is no logical or reasonable progression of events that could illuminate the circumstances of Earle's demise.

Even if we feel we ought to know more than Walter (from our superior vantage point in time, or our ability to make sense of conflicting information), we do not. If historical fiction is prone to adopting the whodunit model of detective fiction (since we are used to regarding history as a series of established facts that are logically connected), here the model is introduced only to be thoroughly undermined. If, for example, Barry Unsworth's novel *Morality Play* uses the pattern to establish the true identity of a murderer the village community thought was long established, the exact cause of Earle's death is never revealed, not even at the end, when Walter finds his body inside the manor house. We remain equally ignorant of the identities or histories of the nameless exotic strangers, the cause of the barn fire, and Willowjack's killer, whereas Walter constructs his story from the start as if he knew precisely who is to blame for what. "I know at once whom we should blame," (2) he states when the story has hardly begun but continues to blame varying people for the same thing as the story progresses. He continuously has 'logical suspicions' (11). "Here's what took place," (6) is a typical turn of phrase which is undermined with expressions such as "it could have been" (65), and "This would have been the moment, I am sure […]" (106).

As it happens, Walter is actually *never* witness to crucial events: on the first day he is asleep when the barn fire starts; and since he hurts his hand while fighting the fire he cannot join the villagers later to find out more about the squatters and join their attack on them; the morning of the second day he misses that one of the newcomers has died on the pillory; he is not there when Kent's horse is killed. Since he is on a mission to aid Earle he is also ignorant of how the four-year-old Lizzie Carr, his neighbour's niece, is tortured by Jordan's men to reveal her alleged entanglement with a witch. He is not there to witness that the two women who try to come to Lizzie's aid receive similar treatment. This is why on day four – the time when Earle goes missing – he can only relate reports as to what went on inside and outside the manor house. The only crucial event he does witness is when some of the villagers take to beating up Jordan's groom (while he takes care not to be implicated in the villagers' act of retribution). Towards the end (evocatively three and a half days after Earle's death), when we are left with more questions than answers, we understand that the novel aims to present the creative arts as servile and historiography as a crippled set of shifting, mostly unethical, or at least questionable, attributions as to why political events and socio-economic change come out the way they do. Walter's example shows that even if we could hear eye-witness accounts of what 'really' took place during the enclosures, they would be tainted by individual conjectures based on vested interests.

Yet just as we sense that the novel questions the ethics of historiography and storytelling in casting an ironic light on Walter's (mis)interpretations as well as those of the aristocrats, who use the witch hunt against the squatters to justify their violent treatment of the community at large, there is an unmistakable hint that Earle's employers may have engineered the mapmaker's mysterious absence, and as is con-firmed later, murder. The narrator himself does not seem to read between the lines however. A while after Earle has gone missing, he asks Master Jordan: "'Has Mr. Earle finished with his charts?' I ask. I cannot see the risk in that. 'Ha, Mr. Earle will never finish it, I think.'" (141) As Walter asks more questions, Jordan responds: "'Your face is very cruelly bruised […]. I hope the injury has no cause to spread […].'" Walter continues his story without acknowledging or recognizing the threat: "'And on those words, as if ordained, the first sunlight finds passage through the red-black canopy of sentry beeches and lays a glossy stripe across the tabletop. At last I understand the hope in Master Kent's face, and his composure in these torrential times. His resignation too. There'll be no trials. There'll be no burning at the stake. There'll just be progress of a sort" (141).

It is as if Walter's blindness to Jordan's implicit threat is a signal for the reader to claim a superior vantage point, to 'know at once who is to blame' for this 'progress of a sort' which occasions the vilification and subsequent destruction of an entire village, and it is striking that the narrative is hiding what is effectively a trap for the reader in terms of a beautifully phrased pathetic fallacy of nature that, too, obeys the narrative rules of inverted creation. Again, first light is evoked; unlike Walter, who associates hope with sunlight finding a passage through darkness, the reader is led to believe that Walter falls prey to the literary tropes he creates and is thus tricked into being optimistic by his love of beauty: If there is beauty in nature, and beauty in art, things must be well, times must be hopeful. Seeing beauty in the light, Walter identifies Kent's features as indicating a positive future for the community rather than as a sign of complicity with Jordan or perhaps of his satisfaction with Walter who, instead of rebelling, continues to be of service to the aristocrats. Walter appears to ignore the cynicism of the thought that there will be no trials, while the reader suspects that both Kent's and Jordan's understanding of 'progress of a sort' translates to severe hardship for the people who, like the family of nameless squatters, will not be welcomed anywhere else. Readers will conclude that they must therefore also be responsible for the absence of the crippled man who previously showed compassion both towards the strangers as well as the tortured Lizzie and the women who tried helping her. If we can trust Walter's account, it is Earle the mapmaker who would have the ethical sensibility to speak up against the injustice Kent's and Jordan's kind of 'progress' entails. It is by the very pathetic fallacy that deludes Walter that we are thus led to apply and detect in ourselves the same questionable politics of blame and 'logical suspicions' that we find implicitly exposed in the novel: Earle's body is eventually found in the manor after all.

We Versus I: Walter as a Middling Hero

As we have seen, Walter's journal exposes how a general politics of blame governs the ideology of progress in systematically undermining the narrator's own, and even the reader's, attempts to apportion blame. Walter's role as witness who fails to witness is crucial here. In this sense, *Harvest* very much explores what has been described as the postmodern focus of historiographical critique: "the interaction between what is 'known' and what is made up, querying, for instance, the deployment of varieties of quoted 'evidence', [...] highlighting the innate textuality of history, to frame a persuasive narrative, and the use of the realist mode to present a story which is clearly fiction" (de Groot, *The Historical Novel* 113). Instead of reconstructing a possible narrative as to what might have happened, *Harvest* illustrates that we know next to nothing about the peasantry's view of their own time.

On the last day of the reported events, the village now almost devoid of people, Walter, in a belated act of insubordination, finally decides to set fire to the manor house and rescues only one item from the flames: the new and clean sheet of 'pauper's vellum' Earle taught him to make during the past seven days. Whilst John the Apostle opens with "In the beginning was the Word, and the Word was with God, and the Word was God", here, at the close of the story of inverse creation, there is at best a promise of more words (and still no God). The end gestures towards historical fiction's necessary paradox, that the novel we have read may evoke a voice from the past but cannot have been narrated by a figure from the past – and never will be; *this* figure's sheet of vellum inevitably has to remain blank. Realistically speaking, the novel thus insists, there is no such thing as pauper's vellum, and if there was, it is certainly not made in seven days.

Walter cannot have written down the story he is in the process of telling, since he owns no writing implements (though he is in fact literate). The narrator's symbolic act of rescuing a blank sheet of vellum he has made when we have just heard the last of his story is the novel's most forceful reminder that many voices from the past remain unheard, especially those of lowly status; many of those that might have been recorded in writing are lost nevertheless, despite postmodern attempts to give voice to the voiceless across time. *Harvest* dramatizes this very 'real' impossibility of representation also in gendered terms through the figure of the nameless female vagrant. The quintessential subaltern of premodernity, lowest of the low, she is routinely objectified either as malicious witch or erotic 'Mistress Beldam' or both The portrayal of her existence, it seems, is entirely the product of Walter's fantasies which are modeled on early modern theatrical discourses of poverty. Her nickname 'Beldam' anagrammatically connotes the figure of the 'Bedlam beggar' and thus refers to early modern theatre where the part is habitually employed as a kind of trickster-troublemaker: "By exacerbating rivalries and fears he overturns all the controlling social hierarchies [...]: household, class status, age, gender, heterosexuality, gender, religion, and law" (Neely, *Distracted Subjects: Madness and Gender in Shakespeare and Early Modern Culture* 29). Walter suggests that Mistress Beldam provokes fear and chaos in the community as her presence stirs rivalries among men across the social spectrum; especially her odd possession of a beautiful shawl disturbs the social pecking order as it makes her even more desirable and incites jealousy among the women. However, in contrast to stage plays, Walter's diary never allows this trickster to speak for herself. While shrouding her character in mysteriousness, *Harvest* represents her identity as a 'living ghost' (Crace, *Harvest* 163) – as inaccessible even to her contemporaries. If it is one concern of the postmodern historical novel to call for a need to represent the nameless of history, *Harvest* elegizes our desire to know what is lost, what cannot be known.

Importantly, Walter is nevertheless cast as a trustworthy observer of the ethical currencies that feed the discourse of socio-economic progress. In moving towards a premodern, allegorical mode of representation, the novel strikingly reinstates Walter's credibility as witness. In a scene that overtly alludes to the medieval tradition of the morality play he becomes less an observer of the 'hard facts' he so unsuccessfully chases, but a spectator of his own and others' ethical performances. It is crucial to remember that up until this scene we have seen him routinely making questionable choices: We have seen him as simultaneously compassionate and complacent, caring for the family of strangers somewhat but being blind to their needs; we have seen how he randomly trusts and mistrusts the motives of the people around him, blaming others while condemning the fabrication of unsubstantiated accusations; criticizing a mistrust of strangers in others and being guilty of such behaviour himself. We have seen him as what could be called the ultimate middling character: Once a stranger to the village himself, he is both an insider and an outsider – torn between the lure of the town (where he grew up and was educated as Kent's 'milk cousin' and later servant) and the pull of the country (where he found Cecily's love and became a farmer). We have seen how, in the face of his village's crisis, he is, in fact, wavering between a personal ambition which would take him back to the city, and his devotion to farming and defending the communal life of his village. On the fifth day he finds himself alone however. He is the only cottager both Kent and Jordan trust, and having advanced to the position of steward, he is the only farmer not to have fled the village. Jordan and Kent are leaving, too, riding with their entourage, as well as their female captives and the injured groom. Watching the procession of horses and men, Walter notices that the aristocrats betray a disturbing alliance of interests that acknowledges "how their futures will be shaped (151). He muses:

> Am I to be the only one to witness and know it all, the only to wonder what this mounted pageant represents? Is that why I've been left behind? To watch this spectacle? It's like a costumed enactment at a fair, a mummer's show. I used to love them as a boy. I'd want to

> be the first to name the parts and identify the players from their garb. Today, I'm seeing Privilege in its high hat. Then comes Suffering: the Guilty and the Innocent, including beasts. Then Malice follows, wielding its great stick. And, afterward, invisibly, Despair is riding its lame horse. [...] It wouldn't take me long to catch up with that mummers' show. I could tag on at the end and follow Despair and his dejected mount as . . . Shame, perhaps. As Servitude.

> (Crace, *Harvest* 152-53)

As allegory invades Walter's narrative of the 'here' and 'now' in the form of an imagined re-enactment of political events in an alternative temporality, Walter is finally able to understand the significance of the confusing events that have befallen his community. The pageant represents the moment in time when he finally comprehends that he – as Servitude – as steward of the wealthy *and* unlikely poetic voice of the poor – has a choice to make. Walter must choose as to which forces he will follow, and his choice is by no means inevitable. He resolves to rebel against 'Privilege' by first working the land one more time with the help of the squatter whom he frees before his sentence is over, then by burning the manor house. Refusing to serve as steward any longer, he, too, takes to the road. His use of pronouns in the novel's last sentence indicates that he has resolved the ethical conflict between serving himself or others: "I have to carry on alone until I reach wherever is awaiting me, until I gain wherever is awaiting us" (208).

Crace's novel persistently draws attention to its own narrative economy, which is both heavily indebted to, and overtly critical of, the traditional historical novel. Letting Jordan make fun of Walter's name – "Water! Thirst!" (140) – the novel ironizes Walter's paradoxical, 'wavering', personality in an unmistakable nod towards Lukács's analysis of Scott's *Waverley* novels. Whereas Lukács's approach identified the middling hero between two opposing, temporally concrete, social forces, one of which would win in the service of inevitable progress, Walter is a character wavering between timeless ethical forces in an allegorical setting where "Profit, Progress, Enterprise" (140) is a catchall excuse of the privileged to make unethical choices that further disadvantage the poor. In contrasting the figures of Kent and Walter, Crace emphasizes that at the root of any clash of opposing social trends are ethical choices. Kent – on the privileged side but less so than Jordan – decides to advance at the cost of the village community; Walter – on the deprived side but less so than his neighbours – eventually chooses to resist siding with those who put their own interests first, and he is open to find out what kind of future will await him instead. Walter's final choice moves *Harvest* away from historical fiction into the temporal sphere of utopian literature. Once the reader has grasped the social determinants of the conditions the protagonists endure, there is no great historical hero who enters the scene to resolve the crisis. Instead, the narrative is future-oriented and presents Walter's future literally as a blank sheet of pauper's vellum. The story, chiefly told in the present tense, thus has a potential Jameson identified in science fiction: "to defamiliarize and restructure our experience of our own present, [...] transforming our own present into the determinate past of something yet to come" (Jameson, *Progress Versus Utopia; or, Can We Imagine the Future?* 151).

Harvest is focused on a devastating intrusion into a hardly Edenic but nevertheless functional community – functional at least until the moment Walter begins to tell his story. Rather than using secularization as a pointer towards modernity, the novel alludes to medieval allegorical theatre and uses the biblical stories of creation and Adam and Eve's expulsion from Eden to provide an effective counter-narrative for the depiction of complex economic change as well as for the evaluation of change as the result of ethical choices. At the same time, the novel allegorically (and paradoxically) enacts its own (in)ability to recreate history by creating a world outside of history. Such an approach could perhaps be mistaken as merely following the lead of postmodern historical meta-fiction. *Harvest* reveals itself however to be an elegy on both the traditional historical novel that was capable of promoting progress and a sense of national belonging no matter how tragically competing forces impacted on individual lives (as in the Scottian model), and on the post-modern attempts to rescue the historical novel through telling the stories of the marginalized and nameless of history. *Harvest* does not reject historical realism altogether: It proposes that realism can no longer be attained unless we truly admit that our urge to unravel historical truth – the historically real – is as undying as it is futile. The novel demonstrates that the historical novel is possible if the political potential of the full spectrum of aesthetic choices is acknowledged. Moving away from an association of realism with the ideology of inevitable progress, and in embracing alternative spaces of temporality, *Harvest* offers a multi-temporal alternative to the politics of time that underwrites much of historical fiction as well as its criticism.

Works Cited

Anderson, Perry. 'From Progress to Catastrophe: Perry Anderson on the Historical Novel.' *London Review of Books* 33-15 (2011): 24-28.

Crace, Jim. *Harvest*. New York: Doubleday, 2013.

Crace, Jim. 'Picador Podcast: Jim Crace', Picador.com, 11 February 2013. Available at: <http://www.picador.com/blog/february-2013/picador-podcast-jim-crace>.

Davis, Kathleen. *Periodization and Sovereignty: How Ideas of Feudalism and Secularization Govern the Politics of Time*. Philadelphia: University of Pennsylvania Press, 2008.

De Groot, Jerome. *The Historical Novel*. Abingdon: Routledge, 2010.

Dinshaw, Carolyn. 'Temporalities.' *Middle English*. Ed. Paul Strohm. Oxford: Oxford University Press, 2007. 107–23.

Dutton, Elizabeth. 'The Croxton *Play of the Sacrament*.' *The Oxford Handbook of Tudor Drama*. Eds. Thomas Betteridge and Greg Walker. Oxford: Oxford University Press, 2012. 55-71.

Felski, Rita. *Doing Time: Feminist Theory and Postmodern Culture*. New York: New York University Press, 2000.

Jameson, Fredric. 'Progress Versus Utopia; or, Can We Imagine the Future?' *Science Fiction Studies* 9-2, Utopia and Anti-Utopia (July 1982): 147-158.

Johnston, Andrew James. *Performing the Middle Ages from* Beowulf *to* Othello. Turnhout: Brepols, 2008.

Leith, Sam. 'Closed Communities [Review of *Harvest*].' *Times Literary Supplement*, 22 February 2013. Web. <http://www.the-tls.co.uk/tls/reviews/other_categories/article1218218.ece>.

Lukács, György. *The Historical Novel*. Lincoln, Neb.: University of Nebraska Press, 1983.

Neely, Carol Thomas. *Distracted Subjects: Madness and Gender in Shakespeare and Early Modern Culture*. Ithaca: Cornell University Press, 2004.

Turner, Michael. 'Enclosures.' *The Oxford Encyclopedia of Economic History*. Vol. 2. Ed. Joel Mokyr. Oxford: Oxford University Press, 2003. 193-96.

Umberto, Eco. *The Name of the Rose: Including the Author's Postscript*. Trans. William Weaver. San Diego, New York, London: Harcourt Brace Jovanovich, 1994 [1983].

Wallace, Diana. *The Woman's Historical Novel: British Women Writers, 1900-2000*. Houndmills, Basingstoke, Hampshire: Palgrave Macmillan, 2005.

Biographical Notes

Ute Berns is professor of English Literature at the University of Hamburg. Her most recent publications comprise the monograph *Science, Politics and Friendship in the Works of Thomas Lovell Beddoes* (2012), the special issue *Theatre and History*, co-edited with Verena Keidel and Janina Wierzoch, in the *Journal of Contemporary Drama in English* (2015) as well as *Figurations of Knowledge in British and German Romanticism*, a cluster issue of the *European Romantic Review*, co-edited with Susan Gustafson (forthcoming in February 2017).

Renate Brosch holds the chair of English Literature at Universität Stuttgart. She has published books on Henry James (2000) and on short story theory (*Short Story: Textsorte und Leseerfahrung*. WVT 2007). Two of her edited collections are concerned with cultural mobility and Australian Visual Culture respectively (2011 and 2014). Her current research interests are in cognitive narratology and reader response (*Anglistik: Focus on Reception and Reader Response* 2013). She is also currently editing a special issue of *Poetics Today* dealing with ekphrasis in the digital age.

Heike Hartung received her PhD in English from the Freie Universität Berlin and her PhD habil. in English Literature and Cultural Studies from the University of Potsdam. While her PhD thesis was devoted to the historical novel, she has also published in the interdisciplinary fields of aging, disability and gender studies. Her research interests further include narrative theory and the history of the novel. She is the author of the monographs *Ageing, Gender, and Illness in Anglophone Literature: Narrating Age in the Bildungsroman* (Routledge 2016) and *Die dezentrale Geschichte – Historisches Erzählen und literarische Geschichte/n bei Peter Ackroyd, Graham Swift und Salman Rushdie* (WVT 2002).

Andrew James Johnston is professor of medieval and early modern English Literature at the Freie Universität Berlin. He studied there and at Yale University and received his PhD from the Freie Universität in 1998 and his 'Habilation' from the Technische Universität Dresden in 2005. His monographs include *Performing the Middle Ages from Beowulf to Othello* (Brepols 2008) and *Robin Hood* (in German, C. H. Beck 2013). He has co-edited *The Medieval Motion Picture* (Palgrave Macmillan 2014, with M. Rouse and Ph. Hinz), *The Art of Vision: Ekphrasis in Medieval Literature and Culture* (Ohio State UP 2015, with M. Rouse and E. Knapp) and *Love, History and Emotion in Chaucer and Shakespeare: Troilus and Criseyde and Troilus and Cressida* (Manchester UP 2016, with R. West-Pavlov and E. Kempf).

Cordula Lemke is professor of English Literature at the Freie Universität Berlin. She is the author of *Wandel in der Erfahrung: Die Konstruktion von Welt in den Romanen von Virginia Woolf und Jeanette Winterson* (2004) and has coedited *Joseph Conrad (1857-1924)* (2007) and *Weeds and Viruses: Ecopolitics and the Demands of Theory* (2016). She has published in the fields of Gender Studies, Postcolonial Studies and 19th to 21st century literature and is currently working on a book project on Scottish hospitality.

Claudia Olk is chair of English and Comparative Literature at the Peter Szondi Institute of Freie Universität Berlin and the President of the German Shakespeare Society. Her main fields of research are medieval and Renaissance literature as well as Modernism. Her publications include a monograph on the development of Fiction in late medieval and Renaissance travel narratives, and one on *Virginia Woolf's Aesthetics of Vision*. She has edited volumes on *The Idea of Perfection in Medieval and Early Modern Literature* and on *Neoplatonism and Aesthetics*. Her edition of one of Virginia Woolf's hitherto unpublished manuscripts was published in 2013 by the British Library.

Margitta Rouse is postdoctoral Fellow at the Collaborative Research Group Discursivations of the New at Freie Universität Berlin. Her research interests include medieval literature, visual culture and the uses of history in contemporary literature and film. She is the author of *The Self's Grammar: Performing Poetic Identity in Douglas Dunn's Poetry* 1969-2013 (Winter 2013), and she has coedited *The Medieval Motion Picture: The Politics of Adaptation* (2014, with Andrew James Johnston), as well as *The Art of Vision: Ekphrasis in Medieval Literature and Culture* (2015, with Andrew James Johnston and Ethan Knapp). She is currently working on constructions of temporality in late medieval Troy narratives.

Helga Schwalm is professor of English Literature at Humboldt-Universität zu Berlin. Publications include *Dekonstruktion im Roman. Erzähltechnische Verfahren und Selbstreflexion in den Romanen von Vladimir Nabokov und Samuel Beckett* (Heidelberg: Winter 1991), *Das eigene und das fremde Leben. Biographische Identitätsentwürfe in der englischen Literatur des 18. Jahrhunderts* (Würzburg: K&N, 2007), articles on eighteenth-century sympathy, life-writing, 20th and 21st century fiction, and literary theory.

Russell West-Pavlov is professor of Anglophone Literatures at the University of Tübingen and a Research Associate at the University of Pretoria. Book publications include *Temporalities* (Routledge 2013) and an edited volume, *The Global South and Literature* (Cambridge University Press, forthcoming 2017).

Kai Wiegandt is assistant professor of English Literature at the Freie Universität Berlin. He has published *Crowd and Rumour in Shakespeare* (Ashgate 2012) and articles on Shakespeare, Modernism, postcolonial literatures and ecocriticism. In 2016, he received his 'Habilitation' from the Freie Universität Berlin. He is elected member of the German Young Academy at the Berlin-Brandenburg Academy of Sciences and Humanities and the German National Academy of Sciences Leopoldina.

Index